THE ENTERPRISE OF ENGLAND
THE SPANISH
ARMADA

THE ENTERPRISE OF ENGLAND
THE SPANISH ARMADA

Roger Whiting

ST. MARTIN'S PRESS · New York

THE ENTERPRISE OF ENGLAND: THE SPANISH ARMADA

St. Martin's Press, Scholarly and Reference Division, 175 Fifth Avenue, New York, N.Y. 10010

Printed in Great Britain

ISBN 0-312-12731-6

Library of Congress Cataloging-in-Publication Data

Whiting, J.R.S. (John Roger Scott)
    The enterprise of England : the Spanish Armada / Roger Whiting.
       p.   cm.
    Bibliography: p.
    Includes index.
    ISBN 0-312-12731-6
    1. Armada, 1588.   2. Great Britain–History. Naval–Tudors,
1485–1603.   3. Spain–History–Philip II.   1556–1598.   4. Spain–
History, Naval–16th century.   I. Title.
DA360.W45   1988 1995
942.05–dc19   88–17443
                                                                        CIP

Cover illustration: English ships and the Spanish Armada, August 1588 (National Maritime Museum, London, BHC0262).

First Edition 1995

Acknowledgements

The author and publisher are grateful to the following for permission to reproduce illustrations: The Mansell Collection, pages 18, 35, 75, 84, 87, 98, 99, 102, 106, 113, 114, 117, 118, 119, 123, 130, 134, 152; The National Maritime Museum, London, pages 47, 60, 77, 88, 89, 108, 121, 136; Colin Martin, pages 214, 222, 223; The Ulster Museum, pages 216, 217, 218, 219; The National Portrait Gallery, London, page 14; The Naval Museum, Madrid, page 43; The Musées Royaux des Beaux-Arts, Brussels, page 22; Berel Feritte, Irish Tourist Board, pages 177, 187, 198, 201; Laurence Flanagan, page 172; Ann Lynn-Wood, drawings pages 63, 103, 115, 132, 170, 178, 179, 213; The remaining pictures are the author's.

Preface

The four hundredth anniversary of the sailing of the Spanish Armada, Philip II's great 'Enterprise of England', is an ideal time to take stock of what is known about this great event in the histories of Spain and England. After centuries of biased writings, or viewpoints voiced when knowledge of the facts was far less available than now, it is possible to offer an objective reassessment of what actually happened and why. Archives have been unearthed, underwater archaeologists have brought new evidence to the surface, and nationalistic bias has been discarded by historians.

In the past English historians had almost a monopoly of Armada historiography and so anglicized the events. This was due to a reluctance on the part of Spanish historians to face up to a subject which seemed to stain the proud record of their homeland. When the Armada's objective was seen purely as the conquest of England, attention was concentrated mainly on the fighting. In turn this led to an assumption that the execution of Mary, Queen of Scots, was *the* event which led to the Armada's sailing, as it opened the way to the deposition of Elizabeth without the immediate succession of Mary. Today it is appreciated that Philip would have agreed to a political settlement which fell short of requiring the queen's deposition for its acceptance.

Philip's main aim was to undermine the threat that the English nation posed to interference in the affairs of Spain, whether it was by Drake's sea-dogs on the Spanish Main, or Elizabeth's aid to the rebels in the Netherlands, or threatened aid to the Portuguese pretender. Philip did not want to have to rule a conquered England, as that would have faced him with the need to run the country with an army of occupation for years to come. He was already having to cope with that very problem in the Netherlands. From a purely military point of view conquest leading to occupation was out of the question. Moreover, France would never have accepted a Spanish presence to the north, south and west, without a prolonged fight. Although the re-Catholicizing of England would have been to his religious and moral credit in the eyes of Rome, freedom of worship for Catholics might well be a reasonable compromise obtainable by negotiation under threat of invasion.

The Armada's role was to cause insurrection in England by either securing an invasion or convincing Englishmen it was imminent. For that reason it had to look as if it would succeed, and consequently its size had to be inflated by the use of any ships available and by exaggerating the numbers of troops aboard. Publicity designed to create panic in England was essential. Whether the fleet would actually land troops in England would depend not only on the logistics involved, but also upon whether Elizabeth bowed to the inevitable and accepted Philip's demands by negotiation. So long as Philip got what he wanted, it was not particularly important whether his conditions were met as the result of negotiations or invasion. Thus both the negotiations and the Armada's sailing had to be convincing in the threat they presented.

The contrast between the hurried mustering of an almost amateur 'home guard' to defend England's shores and the professionalism of much of her navy is now fully known and appreciated by historians. So too are the significant differences between 'Mediterranean' and 'Atlantic' ships in the Armada on the one hand, and the English developments in ship design on the other. Important discoveries have been made about the poor quality of the Spanish gunpowder in comparison to that of England. It is now known just how effective, or ineffective, the firing was on both sides.

Heroic roles played by sea-dogs, such as Drake, are now taken properly in context. The game of bowls is clearly 'not proven', and Drake's privateering, when he should have been leading the fleet up the Channel, now taken note of. Howard's diplomatic handling of this fiery sea-dog and his own generous care for his men after the event was over are to his credit. The Duke of Medina Sidonia is no longer seen as a poor choice for the commander of the mighty Armada. On the contrary, it seems that the king had picked the obvious man for the job. The fatal weakness of the lack of communication between the Duke of Parma and Medina Sidonia is now fully understood. The impossibility of getting the troops out to the Armada in barges without the availability of a deep-water port is now accepted as the major reason for the disaster of the 'Enterprise' at its most crucial point.

In short, a variety of historical research over the years by eminent research historians and underwater archaeologists has enabled a far more accurate narrative of the events to be pieced together. The jigsaw is now as near complete as it is ever likely to be. In this account I have set out to present the picture as best I can, drawing attention to the new evidence and viewpoints as the events unfurl.

Roger Whiting
Cheltenham, 1988

Contents

The Calendar

The dates used in this book are all *New Style*, except on the playing card illustrations, which are *Old Style*. The *New Style* calendar was proclaimed by Pope Gregory XIII in 1582 and most of western Europe was using it by 1587. Naturally England, as a Protestant country, had refused to change, lest it might be thought that the Pope's authority had been re-established. The Gregorian *New Style* calendar had moved the date forward ten days on the *Old Style* calendar in order to make up the short-fall that had occurred over the centuries. Of course the days of the week remain the same in both calendars.

CHAPTER ONE

Prelude to an Enterprise

King Philip II of Spain had been disgusted by the only battle he had ever witnessed. Indeed he had never led any force into battle, nor shown any skill as a swordsman. Yet he was destined to be the greatest religious crusader of his time, planning armada after armada in the name of the Holy Catholic Church against Protestant England. A slow thinker, who dreaded making quick decisions, he had acquired the nickname of 'Philip the Prudent'. But some would argue that he was far from prudent in attempting the 'Enterprise of England', as he called his Armada plan. He thought time would sweep away the problems which faced him. 'Time and I are one,' he used to say. Time, however, was to prove him wrong.

The 'Enterprise' was the design of a man who was not a great intellectual, but one who had the necessary power to carry out his plans. His obstinacy and self-righteousness presented his advisers with a difficult problem when dealing with him. He tended to shut himself away and spend the time writing his instructions rather than having meetings with those who were entrusted with carrying out his grand ideas. He was reluctant to delegate any power, so that the machinery of government depended almost entirely upon him. This reluctance to decentralise was undoubtedly his chief weakness. It forced him not only to deal with momentous decisions in isolation, but also to issue directives on trivial matters. Indeed his espionage system was so elaborate that it still defies historians to fully appreciate all its ramifications. Moreover he did not appreciate that spies sometimes tell their employers what they want to hear, rather than what they should be told.

His daily routine was not a healthy one. He would spend three or four hours in prayer, as well as sitting long hours in his study. He suffered from swollen, painful knees and gout, and as he grew older he found it difficult to sleep. The palace-monastery, El Escorial, which he had had built between 1563 and 1584 at a

King Philip II.

cost of three and a half million ducats, cannot have improved his health. It was a lonely and harsh place, susceptible to the summer heat and the cold winter winds. Dedicated to St Lawrence the Martyr who had died on a gridiron, it was designed like an upturned gridiron, with four 180 ft tall towers representing the legs. Inside the dark grey granite walls it was rich with white and coloured marble. But their richness did not affect Philip whose mind was set on his Maker and His Church.

The relationship between Philip and the Tudor dynasty had begun twenty years before the construction of El Escorial had started. It began on 18 July 1554, when a Spanish fleet of 130 ships, bearing 8,000 troops, arrived off Portland Bill. Two days later Philip stepped ashore at Southampton, which was decorated to receive him. He had come to conquer England's queen, Mary, by marrying her. At the age of twenty-seven, nine years a widower, he was to be king-consort of England. In contrast, Mary was thirty-eight and a spinster. She was not only the first Queen of England in her own right for four hundred years, but half-Spanish herself, as her mother was Catherine of Aragon. In turn Philip could claim direct descendancy from Edward III of England. For a queen who was restoring her country to the Holy Catholic Church, the match seemed ideal in all aspects. Philip, quiet, dignified, splendidly dressed, and with a blond beard too, was all she could desire.

Nevertheless, none of his 8,000 troops were allowed to land. They were sent on to the Netherlands, an ominous portent of 1588, when the aim was to bring Spanish troops from there to England. The couple were married at Winchester with great ceremony. While Philip proved very attentive to his new wife, his followers were disillusioned by the ungentlemanly manners and crudity of their English opposites. They saw England as a land of barbaric heretics, which is not surprising since they were jeered at in the streets, continually overcharged for services rendered and assaulted and robbed on some occasions. Throughout August and September the followers made their excuses one by one, and left. Their intention of offering friendship to their counterparts having been rejected, they were to feel a resentment which their king would in due course satisfy when he planned his 'Enterprise of England'. For the time being Mary was content to take Philip's advice about the need to restore the strength of her navy. In spite of this her privy councillors were suspicious of the influence Philip was likely to have on her, and sought to protect her as best they could.

Then in February 1555, Mary's 3½ year persecution campaign against those who would not accept the Roman Catholic church began. It is sometimes argued that Philip should be blamed to some extent for this campaign as he had once remarked that he would burn his own son if he turned heretic. In fact he continually pressed Mary and her advisers to be moderate in application of this policy.

Although Mary claimed she was pregnant in November 1554, by the following May it was clear that she was wrong. This disappointment, together with news in August that his father, Charles V, was willing to abdicate in his favour, tempted Philip to sail for home on 3 September. He had come to the conclusion that Mary was not going to produce the necessary heir. Had she done so, and had Philip's son by his first marriage died, that heir would have ruled not only England, Wales and Ireland, but also the whole Spanish Empire. Early in 1556 Philip was crowned King of Spain.

After an eighteen months' absence he returned again to England. One of the reasons for this journey was to persuade England to join him in a war against France. When the war began on 7 June, England was completely unprepared for her role in it. This fact, together with Mary's ailing weakness, prompted him to return home once more on 5 July. Within sixteen months Mary was to die at the age of forty-two. It is interesting to note that only a month later Philip was considering the possibility that his duty lay in marrying Elizabeth, Mary's half sister, the new Queen of England. He had met her on his first visit to England, and found her altogether more attractive than his rather tense, plain bride. Moreover, unlike Mary, she was younger than him and marriage with her was more likely to produce an heir. The Venetian ambassador, Giovanni Michieli, had commented of her, 'At the time of the Queen's [Mary's] pregnancy, Lady Elizabeth contrived so to ingratiate herself with all the Spaniards and especially the King, that ever since no one has favoured her more than he does.' So genuine had the attraction between them become that Mary showed signs of jealousy, which might well have proved Elizabeth's final undoing.

Philip sent the Count de Feria to see Elizabeth privately and convey his formal proposal to her. The catch was that Philip saw the marriage as a service he could perform for God in that he could insist that such a union was dependent on Elizabeth becoming a Catholic and the pope giving his dispensation for the marriage to take place as they were in-laws. It was typical of Elizabeth that she kept him waiting for her answer. She waited too long though, for, taking her lack of decision for rejection, Philip married the 14-year-old French Princess Elizabeth of Valois. He also tried in vain to get Mary, Queen of Scots, to marry his 17-year-old semi-insane and deformed son, Don Carlos, in the hope of securing a claim to the throne of England.

Although there was some correspondence between Philip and Elizabeth in the early years of their reigns, it led nowhere as events began to overtake them and they became more firmly entrenched in their policies. Philip, driven on by his hardening religious convictions, sought solutions to the problems of power politics, while Elizabeth regarded solutions as too rare to be worth pursuing and sought compromises as they were more practical.

Prior to the Reformation power politics had been relatively unchanged for some seventy years. On the one hand there was the Holy Roman Empire, consisting of a loose grouping of Spain, Germany, Italy and the Netherlands, to which Henry VII had once linked England by treaty, and on the other hand there were countries like France and Scotland, which felt encircled. The rise of Protestantism had led to a Netherlands revolt, which in turn had drawn sympathetic England away from Spain. Calvinism in Scotland undermined that country's relationship with Catholic France. The Roman Catholic Church stood for the older monarchies, their aristocracies and wealthy landowners, while Protestantism was tempting the new 'middle' class with its aristocratic leaders in many parts of Europe. A combination of a reforming church and an upstart socio-economic class was a danger signal which disregarded national boundaries.

So far as Catholic France was concerned, thirty years of anarchy began dramatically when Henry II died during a tournament to celebrate the marriage of his daughter Elizabeth to Philip II. Subsequently Mary, Queen of Scots, was briefly Queen of France, before her husband died leaving a 10-year-old boy on the throne. Matters were not improved when the pope ordered fireworks and bonfires to celebrate the death of 30,000 Protestants in the Massacre of St Bartholomew's Day, 1572. So delighted at the news was Philip that he wrote to Catherine de Medici to congratulate her on having a son, Charles IX, who could order such a splendid event. In contrast, Protestant England was horrified, the event coming as it did at the time when Elizabeth was considering whether to marry the Duke of Anjou, Catherine's favourite son. This Catholic action by Charles alerted Philip to the fact that he could safely assume that any Spanish army operating in the Netherlands need no longer fear a French army at its rear.

The Netherlands were then Philip's chief concern. In 1567 he had sent the Duke of Alva (or Alba) to reduce the population to obedience by means of a reign of terror. This move had only succeeded in setting all the provinces against him as Alva had caused an outcry with his 'Tenth Penny' tax proposal. At the root of the problem was the fact that the Netherlands were a loose federation rather than a unified country, as well as being a heavily populated trading area. Revenue from them was essential if Spain was to be prosperous, as gold and silver from the New World were proving inadequate. The fact that Elizabeth I was assisting the resistance movement there did not help matters. The year 1567 had marked a

Queen Elizabeth I.

change in relations between Philip and Elizabeth as the employment of Alva's army showed that the Counter Reformation was on the march against Protestants. This soured the relationship of the two prudent sovereigns of Europe.

In 1568 Elizabeth seized four ships carrying 400,000 ducats to Alva, and Philip ordered an embargo on Anglo-Netherlands trade. She retaliated by placing one on Philip's subjects. As the Dutch lost more heavily than the English over the trade embargo, Alva was forced to negotiate with Elizabeth. However, when she demanded more than he had authority to agree to, trade between the two countries declined. Not until after the Massacre of St Bartholomew's Day, 1572, did they sign the Convention of Nijmegen to restore trade relationships and reciprocally not to aid rebels.

Philip was also faced with the pressure the papacy was putting on him to ally himself with its aggressive plans for Catholic revival in England. This he was reluctant to do as it would play into the hands of Mary, Queen of Scots, and France. Twice he stopped the pope from excommunicating Elizabeth – in 1561, after she had refused to receive the papal nuncio – and again in 1563. When the bull was finally issued in 1570, without consultation with Philip, he forbade its publication in his own states and did everything he could to prevent it being delivered to England. He wrote to his ambassador there, it 'will embitter feelings in England and drive the Queen and her friends to oppress and persecute the few good Catholics who still remain there.' To Elizabeth he wrote that no act of the pope had caused him more displeasure. We can conclude that at least up to 1569 Philip's relations with England were not motivated by papal action so much as by commercial provocation by English privateers such as Drake. This important aspect will be considered in due course.

Pope Pius V's Bull of 1570 absolving Elizabeth's subjects from allegiance to her on the grounds of her Protestantism and illegitimacy, could only be seen by her enemies as a licence to assassinate her at the earliest opportunity. Thus the very existence of Mary, Queen of Scots, posed a serious problem to the unmarried Queen of England. It had been intended to time the excommunication with the revolt of the Catholic Northern Earls the previous year, but Philip and Alva had both refused to help the earls in spite of Pius' pleas. Ten years later Cardinal Allen was urging all true Englishmen to purge their sins and save their souls by killing her. Nor was assassination an unused tactic in those days for Francis, Duke of Guise, had died that way in 1563 and Lord Darnley, Mary, Queen of Scots' husband, was to do so in 1567, followed by the Earl of Moray, the Scottish regent in 1570. The 1580s were to witness the assassinations of William of Orange in 1584, Henry, Duke of Guise in 1588, and Henry III of France in 1589. With Elizabeth having passed the child-bearing age, the temptation to replace her with Mary, Queen of Scots, was indeed considerable. Inevitably Mary became the centre of intrigue.

The Ridolfi Plot of 1571 was one such attempt to assassinate Elizabeth in favour of Mary. The plotters hoped that Alva would invade from the Netherlands to aid them. But he thought little of their abilities and only agreed to send Ridolfi to Philip at the pope's request. Philip concluded that the attempt was cheap to mount and might, if successful, bring a profitable return. But when the plot failed, the Spanish ambassador in England was expelled. The post remained unfilled until 1578. This spirited reaction by Elizabeth, as well as English activity in the Netherlands, made Philip realise that England was *the* enemy now that France was rent by civil war. Thus events were pushing England and Spain into conflict, though neither wanted the expense of a war. Already he and the pope were encouraging Jesuit priests to infiltrate their way into England in disguise, although Philip remained largely indifferent to the fate of English Catholics as their weak position could not serve his ends.

The situation was compounded by the growing activity of the up-and-coming sea-dogs, led by Francis Drake. Once John Hawkins' attempt to get himself recognised as an official slave-trader to Philip's New World had failed, the sea-dogs began to turn to privateering. Daringly they raided the ships, then the harbours and finally the mule-caravan routes, which brought the gold and silver of Mexico and Peru to Spain. It became increasingly difficult for Elizabeth to disown their activities. They were setting the pace, and for all her carefulness she barely held them in check. On the other hand she was well aware of the effect the Spaniards were having on the English cloth trade. The Spanish, Portuguese and Flemish markets were closed and the route to Germany blocked by Spanish control of the middle Rhine and diplomacy in Hamburg.

Consequently from 1577 to 1584 relations between Elizabeth and Philip were strained. Although she had stopped aiding the Dutch openly, she did not restrain her subjects from doing so, nor stop them privateering against the Spanish Main. When Drake returned from his world voyage in 1581, having robbed the Spanish on the western coast of South America, she knighted him aboard the *Golden Hind*.

She countered Spanish complaints by arguing that he had gone on an exploring voyage (he had tried in vain to find the western end of the North West Passage on the Californian coast), and that any robbery done was on his own initiative. Only a small amount of the treasure seized was officially landed, the rest being slipped ashore discreetly. As Philip was not prepared to take on England at this time, he persuaded the Spanish merchants who had lost out to sue Drake in the civil courts.

Meanwhile, alert to the growing might of Spain's most Catholic king, Pope Gregory XIII kept pressing him to invade Ireland and from thence cross to England and restore that land to the Catholic church. Don Juan of Austria, Philip's illegitimate half-brother, had told the pope he was prepared to lead the invasion from the Netherlands. In fact, a handsome man, Don Juan harboured thoughts of marrying Mary, Queen of Scots, and putting her on the throne. Philip was slow to approve this plan, and Don Juan died in October 1578, before anything materialised.

Two years later in 1580, Dr Nicolas Sanders led the so-called Papal Volunteers' landing in Ireland. The force was made up of Spanish and Italian volunteers, and in clannish, restless Ireland, it posed a serious threat for a while. A superior force from England suppressed it at Smerwick in 1580.

It was also in that year that Philip annexed Portugal so adding that country's overseas possessions and trade to that of Spain's. This meant he increased the number of his warships and acquired the ports of Lisbon and Oporto. The Marquis of Santa Cruz, Captain-General of the High Seas, was so delighted with this achievement that he offered to seize England and deal with all her sea-dogs. His offer was to be ignored for the time being.

Philip was already finding England a problem so far as his Netherlands policy was concerned. Two years earlier he had posted the Duke of Parma to the Netherlands to repair the damage the Duke of Alva had done in following his royal master's command to use the utmost force to oppress the people. The revolt which had followed needed a man of Parma's calibre to cope with it. He was a strategist and tactician of the first order. A man of great personal bravery, he was ruthless when the need arose. But he was also tolerant and humane to those he conquered, as he saw the value of such a policy. He was skilled at exploiting the human desire for titles, financial rewards, and so on. So with such tactics, as well as using his troops, he was slowly able to regain control of parts of the country. Resistance was led by the iron-willed William of Orange, until, at the sixth attempt, he was

Alexander Farnese, Duke of Parma; oil painting by Otto Van Veen.

assassinated in 1584. Philip had offered 25,000 crowns for his death on the grounds that it would be a 'laudable and generous deed'.

Ghent, Brussels and Bruges fell and Antwerp seemed doomed, when the States General in despair offered the throne to Henry III of France. When he refused on the grounds of the civil war in his own country, they offered it to Elizabeth instead. Although she refused, she did offer to step up her aid to the cause of freedom. Hitherto aid had consisted of money and volunteer troops led by gentlemen volunteers and soldiers of fortune, together with some naval help. Now, on 20 August 1585, by the Treaty of Nonsuch, she agreed to send 6,000 troops, including 1,000 mounted ones, under the Earl of Leicester. In addition she agreed to a loan provided that her army was allowed to garrison the fortifications at Flushing and the Brill, the most likely invasion ports. She accompanied this treaty by a public statement justifying her action, taking care to send a copy to the Duke of Parma. Thus, by signing the treaty three days after the fall of Antwerp to the duke, Elizabeth had changed the scene dramatically. She had saved the Dutch republic and shattered the fiction that the revolt was purely a domestic affair as Philip had maintained. The arrival of Leicester's army amounted to the first official act of English intervention in the war there.

Philip was thus faced with English harassment both in the New World and the Netherlands. When Drake attacked Vigo and Carthagena among other Spanish ports earlier in the year, Philip was alerted to the fact that his economic lifeline was vulnerable. Spanish mercantile interests were clamouring for action. Under these circumstances an attack on England seemed a sensible policy to pursue.

It has usually been assumed that the Armada 'Enterprise' which gradually developed in Philip's mind was solely to effect a military conquest of England. Clearly this possibility was of prime importance, but the over-riding aim of the king's plans was to stop English interference with his empire, in the Netherlands, the Spanish Main and Portugal. This could be achieved by forcing her to keep her fleet on the defensive and involving her in heavy defence costs. Thus the ideal was a diplomatic success brought about by the threat, and if need be the actuality, of war. If the English Catholics rose when the Armada appeared in the Channel, that would serve admirably. To that end the Armada must not only sail, it must be made to look even more imposing than it actually was. The inclusion of every possible ship and the exaggeration of muster numbers could supply excellent propaganda material for this end. In fact, a successful conquest could put Philip in dire straits, as it would mean he would have to cope with an heretical resistance movement such as he already faced in the Netherlands. Whether the papal offer of financial help, and the religious and moral credit he would gain in heaven and on earth, would justify that risk was not easy to resolve. Ideally insurrection in England, leading to the deposition of the queen, would serve his purposes, for it would leave his rival involved in a long civil war such as France was experiencing.

In fact Philip had already taken the preliminary steps necessary for such a policy back in 1583. Following the annexation of Portugal and Santa Cruz's enthusiastic call for a blow against England, he had told his admiral to estimate the forces he would need for the 'Enterprise'. Santa Cruz's response then was to produce a thoroughly detailed memorandum for a considerable force of some 556 ships, including 180 galleons, with 30,000 sailors and 65,000 troops, as well as a further

200 flat-bottomed boats carried by the larger ships. Among his list of ships required were 40 oared galleys and six galleasses, which had sails and oars. Provisions would be needed for 100,000 men for eight months. Again his calculations were precise: 373,337 cwt of biscuit; 22,800 cwt of bacon; 21,500 cwt of cheese; 23,200 barrels of tunny fish; 16,040 cwt of salt beef; 66,000 bushels of pease, beans, rice; 50,000 strings of garlic; 11,200 gallons of vinegar; 20,000 pipes of water; 46,800 pipes of wine. A pipe was a large cask containing 110 gallons, or two hogsheads; thus the wine requirement amounted to 5 million gallons, which in turn meant 55 gallons per person at the rate of 2 pints a day. This was four times the issue for English sailors.

What Santa Cruz was asking for amounted to about twice the requirements which had been necessary for the capture and occupation of Portugal, a task which had itself set new records in its demands on the country's economy and manpower. His expedition would cost about 4 million ducats, a staggering sum when one recalls that this would equal 3½ years' income from Spain's New World. Philip had noted on the estimate, 'The time has not yet come to discuss this . . . but I am ordering provisions of biscuit from Italy, and expediting the construction of galleons and the hire of ships in Vizcaya, and everything else which seems necessary in preparation for a favourable opportunity; and I am also ordering Flanders to be ready for what you suggest.'

Philip had alerted the Duke of Parma in September 1583 to the fact that an army to invade England might be needed. Wisely he had told his general, 'to launch the expedition in the sole expectation of assistance from the Catholics would be hazardous'. Parma replied in November that the Catholics in England were too weak to organise an uprising on the one hand, while the 'English Catholic exiles speak more from a desire to return home than with a sense of reality'. He concluded that Spain would have to assume no effective help would be forthcoming, and that consequently an army of 34,000 troops would be needed. Absolute secrecy would be essential if they were to prevent England organising her defences efficiently, and making alliances too. He pointed out that launching an invasion from the Netherlands would have the advantage, from a secrecy point of view, due to troops movements there being a daily occurence. He ended by stressing that he would prefer to finish the conquest of the Netherlands first as 'the possession of Flushing would facilitate the operation against England'. In mentioning this, he put his finger on what was to become the crisis point of the

Armada, namely a deep-water harbour where the convoy-protecting fleet from Spain could link up with Parma's army invasion barges. The absence of such a rendezvous was to prove fatal in 1588.

In 1584, Philip began to assemble a fleet. In January formal diplomatic relations between England and Spain ended when Ambassador Mendoza was expelled for his involvement in the Throgmorton Plot to assassinate Elizabeth. Gradually the king realised that Santa Cruz's plan to sweep the enemy from the seas and capture England could be linked to the late Don Juan's, which Parma had revised, of deposing Elizabeth by moving troops from the Netherlands. The Armada could sail from Lisbon to the Netherlands, pick up the troops and invade England. This would involve a smaller fleet than Santa Cruz had envisaged and so be more economical.

In April 1586, Parma supplied his estimates for his revision of Don Juan's plan, both elaborating and simplifying them. 'The substance of the England operation,' he wrote, 'consists in three elements; the first and principal one is secrecy; the second is security against France; the third is security in the Low Countries.' Working from these principles, he argued his case for sending veteran troops swiftly across the Channel in flat-bottomed boats on a single night, guarded by some twenty-five warships. Surprise would be the vital element needed in landing 30,000 infantry and 500 cavalry in Kent or Sussex, probably between Dover and Margate. He reckoned the crossing would take between eight and ten hours. As Dunkirk and Ostend were too shallow for embarkation points, he proposed Flushing as the best port. By using the army already in the field money could be saved. He stressed that 'mastery of the sea' was essential, and a powerful fleet from Spain would be necessary if the surprise element could not be guaranteed, otherwise his barges would be vulnerable. Philip's marginal notes on Parma's plan showed that he doubted the surprise element would work as the mustering of so many men would be spotted.

It was the demands of Santa Cruz's plan, and the appreciation that the decade was witnessing a continuous and expanding war policy, that made Philip see to the reorganisation of his Council of War in 1586. This long standing Council had shrunk to two members as no new appointments had been made since 1579. Now the king divided the over-burdened secretary's work between two men. Andrés de Prada, who had served with Don Juan of Austria on his campaigns, was made secretary for land forces, while Andrés de Alva, controller, and subsequently inspector of galleys, became secretary for the navy. When six councillors were appointed, it was significant that the long standing arrangement by which members of the aristocratic Council of State had a right to be on the Council of War as well was ignored. Of the six, only one was a member of the Council of State and two alone came from superior aristocratic families. In contrast, they were all highly respected military men. Together with their secretariat, they represented a significant shift towards professionalism. In 1588 Alva was to be sent to take over personal direction of the preparations at Corunna, while Don Juan de Cardova, a Councillor, was dispatched to Santander to take charge of 'all the affairs of the fleet and the ships, mariners and soldiers at present in the ports of Vizcaya, Galicia and Asturias'.

The Council was to concern itself with general policy, leaving specific matters to ad hoc committees (juntas), made up of some Council of War members, financiers, and other experts. The fact that these changes were made in 1586 shows just how unprepared Spain was for a large scale operation like the 'Enterprise of England'. Given this need for change, it is difficult to envisage the Armada as part of a long term and deliberate policy of imperialism. Instead it looks more like an ad hoc reaction to the hostility displayed to Spain following her acquisition of Portugal. This point is emphasised by the fact that as late as October 1585, when the secretary of the Council of War died, none of the changes thought necessary in the spring of 1586 had even been envisaged. One can conclude that as long as the king had little use for the Council of War he was prepared to leave it in the hands of the higher aristocracy, but that once he was faced with the colossal task of mounting the Armada, he acted in such a way as to show his full appreciation of the need to set up a fresh system based on expertise and careerism. This reform proved essential as from that time onwards the only person Philip dealt directly with was his Secretary of State, Don Juan de Idiáquez. No longer did the king's handwriting appear on Council of War papers. A feudal and proprietary concept of office gave way, almost overnight, to one of professionalism allied to careerism. Without that development it is doubtful that the Armada would ever have set sail at all.

As early as March 1586 Idiáquez had drawn the Duke of Medina Sidonia, Governor-General of Andalucia, into the planning team for the sake of his technical advice. He had alerted the king's secretary to the English tactics of keeping their distance and relying on long-range gunfire, among other things. At the beginning of 1587, the duke asked if the treasure fleets were to sail as usual in view of the priority the king was now giving to the marshalling of an attack fleet. Philip's secretary, Idiáquez, replied,

> The intervention of the English in Holland and Zeeland, together with their infestation of the Indies and the Ocean, is of such a nature that defensive methods are not enough to cover everything, but force us to apply the fire in their homeland, and so fiercely that they will have to rush back and retire from elsewhere . . . They are powerful at sea, and that is their great asset. Therefore His Majesty's Armada should not sail under strength but should be the largest and most powerful one possible . . . The objective of this Armada is no less the security of the Indies than the recovery of the Netherlands.

It was now clear to Philip that the 'Enterprise of England' could be the combined plans of Spain's finest commanders, Parma, the soldier, and Santa Cruz, the sailor. Parma's army was already the most formidable in Europe; some would argue the best since the Roman legions of old. Its professionalism had enabled it to cope with both garrison duty and fighting battles. Its composition was 34 per cent German, 31 per cent Walloon, 18 per cent Spanish, 12 per cent Italian and 5 per cent other lands. If 30,000 of the complete 60,000 strong army could be landed in England, nothing could withstand them. Elizabeth could not afford a standing army, and would only be able to muster emergency forces along the coast. After all, the force she had sent under the Earl of Leicester to the Netherlands had not proved very successful. The Earl had himself returned, leaving Catholic officers in charge of Deventer and Zutphen fort. Sir William Stanley, who commanded the former, took 1,200 Irish troops over to the Spanish side, while Roland York, in charge of the fort, did likewise.

Philip envisaged the Armada's prime function as one of ensuring that the landing force crossed the Channel. It was only to fight the enemy fleet if the necessity arose. Once the landing was achieved, the Armada could secure the army's supply lines to the Netherlands. This would also provide for a retreat in the event of that being unavoidable. The flaw in this plan was the duality of command it assumed. There would have to be perfect liaison between the admiral at sea and the general on land as the Armada sailed up the Channel to escort the army across. Given the problems of communication in those days, such a close liaison was highly risky. Philip was the sole co-ordinator, negotiating with each commander separately. Not only was he based far from the scene of the proposed action, but he never called either commander for interview, let alone did they ever meet as a planning committee. As events were to prove, they were unable to keep up with his frequent changes of mind either. The result was that neither commander really grasped what the other was meant to be doing.

There was also the basic weakness of not having any deep-water port available in the Netherlands area suitable for the Armada to rendezvous with the army in its barges. Parma referred to this problem frequently, and Philip understood it. As early as December 1585, he had written to Parma, 'without a port we can do nothing'. In spite of this admission, the two commanders never discussed the matter with each other, and Philip allowed himself to be satisfied with a mid-Channel rendezvous, or, failing that, at the 'Cape of Margate' itself. This was a foolish assumption as the Dutch and English shallow-draught flyboats would never allow the army barges out of their ports, while the Armada would not be able to sail in close enough to protect them coming out of those ports.

Parma had been thinking in terms of an invasion in October 1586, when in July of that year Philip told him there was no hope of it taking place before the spring of 1587. As it turned out, by that time Mary, Queen of Scots, would be dead and Drake would have sailed into Cadiz harbour itself. These two events were to spur Philip on even more with his grandiose 'Enterprise'.

CHAPTER TWO

The Armada is Prepared

It was in 1587 that Philip became more involved in the plight of Mary, Queen of Scots, then a prisoner in England. He had already persuaded her to write a letter to him disinheriting her son, James, in favour of himself on the event of her death. Plots to assassinate Elizabeth and Mary had failed. If such a plot had succeeded, France might have benefited from having Mary on the throne of England. Philip had not wanted to risk this. Her execution, however, favoured him. It meant that the two main claimants to the throne of England on Elizabeth's death would be himself and Mary's son, James.

Philip claimed that his family was related to Edward III, to say nothing of the fact that he had been Mary I's consort and possessed the letter disinheriting the Protestant James. To Philip's way of thinking, God's wishes and his own coincided. Now, just when papal support would have helped, Philip was faced with a new pope, Sixtus V (elected April 1585), an energetic and independent-minded character. Their dislike of each other was mutual. Sixtus once muttered that he found it strange that the King of Spain, who ruled half the world, could not tackle Elizabeth, who ruled half an island. Whereas Sixtus' policy towards England until Mary's execution had been a peaceful one, in the belief that Elizabeth could be persuaded to turn Catholic, Philip had noted, 'He is deceived about England and labours under a delusion.' Although he continued to admire Elizabeth more than Philip, the pope did make a guarded financial offer and give moral support to the Armada, when pressed, in July 1587. This offer will be considered further later on. But, looking ahead a little, it is interesting to find the Venetian ambassador at Rome reporting to Sixtus, 'The king and his Armada are becoming ridiculous, while Queen Elizabeth knows how to manage her affairs. If that woman were only a Catholic, she would be loved by us more than any other sovereign, for she has great qualities . . . That Spanish Armada gives us anxiety. We have strong presentiments that it will not succeed.'

If the Armada was to succeed, Parma had stressed the need to immobilise France first, lest she invade the Netherlands while his veterans were in England. The problem could be solved and he set about doing so. His method was to sow civil disorder by playing the Protestant Henry of Navarre off against the Catholic Henry III. On 31 December 1584, Parma made the secret Treaty of Joinville with the Guise family, so reviving the Holy League in France by giving it Spanish subsidies and outlining his programme for stamping out Protestantism in France and Henry of Navarre's hopes of succeeding to the throne. In the months which followed Mendoza made contact with Catholic revolutionaries and acted as Parma's paymaster to the League. So skilful was Mendoza at exploiting the religious and political divisions in France that the danger of France invading the Netherlands was nullified.

In September 1585, the pope interfered by issuing a bull denouncing Henry of Navarre as a lapsed Catholic and therefore incapable of inheriting the throne. For two more years the Huguenots fought for their survival. At the same time, Mendoza made Henry III more and more dependent on the Guise and Catholic party. He appreciated that timing was all-important, so he had to make sure that immobilisation reached its peak when the Armada arrived to escort Parma's forces across the Channel. In the event the Armada's delay added to this problem. But he did succeed in bringing matters to a head, when, on 12 May 1588, by a *coup d'état*, Henry of Guise took over in Paris and Henry III fled to Chartres. Thus Parma's western flank was secure when he marched his men down to their barges for embarkation.

Parma had also insisted that there must be security in the Netherlands before he could risk crossing the Channel. He planned to do this by leaving as large an army as he already had stationed there while the invasion was on. Provided he had sufficient money he could recruit enough men to make this possible. The real problem was securing a deep-water port. In the summer of 1587 he attacked Sluys on the Flemish coast. Although its harbour facilities were not deep enough, it did have the advantage of linking the network of waterways between Bruges and the east Flanders coast, along which he would have to move his troop-carrying barges. He had 200 boats at Sluys and a further 70 already at Dunkirk. He sent recruiting agents to north German seaports to get crews capable of handling them. Then, as soon as Sluys fell on 5 August, he began the construction of 15 miles of new canals to link it with Nieuport. In this way the barges would be able to pass from the

Scheldt above Antwerp to Dunkirk, where his troops would embark. The passage from there to Deal was 40 miles, and was possible in a single night. Anticipating the Mulberry Harbour preparations of World War II, he collected 20,000 empty casks at Gravelines to take across the Channel to make temporary piers on the English beaches.

He became increasingly of the opinion that good as this plan was, it was still essential to get a deep-water port. Flushing was the obvious target. But he was faced by Philip's decision to save on resources while the Armada was being prepared. In effect this meant temporarily running down the army in the Netherlands. The result was that Parma's army, which had been at its peak of 30,000 in September 1587, was reduced to a mere 17,000 by March 1588. Admittedly this was partially due to sickness and death. Once more he pressed Philip to give him the resources to capture Flushing, without which a direct co-operative rendezvous with the Armada would be impossible. Unless the Armada made that connection its role could only be a diversionary one. No doubt it would be able to keep the English fleet at bay, but that would still leave the Dutch flyboats free to sail inshore and attack the barges as they left the Flemish coast. Given that the construction of an Armada was known to England, he argued, only a false trail of peace negotiations would give them any hope of success when the hour came.

It should not be overlooked that the Duke of Parma was Philip's nephew, and a very ambitious man. With ten years' service in the Netherlands, he was undoubtedly the greatest general of his age. He personally resented the fact that Philip never allowed him to visit the Italian dukedom which he had inherited in 1587. Probably, he never believed the Armada would succeed and so did the minimum towards it. Inevitably he was directly involved in the peace negotiations which continued with England while the invasion preparations went ahead. So far as Philip told him, the negotiations were not intended to succeed, but merely to mislead Elizabeth. On the other hand, Parma knew the queen wanted to detach him from his royal master, and might even support him as King of the Netherlands should he want that prize. Moreover, his own claim to the English throne was as good as Philip's.

Meanwhile, from April 1587 onwards, instructions and letters poured from El Escorial. Philip had abandoned prudence in favour of impatient action. When Pope Sixtus, a shrewd but tactless man, made a casual offer of one million ducats if

Spanish troops landed on English soil, God's support seemed overwhelming. Parma hastened to press him not to break off peace negotiations with Elizabeth, but to continue them as a disguise for his invasion preparations.

> One cannot help feeling, and I for my part firmly believe, that this cruel act [Mary's execution] must be the last of many which she of England has performed, and that Our Lord will be served if she receives the punishment which she has deserved for so many years . . . For the reasons I have so often put before your Majesty we must be able to achieve our aims if we are called on to undertake any of the many parts which fall to us. Moreover, the aims of your Majesty as a most powerful and Christian king oblige you to try to end this affair as the service of God requires . . . Above all, I beg your Majesty that neither on this nor on other occasions will you relax in any way in regard to your preparations for the prosecution of this war.

So Philip pestered Santa Cruz to get the fleet ready. Ships and guns were ordered from Carthagena, Malaga, Naples, Genoa, the Adriatic and Biscay ports. Lisbon was the centre of all the activity which followed. Supplies were bought where they could be. The toll-fortress records of Elsinore show 377 shipping movements connected with ships from the powerful Hanseatic free-trading port of Rostock alone. In June 1586, for example, twenty-five Baltic hulks with shrouds, pitch and sails left Hanseatic ports for Spain. It is significant that they took the Northern route round Scotland for security reasons. They were followed by nine hulks from Hamburg with similar cargoes. But, by then, the English were alert to what was going on and they were all captured. The Hanseatic towns of Hamburg, Rostock, Lubeck, Wismar, Bremen and Danzig all played a vital role in supplying equipment. Their Catholic communities were only too keen to court Spanish favour as they felt isolated in the Protestant north. The greater the counter-Reformation effort by Spain, the more they would gain. Moreover, if Spain undermined Dutch and English trade this would be to their advantage. Already the Hanse merchantmen carried the German grain needed to feed the Spanish troops in the Netherlands. Norwegian pines for masts and Baltic iron ore were all essential.

Everywhere the king's agents made contracts for rope, sails, timber, food and everything else that was needed. All Europe was scoured for cannons, shot and powder. A price of £22 per ton was even offered for good quality Dutch guns. A lot of arms were bought in England, much to the annoyance of Sir Walter Ralegh.

But the Privy Council was powerless to do anything about it as no licence was needed to ship goods from port to port along the English coast. Ships could easily divert once their cargoes were loaded. Bristol merchants happily sold nine shiploads of culverins cast in the Forest of Dean, together with powder, musket and shot, routeing the equipment through Naples and other places. One Sussex ironmaster sold the Spaniards a hundred cannons. Gunmaker Ralph Hogge of Buxted in Sussex wrote to tell Walsingham that 'they say . . . that your enemy is better furnished with them [weapons] than the ships of our own country are'.

Nor was Philip above subterfuge in the way he acquired ships. When grain was short in Spain in 1585, he gave safe conduct to English merchants to ship supplies to Spain. When the ships arrived at Bilbao, he took the ships and their crews, as well as the corn. But one Foster, Master of the *Primrose* of London, suspicious of several boats full of 'merchant seamen' offering cherries to his crew, opened fire on them. He was right to do so for they turned out to be soldiers in disguise. In a stiff fight his twenty-eight crew fought off ninety-seven Spaniards, before escaping. Some way out to sea they found the sheriff of Biscaya clinging to the side of their ship. So they brought him home as evidence of Philip's treachery. As a result of the anger aroused in England, Drake was allowed to go on a joint-stock venture, which amounted to a warlike attack on Vigo Bay, San Domingo and Carthagena.

Then in December 1586 Philip ordered the requisitioning of large ships which put into Spanish ports, regardless of who owned them. Foreign ships were simply impounded when they arrived from Denmark, Germany, Naples and elsewhere, while others were chartered. Venice and Florence objected strongly to this high-handed action, but Hanse merchants were willing to allow their ships to take part in the Armada. The requisitioning did not deter twenty more German ships from entering Spanish ports. When the Armada finally sailed from Lisbon in 1588, twenty-three hulks formed part of it. They proved a mixed blessing as their clumsy design meant they could not sail close to the wind. Thus the Armada's speed had to be restricted to theirs, as well as sailing manoeuvres done which suited them. Medina Sidonia's General Instructions bore this out, ordering: 'Great care and vigilance is to be exercised to keep the squadron of hulks always in the midst of the fleet.'

Meanwhile it was decided to give a liberal gift of money to Scottish Catholics to rise up against the Protestant James. The Count of Olivares was told to get the pope's rather vague offer of a million ducats properly confirmed and add his blessing to the enterprise. In July 1587 the count wrote to say he had succeeded. The pope had signed a document to pay the money, but not until the Spanish army had actually landed. The count had managed to insert a clause in the middle of the agreement to the effect that Philip was to have the right to decide who England's next ruler should be. The pope had not spotted the clause when he signed it. It seems likely that Philip would have nominated his eldest daughter, the 21-year-old Infanta Isabella, as queen in the event of the Armada succeeding.

Besides Parma in the Netherlands and Santa Cruz at Lisbon, Philip made good use of Don Bernardino of Mendoza, his ambassador in Paris. Mendoza was the spider at the heart of the web, as we have already seen in connection with Parma's plan to neutralise France. Although the three had considerable correspondence with their king during the planning stages, none of them met each other at any time. Philip never saw his Armada fleet nor the army that sailed with it, nor any of his commanding officers. The fact that the post from El Escorial to Lisbon took a week, and that to the Netherlands a month, played its role in the events which were to follow.

Mendoza, the master-spy, was the only one of the three who was content with his role. He had a passionate hatred of the English, having been ambassador there before he was expelled for his part in the Throgmorton Plot to kill Elizabeth in 1583. He even paid 10,000 golden ducats from time to time to the English ambassador in Paris, Sir Edward Stafford, for bringing him his dispatches. He also had his contacts in England. But he felt he could trust no one, referring in his letters to his messages being intercepted by horsemen on the road, his agents being knifed in dark alleys, and others having to be put ashore in rowing boats in the night. Every week he sent three or four messengers to Philip. In his desire to gain revenge on Elizabeth, he was only too ready to believe what he wanted to hear. His paid informers sensed this and played on it. One weakness in his information system was that he only knew English Catholics who wanted to return home, who kept assuring him the time was near at hand. Consequently he kept impressing on Philip that the Protestants were no more than a minority in England, and that the majority, as Catholics, would rise when the Armada arrived.

In 1586, when the King of Denmark tried to mediate between Philip and Elizabeth, Philip wrote back to him, 'One should not ask me a thing like that. For if it is clear that other sovereigns do not allow their subjects to have a religion, other than the one they themselves profess, for reasons of state as well as for religious motives, why then should this attitude be denied to me?'

Santa Cruz was by now an elderly man. He had spent his lifetime at sea. In spite of this, Philip bullied him as if he was incompetent and obstinate. This was unjustified, as Santa Cruz was faced with the daunting task of creating an armada capable of the task required of it. He was to be frustrated in his first attempt by 'El Draque', as Sir Francis Drake was called by the Spaniards.

In 1587 Walsingham used some of the year's £3,000 secret service funds to send Anthony Standen, known as 'Pompeo Pellegrini', to Spain. Not only did Standen succeed in getting the latest facts on the state of the Armada, but he also discovered

Sir Francis Drake.

that Genoese bankers would not lend Philip any more money. This meant that Philip was dependent on the arrival of the treasure fleet. In fact that fleet did arrive safely in August with 16 million ducats aboard, equivalent to a contemporary value of £4 million. Before then a dramatic turn of events had taken place.

In April 1587, Drake set sail with 21 ships and 2,200 men 'to prevent or withstand such enterprises as might be attempted against her Highness' realm or dominion'. This voyage was soon to be known as the *Singeing of the King of Spain's Beard*, as in effect his instructions gave him licence to destroy as much of the Armada as possible while it was still in harbour under preparation. A fortnight later he attacked Lisbon, the port where the Armada was destined to gather before setting sail. At that time not many of those ships were there, and as Lisbon's defences were strong and he had heard there were more ships at Cadiz, Drake sailed on. So fast did he sail that when he arrived in the afternoon three days later, he found that only part of his squadron had kept up with him. He held a hurried council aboard his flagship, the *Elizabeth Bonaventure*, and decided to sail straight into the harbour at once. His vice-admiral, William Borough, strongly objected on the grounds that not only were the port's defences too strong, with enemy guns covering the narrow entrance into the harbour, but there were also a dozen oared galleys renowned for their skill at ramming their foes. But Drake ignored him, even to the extent of brushing aside his suggestion that they wait until nightfall.

At about 4 p.m. they sailed into the harbour where about eighty to a hundred ships, large and small, were being prepared. Some had still not got their guns or crews, while commandeered foreign ships were without their sails lest they try to escape. Thus, many were sitting targets for Drake's guns. Not so the galleys, two of which moved in to attack his ships as soon as they were sighted. In the open sea, before the narrow entrance was reached, it was not difficult to drive them off. But in the narrows and harbour itself, these galleys were bound to be formidable since they could turn in their own length and outmanoeuvre any sailing ship. As the guns of Matagorda Fort opened fire, five of Drake's ships sailed in through the narrow entrance. The majority of ships were anchored in the outer harbour, and many cut their cables to try and get clear of him. Ten galleys appeared to stop him. He quickly ordered his armed merchantmen to deal with the Armada ships, while he turned his four warships against the galleys. The fire power of the English ships proved greater than that of the galleys and in fifteen minutes it was all over. One galley was sunk and the other nine retreated.

Those enemy ships which were fully equipped were taken as prizes, while the others were set on fire. Drake's ships then anchored overnight and sailed into the inner harbour the next day. They destroyed one of the largest galleons of the day, belonging to Santa Cruz himself. This was not a difficult task as the ship had no guns at the time. During the two-day attack they had destroyed thirty ships and captured six. The Spaniards admitted the loss of twenty-four, while Drake claimed thirty-seven.

Just as he was about to leave the wind dropped. This was the chance for the galleys to come into their own, to say nothing of the masses of troops being hurried to the shore. But once more the firepower of the English galleons outmatched the galleys' single-gun platforms. A desperate attempt to tow fireships in amongst the English failed as their crews abandoned them before they were close enough to be effective. At midnight a sufficient breeze blew up to enable Drake to escape.

Drake then went on to Cape St Vincent and, among other destruction he wrought in that area, he destroyed many seasoned barrel-staves being carried in coastal vessels. As a result, good barrels were one of the deficiences of the Armada which sailed the following year. Finally, after another appearance opposite Lisbon, he captured the *San Felipe*, a huge Portuguese carrack, carrying ivories, spices, silk and gold to the value of £114,000. The total profits amounted to some £140,000, of which the queen took £46,672, London merchants £44,787 and Drake £18,235.

Although the 'head' of the Spanish peninsula had been given a 'close shave' by this *Singeing of the King of Spain's Beard*, it should not be forgotten that a beard can quickly grow again. Philip lost no time in seeing that it should, although the task of rebuilding the fleet was a gigantic one. By 1588 the monthly expenses of doing so had reached 900,000 ducats. Philip was helped by the extraordinary generosity of Archbishop Gaspar di Quiroga of Toledo who had given him 200,000 ducats in 1586, and a further 100,000 in February 1588. In fact, the archbishop was so devoted to the concept of the 'Enterprise of England', that he gave another 10,000 ducats in 1589 for a second Armada. One source of income for Philip was the 400,000 ducats a year provided by the *cruzada*, the 'crusade subsidy' which successive popes had made available to Catholic kings. Initially devised to deal with the Moors, it had become an anti-Protestant contribution from the faithful laity in return for spiritual benefits from the papacy. In 1585 the pope granted it for a further seven years to Philip. In addition, back in 1571, Pius V had renewed the tax on Spanish clergy for five years provided Philip maintained 60 galleys to fight the church's enemies.

The high cost of materials and labour was partially due to a contemporary price revolution, and to the Basque region being unable to supply sufficient raw materials for shipbuilding. Persistent inflation was most marked in the supply of timber and other raw materials due to their scarcity. Also, between 1580 and 1596, wages went up more steeply than prices, causing a double increase in shipbuilding costs. Moreover, raw materials from Scandinavia had to be imported in foreign ships as the Spanish ones proved unsuitable for transporting such supplies. The contracts were made more costly by the need to pay 'danger money' to the ship-owners who ran the risk of being intercepted by English patrols. Fearing the commandeering of any new vessels built, Spanish ship-owners had cut back on their personal building programmes. Consequently Spanish shipbuilding costs rose more steeply than those of her enemies. Both sides appreciated this. In July 1584, Sir John Hawkins reckoned them to be three times those of England. In turn this meant that English and Dutch offensives could be based on less expensive naval economies, and so the cost of attack was cheaper than that of defence. Privateering was the tactic used and it seriously affected Spain's war potential. On the other hand, these drawbacks were offset by the fact that the years 1582–5 had been the most favourable for trade expansion and the large financial surpluses of those years could be used. The acquisition of Portugal's ports and navy was valuable too.

From September 1587 onwards, Philip sent letter after letter to get Santa Cruz to sail. Conflicting orders poured forth leading to ever more confusion. In December he was even trying to get his admiral to divide his fleet into two Armadas. The first was to go straight to Parma with troops on board, before returning to join up with the second. When he discovered Santa Cruz was not ready, Philip simply ordered Parma to sail on his own. He then received the blunt reply to the effect that while Parma himself was prepared to cross the Channel in a longboat if need be, he was not prepared to send his troops to certain death, which would be their portion if they set off unescorted. Philip took his point and delayed matters.

When February came round, and the Armada was due to sail, Santa Cruz pointed out that he could not set out unless his men were paid. He had little chance to say more, for he died on 9 February. A few days later, his vice-admiral died too. It was a startling climax to two years of mismanagement and a mounting morass of administrative chaos. Though Santa Cruz was an excellent admiral in battle, he was no staff officer. Consequently many of his ships were still unseaworthy, the supplies rotting and his men disillusioned. The decision to go for a February sailing had led to a last minute chaotic loading of ships. Officers had grabbed what stores and guns they could for their ships, regardless of the fleet as a whole. If order was to be restored and the Armada sail at all, it was essential for the king to appoint an outstanding administrator, whose rank would put him clearly above his fellow officers. The problem was now an administrative one rather than one requiring a flag-waving admiral.

Who was Philip to choose? Naturally a nobleman was essential. But all leading naval officers were noblemen, though that could mean little as younger sons were entitled to the status of hidalgo. Santa Cruz, a minor noble, had started as commander of Mediterranean galleys before rising to the level of grandee in 1584. The natural authority of the higher nobility had been eroded over the years, but it remained where it suited the king that it should. Eminence did not automatically entitle one to the position of commander, as the Duke of Medina Sidonia had found in 1574 when he sought a high military post.

Juan Martinez de Recalde, a sea-dog and Admiral of the Armada, proposed himself for the post. He had served as second-in-command to Santa Cruz in a number of actions, and logically would be the obvious man to choose. But his pride was overbearing and he had had to be replaced on one occasion already. Moreover he lacked the necessary standing and his honesty was questionable. For rank and experience, the Prior Don Hernando de Toledo, natural son of the Duke of Alva, seemed the best choice. He had seen honourable service as Captain-General of Catalonia before becoming a Councillor both of State and of War. The drawback was that he would not have served willingly with the Duke of Parma, no doubt due to his previous experience in the Netherlands. Moreover the fact that he led the old-guard faction at Court which resisted the influence of chief ministers, such as Moura and Idiáquez, told against him. Another name put forward was that of the Adelantado Mayor of Castile, Don Martin de Padilla y Manrique de Lara, who had been Captain-General of the galley squadron in 1585. He had had both land and sea fighting experience and was recommended to Philip by Medina Sidonia. Perhaps it was the Adelantado's fiery temper which the king feared would jeopardize the tricky enterprise. There was even the danger that he might rush into a fight before joining forces with Parma.

Don Alonso de Bazán, Santa Cruz's brother, might have been chosen, for in the winter of 1587–8 the king had decided to appoint him commander of a second Armada of thirty-five ships that would be sent ahead to ferry 6,000 men to Flanders, if it was needed. But to promote the brother of the deceased commander would not be tactful and might lead to feelings of jealousy among other officers. When Santa Cruz died, his chief subordinate officer, Don Alonso de Leyva (or Leiva) was at Court. Earlier he had attracted the king's enthusiasm by offering to take the Armada to sea when Santa Cruz had declined to do so before 15 February due to the lack of time needed to prepare it. But it was the fierce debate which had followed his willingness to sail that now prevented his appointment. The President of the Council of War and Medina Sidonia had both sided with Santa Cruz in insisting that more time was needed. However the king did sign a secret commission giving him command should anything happen to Medina Sidonia, upon whom his choice finally fell. Because of the Armada's subsequent failure, this choice was to come in for much criticism from historians until relatively recently. Nowadays the reasons for Philip's decision are better understood and more appreciated.

Matters were now urgent for the king could not afford to lose a third fighting season. April was the ideal month for winds as August was too late due to the approach of autumn. The longer the delay the more Elizabeth would be able to strengthen her position, both at sea and on land. There was even the danger that the English ambassador in Constantinople might persuade the Sultan of Turkey to start a diversionary attack on the Spanish empire. James was not likely to resist English offers which would be fulfilled while Spanish ones 'merely entertained [him] with promises'. France was neutral for the time being and the Netherlands situation would be eased the sooner Elizabeth's aid to the rebels could be ended. Every month the Armada was delayed cost 700,000 ducats, and had the spin-off effect of depriving the Indies trade of necessary support. In 1587 the tonnage going out to the Indies was a mere 9 per cent of that of 1586. The ten million gold ducats poured into the Armada during the first three quarters of 1587 were simply going to rot as corruption, decay and disease bit into the Armada while it waited to sail. If Spain did not continue with her aggressive policy, a domino effect could result if it was felt in Portugal, in particular, that resistance would pay handsome dividends. Memories of better times under their own king, Dom Sebastian, were uppermost in Portuguese minds. Nor should Elizabeth's support of the Portuguese pretender be forgotten. Consequently a first-class administrator, with sufficient social standing and wealth, was essential if the chaos was to be overcome and the fleet set sail. Medina Sidonia was the obvious choice.

CHAPTER THREE

A New Commander

The peaceful life of Don Alonzo Pérez de Guzmán el Bueno, seventh Duke of Medina Sidonia, was shattered one February morning in 1588 when a courier from the King of Spain burst in upon him at his modest palace near Sanlúcar. The letter from the King's secretary was terse and to the point. The Marquis of Santa Cruz, present commander of the Armada, was dying and so the King had appointed Medina Sidonia Captain-General of the High Seas. He was to ride at once for Lisbon and sail to conquer England.

That so great an enterprise should be suddenly thrust into unwilling hands at such short notice demanded a reply. The unlucky duke appeared thunderstruck as he promptly wrote a lengthy letter to the king's secretary, stressing his inadequacy for the post.

I first humbly thank his Majesty for having thought of me for so great a task, and I wish I possessed the talents and strength necessary for it. But, sir, I have not health for the sea, for I know by the small experience that I have had afloat that I soon become seasick, and catch cold. Besides this, your worship knows, as I have often told you verbally and in writing, that I am in great need, so much so that when I have had to go to Madrid I have been obliged to borrow money for the journey. My house owes 900,000 ducats, and I am therefore quite unable to accept the command. I have not a single coin I can spend on the expedition.

Apart from this, neither my conscience nor my duty will allow me to take this service upon me. The force is so great, and the undertaking so important, that it would not be right for a person like myself, possessing no experience of seafaring or of war, to take charge of it. So, sir, in the interest of his Majesty's service, and for the love I bear him, I submit to you, for communication to him, that I possess neither aptitude, ability, health, nor fortune, for the expedition. The lack of any of these qualities would be enough to excuse me, and much more the lack of them all, which is the case with me at present.

The Duke of Medina Sidonia in old age.

This letter, stressing as it does the duke's seasickness and inadequate experience for the enterprise, only underlines what seems, at first sight, the oddity of the king's decision to appoint him. Why choose a man who had such a low opinion of himself and who had a tendency to melancholia? Was the duke as weak as his own letter suggested? His portrait at first glance seems to underline this suspicion. But the fact that it was painted much later in life, after the failure of the Armada had broken both his reputation and his health, must not be overlooked. In 1588 he was thirty-seven, sturdily built, with dark eyes which showed a degree of determination even if they did not exude the confidence of a natural leader.

More likely the letter was one written by a man of wisdom and courage who saw the impossibility of fulfilling the task demanded of him. He knew that the authority of a commander in those days was too often seen to lie in the degree of his aristocracy, rather than his professional skill, and suspected that it was his dukedom, rather than his personal qualities, which had led to his appointment. But he had not finished yet for he went on:

> Besides all this, for me to take charge of the armada afresh, without the slightest knowledge of it, of the men who are taking part in it, of the objects in view, of the intelligence from England, without any acquaintance with the ports there, or with the arrangements the marquis [Marquis of Santa Cruz] has been making for years past, would be simply groping in the dark, even if I had the experience. Suddenly and without preparation I would have to begin a new career. So, Sir, you will see that my reasons for declining are so strong and convincing, in His Majesty's own interests, that I cannot attempt a task of which I am sure I should give a bad account. I would be travelling in the dark, and would have to be guided by the opinions of others, knowing nothing of their good or bad qualities or which of them might seek to deceive and ruin me.

It can be argued that in his wisdom Medina Sidonia had spotted the danger that a man as inexperienced in such matters as himself would run the risk of making a fool of himself. His words give this impression, whereas they do not hint at the fear of battle or sudden death. In fact he had served with some distinction in battle, and had been responsible for fitting out fleets which sailed to the Spanish Main. From 1578 to 1580 he had been involved in the capture of Portugal, raising an army of 6,000 in Andalusia and helping Santa Cruz prepare a fleet at Cadiz, before taking part in the campaign itself. In January 1588 he had been appointed Captain-General of the Coast of Andalusia, which was a signal honour giving him considerable authority. For a dozen years he had been one of the king's principal advisers on maritime matters. His claimed ignorance of the Armada fleet needs to be offset by the fact that he had been helping behind the scenes with its preparations from early on in 1586. This work had involved him in inspecting shipping, making decisions as to which ships would be serviceable and which not, and ordering necessary repairs. He had also to ensure that they would be fully manned.

His virtual 'feudal' position in Andalusia was an asset so far as manpower was concerned, for his clients and relatives, and theirs in turn, would sail with him if he was in command. Troops and sailors would see his appointment as one in which a 'general of gold' had replaced a 'general of iron', thus ensuring their pay-packets would be forthcoming. This point is borne out by the king's letter appointing the duke when it referred to recruitment problems. Philip had written,

> The last few days everyone has agreed that we should announce that the galleons are to sail to the Indies, so that the men, especially the sailors, sign on with greater alacrity. *But now that you are to sail in the Armada* [my italics], it could be that things will take a different turn. Knowing that they would be serving with you and under your command, both soldiers and sailors might prefer to join up for the Armada rather than for the Indies.

The duke was already advising the king on naval warfare, arguing that galleys should sail with the Armada, and pointing out the English tactics which relied on speed, manoeuvrability and long-range guns. Thus he appreciated the need for an Armada which was overwhelmingly superior to the enemy's fleet. Indeed he was busily attending to the preparations of the Indian Guard galleons for the Armada when he received his king's letter of appointment. There could be no doubt that he was an expert in all kinds of staff work, both naval and military, having dealt with so many logistical matters and procurement problems.

His administrative ability had been proven by the fact that his advice on provisioning, recruitment and financing the fleet had been accepted by King Philip. Moreover he was the richest feudal landowner in the country. Wealth was an essential requisite of military command in those days. In 1574 a contract had nearly been arranged for him to maintain the galley squadron of Spain. He had been willing to accept payment on the bullion fleets, and not charge interest on any delays in their arrivals, which certainly favoured the crown. It was noted then that he was just the person to be relied upon to keep the galleys in good order and draw gentlemen from Andalusia to accompany him when he sailed. Subsequently he had contributed something approaching eight million maravedís to the 'Enterprise'. That had not been matched by any other Spanish aristocrat. However his estates did give him serious cash-flow problems which explains his reference to money difficulties in his letter. But the king too was faced with a cash-flow problem, and finding his credit was not being trusted. He had let his bankers down on several occasions and his unpaid bills were circulating with discounts of up to thirty per cent. Medina Sidonia's rent roll of 150,000 ducats a year would be valuable credit.

Moreover, the duke was unusual by the aristocratic standards of his day, for he was a gentle, polite and peaceable man, who disliked the political intrigues and violence of his peers. Thus while other Spanish men of good stock were keen to join the Armada for the honour and adventure of such a popular crusade, Medina Sidonia reacted to the challenge in a wiser, more realistic way as became his nature.

Spain's greatest admiral, the Marquis of Santa Cruz, died on 9 February, to be followed within days by his vice-admiral, the Duke of Paliano. The Armada's future was in jeopardy. It was not only the religious aspect of saving England from Protestantism which made Philip persist, but the continued English attacks on the Spanish Main, and hence his country's economy, which necessitated the invasion. An aristocrat had to be appointed, and Philip's choice was firmly made.

One reason for his choice was almost certainly the fact that Medina Sidonia was popular abroad. Whereas Santa Cruz had been associated with the annexation of Portugal, the duke was linked with that country's independence in the 1580s. He was welcome as his wife was half Portuguese and his family had had friendly relations with the Portuguese royal family in the past. Portuguese ports and ships were essential for the Armada's success, and if anyone could gain the good-will of that country it was Medina Sidonia.

He even had his contacts in England, having friends in both the merchant and Catholic communities. He had long taken care to protect the English merchant colony in Andalusia, which his ancestors had fostered, and had made indirect contact with the Earl of Leicester about buying tin and copper for his own artillery. Only a few years before the Armada sailed, he still had agents in England arranging the purchase of wheat, among other things. Much of his income depended on the prosperity of Sanlúcar, which in turn relied on trade with England. Periodically during the war the duke was accused of conniving at illicit trade with the enemy for his own profit. His Catholic contacts would help enormously when England was captured and he would have to represent the King of Spain. For either he would have to be regent in England, allowing Parma to return to the Netherlands or, more likely, vice versa. The long term view of the appointment to command the Armada was just as important as the immediate one of getting it to sea.

Philip's letter to the Duke of Medina Sidonia, 20 February 1588. The last eight lines are in the king's hand. They translate, 'I can but think that this letter will find you nearer Lisbon than San Lucar, since the confidence I place in you forces you to do no less. I trust in God that with this aid, through you, the task which is our desire and purpose to do will be accomplished. I, the King.'

It should not be forgotten that the main purpose of the Armada was to protect the amphibious landing of the Duke of Parma's forces in England, after collecting them in the Netherlands. Parma was to be in supreme charge when the fleet picked him up. But the king had become rather suspicious of Parma's keenness for the enterprise. Indeed he had feared that the unpredictable Santa Cruz might have challenged Parma's authority. With some relief Philip could now entrust it to the reliable Medina Sidonia. After all, his modesty would enable him to take orders from Parma when the time came. Finally he could be entrusted with secret orders should Parma prove unreliable in the event.

Why then had Medina Sidonia written such a letter? Partially because he wanted nothing to do with an expedition which he thought was a mistake, and was bound to fail; he would lose his reputation if it foundered. Also, he had long wanted to restrict his ambitions to his Andalusian estates. To command the Armada would take him from them and cost him dear financially. He must have sensed that Philip was pursuing his policy of breaking the greater nobles by taking them from their estates and dissipating their finances by the tasks he gave them. Medina Sidonia's power in Andalusia, the expansion of his personal military forces in Sanlúcar, which he had achieved by getting foreign residents to enlist to obtain tax exemptions, and his concessions to merchants which had drawn trade away from royal ports, had all posed a threat to Philip's power in the land. As early as 1582, Dr Santillan of the Council of the Indies had told the king, 'I am told the duke is making use of the authority he has from Your Majesty very much to his own advantage and to that of his vassals.' He went on to suggest he be employed away from Andalusia lest he become a threat to the king.

But the reply to the duke's impassioned letter was a further instruction to take command. 'I am certain that you will enjoy every success . . . that there is no reason for you to worry, and if you should die in this expedition I shall take care of your children.' The king added a postscript to the effect that he would have led the Armada himself if he had not been so busy! He encouraged the duke with the thought that the mission could not fail as it was in God's service. This letter reached the duke as he rode with his retinue of twenty-two gentlemen and forty servants along the dusty road from Sanlúcar to Lisbon, the road which was to assure him a place, heroic or foolish, in history.

In fact his appointment was generally welcomed. Hieronomo Lippomano, the Venetian Ambassador, wrote,

This nobleman is the first grandee of Spain; he has excellent qualities and is generally beloved. He is not only prudent and brave, but of a nature of extreme goodness and benignity. He will be followed by many nobles and all Andalusia. One might only desire in him a wider experience at sea, but all other possible appointments presented greater difficulties.

French Ambassador de Longlée commented that in spite of his lack of naval experience, 'he is one of the most capable subjects they have'. The Duke of Parma wrote to Philip to say that 'the choice your Majesty has made . . . is a good one'. No doubt the Court was surprised at Medina Sidonia's reluctance to take command, and Idiáquez had hastened to assure him that 'no one [has] more knowledge of matters of the sea than your Lordship'.

On arrival at Lisbon the duke found affairs in confusion. Arguments, abuses, lack of supplies, recruitment problems had all to be tackled. Just before Santa Cruz died orders had been given to prepare to sail so stores had been rushed on board. Some soldiers had no weapons or proper clothing, while some ships had more guns than they needed and others too few. Eager captains had hopelessly overloaded their ships as they seized what they could. One ship even had several expensive new bronze cannons stowed away as cargo, while others had shot but no guns.

Yet in a few months Medina Sidonia was to achieve more than anyone thought possible. He quickly formed his own council of war with leading officers such as Recalde, Oquendo and Valdés. Together they drew up a set of signals, sailing directions, fighting instructions and the formation to take up when attacked.

All the while Philip bombarded Medina Sidonia with instructions and advice from his monastic-style palace of San Lorenzo del Escorial in the mountainous country beyond Madrid. There in isolation the King worked out what he conceived as his Christian mission and detailed plans to achieve it. The building still houses the thousands of letters and documents he wrote and received about the Armada among its 33,000,000 documents. It seems almost unbelievable that Philip could be satisfied that he had devised and organised such a huge operation without leaving his palace, which in turn meant that he never saw the ships, the men or even the commanders. Never having commanded a ship, it was only too easy for him to make planning mistakes which simply had to be obeyed as royal commands inevitably were.

On the subject of recruiting seamen, he wrote to the duke,

The general opinion here lately has been that it would be as well to spread the report that the galleons are bound for the Indies, so as the more easily to recruit the necessary men, particularly seamen. Now, however it may be that recruits will respond more readily to the call of the Armada, than to that of the Indies, yet, as far as the sailors are concerned, I feel it would be well that they should believe the report of the Indies.

In spite of all the difficulties and the daily messages from Philip, the duke was able in four months to create the necessary central administration of key officers and prepare the fleet for sea. A big effort to careen and tallow the hulls of as many ships as possible was made, and all the available seasoned wood used to replace rotten timbers.

Hurriedly orders were issued to cast a large number of new brass cannons while others were bought from foreign ships which were in Spanish ports. Armour and hand weapons were secured and stowed aboard, and the gunpowder allowance almost doubled. The firepower of each ship was assessed, and then the available cannons and ammunition was distributed rationally. Santa Cruz had ordered an average of thirty rounds for each cannon, Medina Sidonia insisted on sixty for the Castile squadron and the galleys and fifty for the rest. Where necessary fighting castles were added, while new masts, rigging, sails and anchors were supplied for the ships which needed them.

Finally the ships were searched to see that no women were aboard. Thirty were found disguised in men's clothing. It seems likely that the outcome of this ploy was simply to result in the 'camp followers' chartering their own ship! There is mention of the *Urca de las Mujeres* being found on 30 June near the Scilly Islands rendezvous after a storm had separated many of the ships. Other references are made to such a ship in contemporary documents.

Then the consecrated banner, depicting the royal arms of Spain with Christ on the Cross and the Virgin Mary as supporters and the inscription, *Exsurge Deus et vindica causam tuam* ('Arise, O Lord, and avenge thy cause'), was borne between the kneeling ranks of sailors and soldiers as the papal pardon and indulgence for all partakers in the crusade was read out by friars. A homily was read aboard each ship denouncing all the offences of Queen Elizabeth and her countrymen, stressing that there were really but few heretics in England and that the majority were Catholics awaiting their liberation.

> Onward, gentlemen, onward! . . . Glorious to God, to His Church, to His saints, and to our country. Glorious to God, who for the punishment of England has allowed Himself to be banished from the land, and the holy sacrifice of the Mass to be abolished . . . Glorious to the saints, who have there been persecuted, maltreated, insulted and burned. Glorious to our country, because God has deigned to make it His instrument for such great ends. Necessary for the prestige of our king, necessary for the preservation of the Indies, and the fleets and treasures that come from them. Profitable because of the plunder and endless riches we shall gather in England . . . We go on a task which offers no great difficulty, because God, in whose sacred cause we go, will lead us. With such a Captain we need have no fear . . .

In fact a papal emissary reported that a senior officer had told him that 'we are sailing against England in the confident hope of a miracle'; he had made it plain to the emissary that such a miracle would be essential if the English, with their more effective ships and longer range guns, were to be defeated. However, the homily went on to say that

> There also will await us the groans of countless imprisoned Catholics, the tears of widows who lost their husbands for the faith, the sobs of maidens who were forced to sacrifice their lives rather than destroy their souls, the tender children who, suckled on the poison of heresy, are doomed to perdition unless deliverance reaches them in time . . .

Perhaps it was this homily which prompted an Andalusian army captain to write home,

> Pray to God for me that He will grant me in England the house of some very rich merchant. I shall raise my standard on it, and he will ransom it from me for thirty thousand ducats, so that I shall be able to repair my own house at home and live at ease.

Besides the priests' homily, two official documents were issued to each ship. The first listed the daily rations. Each man was to have 1½ lb. of biscuit or 2 lb. of fresh bread a day, and on Sundays and Thursdays, 6 oz. of salt pork and 2 oz. of rice; on Mondays and Thursdays, 6 oz. of cheese and 3 oz. of beans; on Wednesdays, Fridays and Saturdays, 6 oz. of dried fish or 5 sardines, with 3 oz. of beans, 1½ oz. of oil and ¼ pint of vinegar. The wine ration was approximately a modern bottle per man a day, while 3 pints of water per day were used for cooking, washing and drinking purposes. Such orders assumed the food on board was edible, which it was soon discovered not to be.

The second document gave the king's orders. Pointing out that all victories were God's gift, the king stressed that

> You must . . . exercise special care that such cause of offence [sins] be avoided . . . and especially that there shall be no sort of blasphemy. This must be severely enforced, with heavy penalties . . . With regard to . . . less serious oaths, the officers . . . to repress their use, and . . . punish offenders by docking their wine rations . . . As these disorders usually arise from gambling, you will endeavour to repress this as much as possible . . . and allow no play at night on any account.

While they were delayed by a strong head wind at the mouth of the Tagus, the duke took the opportunity to issue further orders:

> Gambling is a prohibited, forbidden game in particular and especially at night. It is well known what inconvenience and offence to God is caused by the presence of public or private women, I therefore forbid that any be taken on board. Every morning, according to custom, the ships' boys will say the morning salutation at the foot of the mainmast, and at vespers they will say the Ave Maria . . . and, on Saturdays at least, the litany as well . . . Brawls and other disgraceful activities . . . will be prohibited and no one is to wear a dagger.

The need for personal hygiene was stressed and clerics, servants and 'non-combatants' told they must put out fires and stop leaks in the event of battle. Signals between ships were listed, bad-weather watchwords (Sunday, *Jesus*;

The Spanish Fleete weighing Ancor from the River Tagus the 20th of May 1588.

Eight of hearts. The Armada sets sail; *Spanish Armada* playing cards.

Monday, *Holy Ghost*, &c.) were issued, and a rendezvous established if the ships became scattered. With the duke sailed his spiritual adviser, his confessor, and some sixty servants.

Within days a strong NNW gale was blowing them towards Africa. When the king heard of this he acted at once. Religious procession after procession was ordered. 'Our Lady of Atocha' was taken round Madrid three days running. Penances, fasts and sermons were organised, for which the king's monks were relieved of all other duties to carry out. The divine response was to make the wind fluctuate again and again until on 9 June it became favourable at last.

These religious observances were not only arranged as a petition for divine assistance, they were also part of the publicity campaign that Philip organised to unnerve England. For this reason he had a highly detailed summary of the fleet and its manpower issued, which will be examined below. Although some would regard such a document as 'top secret', with its exaggerated presentation of facts, its value as propaganda was greater. Indeed all this publicity led the historian Dr Colin Martin (in his *Full Fathom Five*, 1975) to argue the theory that the very sending of the Armada was a gigantic bluff. In doing so he paid tribute to the work of Dr I. A. A. Thompson, who had stated,

> Philip's overriding objective was not to conquer England but to stop English interference in his affairs . . . The *first* task of the Armada was to parade, to sail up the Channel and beat its chest before England's gates. What mattered most was that it should look imposing, hence the inflation of its size by including as many ships as possible, however unserviceable, and exaggerating the number of troops by issuing false muster rolls, all duly printed and publicised by an official propaganda machine.

This led Dr Martin to pose the question, did Philip really expect the Armada to succeed, or did he see its sailing merely as a means of forcing England to submit to certain negotiated conditions?

The fact that Philip gave Medina Sidonia sealed instructions to hand to Parma makes this bluff theory attractive. For those instructions were to be returned, unopened, if the two did not meet. They read:

> If the result be not so prosperous that our arms shall be able to settle the matter, nor, on the other hand, so contrary that the enemy shall be relieved of anxiety on our account, and affairs so counter-balanced that peace may not be altogether undesirable, you will endeavour to avail yourself as much as possible of the prestige of the Armada, bearing in mind there are three principal points upon which you must fix your attention:
>
> First, that in England the free use and exercise of our holy Catholic faith shall be permitted to all Catholics, native and foreign, and that the exiles may return.
>
> Second, that all places in my Netherlands which the English hold shall be returned to me.
>
> Third, that the English shall recompense me for the injury they have done to me, my dominions and my subjects; which will amount to an exceedingly great sum. (The third point may be dropped; you may use it as a lever to obtain the other two).

If this theory is correct, it follows that Philip had to convince Elizabeth that the threat of invasion was a real one. Hence the publicity campaign, including the 'leak' of the Armada's statistics. He also had to ensure that Medina Sidonia believed his mission was a genuine one. Probably the duke saw through the bluff. However, there is evidence that Philip regarded the *negotiations*, not the Armada, as bluff, as we shall see in due course, when we examine his letters to Parma telling him to drag out those negotiations until the Armada's arrival enabled him to invade England.

The late Marquis of Santa Cruz had been full of enthusiasm for the enterprise, envisaging a fleet of 500 ships and a total manpower of some 94,000 men. But no fleet of that size ever sailed. A publicity campaign was needed to compensate for this so, to unnerve the English, a document giving details of the fleet was released.

LA FELI
CISSIMA AR-
MADA QVE ELREY
DON FELIPE NVESTRO
Señor mandó juntar enel puerto
de la Ciudad de Lisboa enel
Reyno de Portu-
gal.

El Año de mil y quinientos y
ochenta y ocho.

HECHA POR
Pedro de Paz
Salas.

General Iventory of the Most Fortunate Fleet. The frontispiece, printed in Lisbon, 1588
for Pedro de Paz Salas.

❧SVMARIO❧
GENERAL DE TODA
EL ARMADA.

	Numero dNauios	Toneladas	Géte dguerra.	Géte dmar.	Numero d todos.	Piecas de artilleria.	Peloteria.	Poluora	Plomo quitales.	Cuerda quitales.
¶ Armada de Galeones de Portugal.	12.	7.737.	3.330.	1.293.	4.623.	347.	18.450.	789.	186.	150
¶ Armada de Vizcaya de que es General Iuan Martinez de Ricalde.	14	6.567.	1.937.	863.	1.800.	238.	11.900.	477.	140.	87
¶ Galeones de la Armada de Castilla.	16	8.714.	2.458.	1.719.	4.171.	384.	23.040.	710.	290.	309
¶ Armada de naues del Andaluzia.	11.	8.762.	2.325.	780.	3.105.	240.	10.200.	415.	63.	119
¶ Armada de naos de la Prouincia de Guipuscua.	14.	6.991.	1992.	616.	2.608.	247.	12.150.	518.	139.	109
¶ Armada de naos leuantiscas.	10.	7.705.	2.780.	767.	3523.	280.	14000.	584.	177.	141
¶ Armada de Vrcas.	23.	10271.	3121.	608.	3729.	384.	19.200.	258.	142.	215
¶ Pataches y zabras.	22.	1.221.	479.	574.	1093	91.	4550.	66.	20.	13
¶ Galeaças de Napoles	4.		873.	468.	1.341.	200.	10.000.	498.	61.	88
¶ Galeras.	4			362.	362.	20.	1.200.	60.	20.	20.
	130	57.868	19295.	8050.	27365.	2.431	123.790.	4.575.	1.232.	1.151

Gente de remo.

En las Galeaças.	1.200.
En las Galeras.	888.
	2.088.

De mas de la dicha poluora se lleua de respecto para si se ofreciere alguna bateria 600. qs. ——— 600.

POr manera que ay en la dicha armada, segun parece por este sumario, ciento y treynta nauios, que tienen cinquenta y siete mil ochocientas y sessenta y ocho toneladas, y dezinueue mil dozientos y nouenta y cinco soldados de Infanteria, y ocho mil y cinquenta y dos hombres de mar, que todos hazen, veyntisiete mil trezientas y setenta y cinco personas, y dos mil y ochenta y ocho remeros, y dos mil y quatrocientas y treynta y vna piezas de artilleria, las mil quatrocientas y nouenta y siete de bronze, de todas suertes en que ay muchos cañones, y medios cañones, culebrinas, y medias culebrinas, y cañones pedreros, y las nouecientas y treynta y quatro restantes de hierro colado de todos calibos, y ciento y veyntitres mil ciento y nouenta balas para ellas, y cinco mil ciento y setenta y cinco quintales de poluora, y mil y dozientos y treynta y ocho de plomo, y mil ciento y cinquenta y vn quintales de cuerda, y los generos de los nauios son en esta manera.

A 9

The summary of the *Inventory* - 10 squadrons, 130 ships, 30,000 men.

Via his Flemish correspondent, Meteran, it enabled the Revd Richard Hakluyt, the most famous geographer and raconteur of sea voyages of the day, to write at the time:

A very large and particular description of this navie was put in print and published by the Spaniards; wherein was set downe the number, names, and burthens of the shippes, the number of mariners and soldiers throughout the whole fleete; likewise the quantitie of their ordinance, of their armour, of bullets, of match, of gun-poulder, of victuals, and of all their navall furniture, was in the saide description particularized. Unto all these were added the names of the governours, captaines, noblemen, and gentlemen voluntaries, of whom there was so great a multitude, that scarce was there any family of accompt, or any one principall man throughout all Spaine, that had not a brother, sonne, or kinsman in the fleete; who all of them were in good hope to purchase unto themselves in that navie (as they termed it) invincible, endless glory and renown, and to possess themselves of great seigniories and riches in England, and in the Low Countreys. But because the said description was translated and published out of Spanish into divers other languages, we will here only make an abridgement or brief rehearsal thereof.

Portugal furnished and set foorth under the conduct of the Duke of Medina Sidonia, generall of the fleete, ten galeons, two zabraes [pinnaces], 1,300 mariners, 3,300 souldiers, 300 great pieces [cannons], with all requisitie furniture.

Biscay, under the conduct of John Martines de Ricalde, admiral of the whole fleete, set forth tenne galeons, four pataches [dispatch ships], 700 mariners, 2,000 souldiers, 260 great pieces, &c.

Guipusco, under the conduct of Michael de Orquendo, tenne galeons, four pataches, 700 mariners, 2,000 souldiers, 310 great pieces.

Italy with the Levant islands, under Martine de Vertendona, ten galeons, 800 mariners, 2,000 souldiers, 310 great pieces, &c.

Castile, under Diego Flores de Valdez, fourteen galeons, two pataches, 1,700 mariners, 2,400 souldiers, and 380 great pieces, &c.

Andaluzia, under the conduct of Petro de Valdez, ten galeons, one patache, 800 mariners, 2,400 souldiers, 280 great pieces, &c.

Item, under the conduct of John Lopez de Medina, twenty-three great

The Ships of Andeluzia, Comanded by Don Pedro Valdes which were 10 Galleons, 1 Pinace havinn in them 2400 Souldiers 800 Mariners, 260 Canons. &c

The Fleet caled Vrtas whose Generall was Lopas de Medina, had 25 Ships, 3221 Souldiers 708 Mariners, 110 Cannons &c:

The Fleet of Guypuscea Comanded by D: Mich: deQueur Consisting of 14 Vessells, and had in itt 2800 Souldiers 807 Mariners 311 Canons &c

The 4 Gallies of Portugall under the Comand of Don Diego de Medrana w:th 220 Souldiers, 212 Mariners, 200 Slaves, 100 Canons .

Four, two, three of hearts; nine of diamonds, five of hearts. The Armada as recorded on playing cards.

The Fleete of Castile whereof Diego Flores de Valdes was Generall, consisted of 14 Galleons and 2 Pinnaces, having in it 2485 Soldiers 1719 Mariners, 384 Canons.

Flemish hulkes [*urcas*, stores ships], with 700 mariners, 3,200 souldiers and 400 great pieces.

Item, under Hugo de Moncada, foure galliasses, containing 1,200 gally-slaves, 460 mariners, 870 souldiers, 200 great pieces, &c.

Item, under Diego de Mandrana, foure gallies of Portugall, with 888 gally-slaves, 360 mariners, twenty great pieces, and other requisite furniture.

Item, under Anthonie de Mendoza, twenty-two patches and zabraes, with 574 mariners, 488 souldiers, and 193 great pieces.

After this list he went on to give further information.

Besides the ships aforementioned, there were twenty caravels rowed with oares, being appointed to perform necessary services under the greater ships, insomuch that all the ships appertayning to this navie amounted unto the summe of 150, eache one being sufficiently provided of furniture and victuals.

The number of mariners in the saide fleete were above 8,000, of slaves 2,088, of souldiers 20,000 (besides noblemen and gentlemen voluntaries), of great cast pieces 2,600. The foresaid ships were of an huge and incredible capacitie and receipt; for the whole fleete was large enough to contain the burthern of 60,000 tunnes.

The galeons were 64 in number, being of an huge bignesse, and very flately built, being of marveilous force also, and so high, that they resembled great castles, most fit to defend themselves and to withstand any assault, but in giving any other ships the encounter farr inferiour unto the English and Dutch ships, which can with great dexteritie weild and turne themselves at all assayes. The upperworke of the said galeons was of thicknesse and strength sufficient to bear off musket-shot. The lower worke and the timbers thereof were out of measure strong, being framed of plankes and ribs foure or five foote in

An Armada galleass is shown in the foreground.

thicknesse, insomuch that no bullets could pierce them, but such as were discharged hard at hand; which afterward prooved true, for a great number of bullets were found to sticke fast within the massie substance of those thicke plankes. Great and well pitched cables were twined about the masts of their shippes, to strengthen them against the battery of shot.

The galliasses were of such bignesse, that they contained within them chambers, chapels, turrets, pulpits, and other commodities of great houses. The galliasses were rowed with great oares, there being in eche one of them 300 slaves for the same purpose, and were able to do great service with the force of their ordinance. All these, together with the residue aforenamed, were furnished and beautified with trumpets, streamers, banners, warlike ensignes, and other such like ornaments.

Their pieces of brazen ordinance were 1,600, and of yron 1,000.

The bullets thereto belonging were 120 thousand.

Item of gun-poulder, 5,600 quintals [100 lbs]. Of matche, 1,200 quintals. Of muskets and kaleivers, 7,000. Of haleberts and partisans, 10,000.

Moreover they had great store of canons, double-canons, culverings and field-pieces for land services.

Likewise they were provided of all instruments necessary on land to conveigh and transport their furniture from place to place; as namely carts, wheeles, wagons, &c. Also they had spades, mattocks, and baskets, to set pioners to worke. They had in like sort great store of mules and horses, and whatsoever else was requisite for a land-armie. They were so well stored of biscuit, that for the space of halfe a yeere, they might allow eache person in the whole fleete halfe a quinatall every month; whereof the whole summer amounteth unto an hundreth thousand quintals.

Likewise of wine they had 12,000 pipes, sufficient also for halfe a yeeres expedition. Of bacon, 6,500 quintals. Of cheese, three thousand quintals. Besides fish, rice, beanes, pease, oile vinegar, &c.

Moreover they had 12,000 pipes of fresh water, and all other necessary provision, as, namely, candles, lanternes, lampes, sailes, hempe, oxe-hides, and lead to stop holes that should be made with the battery of gun-shot. To be short, they brought all things expedient, either for a fleete by sea, or for an armie by land.

This navie (as Diego Pimentelli afterward confessed) was esteemed by the king himselfe to containe 32,000 persons, and to cost him every day 30 thousand ducates.

A more detailed examination of the muster taken on 9 May 1588, and published in Lisbon that year, shows how much roundshot, gunpowder, lead and match was issued to each ship. Front-line ships got over 65 quintals of powder each, while support ships got below that figure. Using these figures as a guide, Colin Martin has shown that twenty-three ships could be classed as 'front-line' vessels. They amounted to a mere 18 per cent of the total fleet; 37 per cent of the tonnage. This meant that they carried 43 per cent of the total of gunpowder taken. Strikingly, these same ships had 78 per cent of the 'gentlemen volunteers' aboard, the flower of the young Spanish nobility. This is not really surprising as it was obvious that they would want to be where the thick of the fighting would be. As a result they were in the ships which bore 57 per cent of the battle losses, compared to the Armada's overall battle loss of some 30 per cent. Some examples will suffice:

Ship	Tons	Soldiers	Mariners	Guns	Shot	Powder (in quintals)	Lead	Match
San Martin	1,000	300	177	48	2,400	140	23	18
Nuestra Señora Del Rosario	1,150	304	118	46	2,300	114	21	10
El Gran Grifon	650	243	43	38	1,900	48	19	15
Zabra Julia	266	44	72	14	700	10	4	3

Archaeological investigation of the wrecks off the Irish and Scottish coasts has recently confirmed that between 1586 and 1588 the forty ships of the auxiliary squadrons of Guipuzcoa and Biscay were replaced. Originally the squadrons were made up of ships designed for Atlantic weather conditions, but they were replaced by 'Mediterranean' ships because they were larger, more impressive and better for carrying troops and heavy field guns. In turn this reflects a change in the fighting plans, as in 1586 these squadrons were to carry light, mainly defensive armaments, but in 1588, heavy, offensive guns, including 50-pounder cannons. Consequently these ships did not have planks and ribs of four or five foot thickness, but were 'eggshells' in comparison. They were also 'over-masted' for Atlantic use. The result was that the battering the sea gave them was to pull their planks and hulls apart during the course of the long voyage.

The urcas, supply hulks, had largely been requisitioned when they sailed into Spanish ports, regardless of their owners' rights and wishes. Baltic-made urcas with two lateen mizzen masts were unable to sail close to the wind. They were also no good for fitting fighting 'castles' to. Some urcas came from Hanseatic ports. In all there were 23 urcas in the fleet.

The 19,295 troops aboard can be divided into a 'main body' and a 'remainder'. The former were arranged in five brigades (tercios) of heavy infantry (pikemen, arquebusiers, musketeers), made up of 3,000 men each under a brigadier (maestre de campo). The remaining 5,000 were for light skirmishing, pioneering work. The commander-in-chief was Don Francisco de Bobadilla. Besides his corps of regular officers, there were 214 entretenidos, who might be described as young men looking

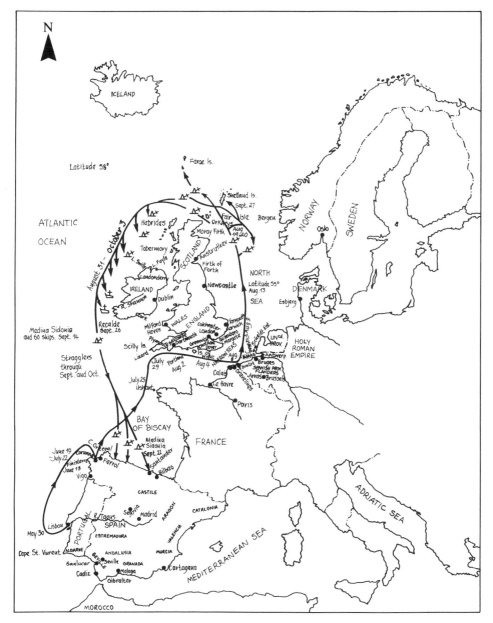

The course of the Armada.

for posts and receiving reduced pay, and 123 *aventureros*, young adventurers from noble families. During archaeological searches on Armada wrecks, 100 lb. lead ingots have been found. These would have been sliced up and distributed among soldiers for them to make bullets with their moulds.

The massive ships of the Levantine squadron, headed by *La Trinidad Valencera*, were crucial to the invasion plan. They have been described as mobile fortifications filled with troops, which were designed to combine the naval warfare techniques of the Mediterranean with those of Parma's professional forces. They were not so much warships as armed invasion transporters.

In short, the Armada as a whole was a cosmopolitan collection of ships drawn from the shipyards of most of Europe.

Within days of leaving harbour the Armada had demonstrated that it could not make any progress to windward. Tacking for three days, they had made but five miles. This was due to the high castles (fore- and after-castles) on the bows and sterns of the ships which were suited to a navy which saw sea-fighting as a soldierly business involving 'land' battles between ships right alongside each other. These castles did not affect the ships when the wind was astern – and voyages to the Spanish Main involved making use of routes allowing for winds astern – but with the winds hitting the castles at any other angle the effect of the sails was seriously impeded. Galleasses and galleys could use their oars, and pinnaces had fore-and-aft rig to aid them, but the rest, galleons and storeships (with temporary castles), were at a major disadvantage. The mixed fleet was faced with serious seamanship problems when sailing in formation. While some had to strain to keep up, others had to make an equal effort not to leave them astern.

Meanwhile below decks the soldiers, most of whom had never been to sea before, coped with boredom and seasickness in airless, stinking and dark conditions. The water was green, slimy and undrinkable. Dysentery was inevitable. The fact that most of the food was found to be rotten due to long storage aboard only added to their misery. The stores had been loaded when Santa Cruz was in command. The duke wrote of this to the king, begging him to send out further supplies as a matter of urgency. He said that he had written to the governor at Corunna for food supplies of all kinds.

The Armada waited off Cape Finisterre, which it had reached on 14 June, for days for the supplies to be ferried out. Nothing appeared and, with the wind being hopelessly against them, the duke finally decided to enter Corunna with some forty ships. The rest, due to enter the next day, were scattered by a violent storm which struck that night. To date, the voyage had lasted three weeks. However the loading of supplies could begin and the 500 sick be tended. As it was, recruitment to replace the sick and dead was essential. But when a collection of old labourers were rounded up, the duke was besieged by their women, demanding their release. Recognising the uselessness of such men, the duke acquiesced.

The state of the weather concerned the duke, who wrote of his anxiety to the king. He could not understand why God was allowing such bad conditions at the time of such a holy enterprise, 'considering how fervently the enterprise has been commended and devoted to Him'. Meanwhile two oared pataches were sent to the Scilly Isles to see if any of the scattered ships had collected there as the duke had said they should be used as a rendezvous point. On 30 June nine ships were found there and told to return to Corunna.

CHAPTER FOUR

The Armada at Corunna – The English Prepare for the Worst

On 24 June the Duke of Medina Sidonia wrote from Corunna the third of his letters to the king, and it is on this letter that historians have often judged him. While some refer to him as showing 'courage, intelligence, lucidity and honesty', others, especially Spanish historians, have seen signs of 'cowardice and defeatism' in its words. He chose his words carefully as the opening sentences show.

> What I am about to say is not an expression of my own personal wishes. I am not looking for any last minute excuse. Your Majesty is well aware of my determination and zealous desire to serve him . . . but this is what my allegiance to Your Majesty, my duty and my conscience force me to say . . .

It was clear that the weather had severely strained his faith in what the king interpreted as God's will.

> I am very anxious about the weather. In any summer, it would be remarkable at the end of June, but at this moment, on such a great occasion in the service of our Lord, it is even more extraordinary, considering how fervently the enterprise has been commended and devoted to Him. We must therefore conclude that what has happened has some good and just reason.

After reminding the king of his reluctance to take on the command, the duke stressed the terrible state his fleet was now in with regard to supplies, sickness and damage.

> I can see no means whatever of recovering from any disaster we may meet,

he declared. To collect enough ships to replace the lost and damaged ones would mean using unsuitable merchantmen, which in turn would leave Biscay, Portugal, Andalusia, the Indies and the Netherlands at risk. To emphasise this, he went on,

> I see very few men in the armada with any knowledge, or ability to perform, the duties entrusted to them. I have tested and watched this point very carefully . . . Sir, do not let yourself be deceived by anyone who may want to persuade you otherwise.

He made a sound point when he reminded the king of the great forces which had been needed to capture Portugal a few years earlier, in contrast to the force he now had at his disposal for taking the mightier England. He even went so far as to suggest that the pause in Corunna was an opportunity for the king to reach honourable terms with the enemy.

The duke's point about the ignorance of those entrusted with duties was echoed by Recalde in his letter to the king.

> I hear great complaints about the command of companies being given to young fellows just because they are gentlemen. Very few of them are soldiers, or know what to do.

It is impossible to tell today what the king's reaction was on reading of the duke's call for an agreement with the enemy. He simply re-emphasised his determination that the Armada should proceed. In so doing, he was also ignoring the Duke of Parma's recent report to the effect that his army was rotting away inside its cold, damp tents, as the increasing numbers of sick and dying made plain. He too called for serious peace negotiations.

Meanwhile, on 27 June, the duke held another of his carefully minuted council meetings. He put some positive questions to the members. First, should they wait in Corunna for the missing ships or go out to look for them? On this they all agreed: they should wait. Secondly, should they pursue their allotted task at once, without waiting for the rest? Wisely they listened to their statistician Don Jorge Manrique's analysis of the position. Twenty-eight ships with 6,000 men were still missing. Only 24,500 men were fit, assuming one deducted such people as senior officers, gentlemen adventurers, hospital staff, priests, cabin boys and oarsmen. If another 6,000 were deducted, it left them with only 16,000 fit sailors and soldiers. Furthermore some of them were sick or dying, while others had simply 'gone away'. Thus nearly a third were missing. The duke had already written that he had 'posted guards at all the landing stages and on all the roads by which the men might try to escape'.

Don Jorge concluded that it would be folly to proceed and all agreed, except Pedro de Valdes, that they should await the remaining ships. None dared voice the corollary that, if the missing ships did not return, the Armada would have to be abandoned.

The duke's third question was, would they estimate how long the food would last and what should be done if there was not enough for 90 days. He had told the king that

> Water, which has been my biggest worry, is being loaded as carefully as possible. I have twenty-six coopers working day and night to repair the casks that were completely wrecked in the storm.

Most of the food had been aboard far too long to be edible. They agreed that at the very most the stores would last 80 days, and recorded that a full report should be sent to the king.

On 5 July twelve missing ships, mainly from the Scillies, returned, and on that very day the king wrote insisting that they sail on 10 July, if they had arrived. But on 12 July he wrote more firmly still,

> It is my wish that you leave port and start your voyage, the day you receive this letter, without so much as an hour's delay, and even if it means leaving some twelve or fifteen ships behind.

The folly of such an order can be judged from the report of the ships returning from the Scilly Isles as they told how they had learnt of the great preparations being made for England's defence, to say nothing of Drake having 180 ships in three squadrons based at Plymouth and beyond Dover.

It was decided that the hundred-and-ninety-eight priests on board should hear every man's confession. Dozens of tents and altars were put up on a nearby island so that no one could desert after attending confession. In all some 8,000 were ferried to the island for a veritable 'penitent production line' absolution, for it was considered vitally important to renew God's approval for the 'Enterprise'. This corporate act of penitence the duke referred to as 'the most precious jewel I am taking with me in the whole Armada'. In a desperate attempt to make up for the sick and dying, the local nobility were pressed into rounding up spare manpower in the vicinity. Naturally those produced turned out to be old and feeble and, when their womenfolk came pleading for their return, the duke was forced to concede defeat.

Then, on 20 July, he reconvened his council and asked the thirteen commanders present if the weather was settled enough for them to sail. In spite of the food problem remaining unsolved – indeed it was not even discussed – they decided they had better sail. At dawn the following morning they did so, insofar as the feeble wind allowed. Not until the night of 23 July did the wind pick up sufficiently for them to leave Corunna finally behind them.

A confidential report shows that 131 ships carrying 24,607 soldiers and seamen set sail, with 1,338 officers, 1,549 volunteers, gentlemen adventurers and artillery officers, together with some 800 clerics, valets and servants. The food situation was better and hence morale was higher than ever before. If the chief victualling officer Francisco Duarte's instructions were carred out correctly, rations were 'handed to each man in person, in the presence of the ship's clerk, who would make a note of it in his books'. Count Olivarez, on the king's orders, saw the pope again in yet one more attempt to get him to hand over the money he had promised for the crusade. After pointing out that the fleet had now sailed, and that the expenses, already enormous, would go higher, he pressed Sixtus V for action. His report to Philip was one more blow. 'I shall not mention the question of money again to His Holiness. It only irritates him. He turns his back on me at the table and chatters away with less sense than a two-year-old . . . He has neither charity, breeding nor intelligence'.

In fact the pope was only too alert to the real situation for he had told the Venetian Ambassador, 'Philip's ships are worthless . . . For every step forward . . . they take two back'. He thought the duke was merely 'a fool'. Sometime later, when Mendoza, Spain's ambassador in Paris, had relayed countless rumours of the Armada's successes to Philip, the Count sought another audience. Full of the news of Drake's cheek and leg wounds and narrow escape, of seventeen, then forty,

Knave of hearts wrongly suggests that
the pope actually handed over the gold.

English ships sunk, followed by a Spanish landing in England and the 'Battle of New-Castle', he called on August 28 to persuade him to illuminate the Vatican and have the *Te Deum* sung. But Sixtus was not to be stirred. When the truth eventually emerged, Olivarez reported,

> Judging by His Holiness' attitude . . . one would hardly credit him with the sort of apostolic zeal for the suppression of heresy and the salvation of souls that his position should demand . . . Once the truth was known he turned haughty . . . and treated me like a slave . . . His ill will, and that of the cardinals, is such that under the circumstances it is positively heretical.

Meanwhile in England rumours, mixed with fact, were spreading. It was said that the Armada had orders to kill all males over the age of seven years, and that it carried torture gear for the Inquistadores to use, to say nothing of some 2–3,000 'wet nurses' to suckle the infants orphaned by the proposed massacre.

But England was far from defenceless. On 7 June Lord Howard, naval supremo, wrote from Plymouth to Lord Burghley,

> My good Lord, there is here the gallantest company of captains, soldiers and mariners that I think ever was seen in England. And God send us the happiness to meet with them [the Spaniards] before our men on land discover them, for I fear me a little sight of the enemy will fear the landmen much.

Before turning to an analysis of England's fleet, we would do well to consider whether Howard's remarks about 'landmen' were justified. In February the government considered 2,990 men on land and 2,900 at sea would suffice. But at the March War Council meeting it was decided that the Armada might land at any one of a number of places, including Plymouth, Milford, the Thames estuary and Margate, to say nothing of a possible invasion of Scotland from Flanders. Burghley thought the nobility and gentry could produce sixty men fit to be army captains and forty-five naval commanders.

If we are to understand what chance England had of defending herself in the event of an invasion, we would do well to look back to the general muster figures of the previous decade:

Source	1574	1577
English counties	271,578	298,068
English cities	11,193	7,570
Welsh counties	10,563	18,056
Total	293,334	323,694

In contrast to the statutory royal navy, with its permanent headquarters, ships and sailors, there was no standing army in Tudor times. Nevertheless the muster figures show that a third of a million men could be raised. So early in 1587 the Privy Council put the nation on a war footing. Lord lieutenants of counties were told to muster the men and start training. The actual work was left to deputy lieutenants to perform. The instructions given were precise and meticulous, though they varied from district to district. On 10 March 1587, a special warrant was issued to the Earl of Warwick, Master of Ordnance, to supply them with guns, ammunition and other equipment, from the Tower's Queen's Store. Thus the Earl of Sussex, who was Captain of Portsmouth, received,

25 cast-iron demi-culverins, mounted and furnished with ladles, sponges and rammers; 7 cast-iron sakers mounted and equipped with similar furniture of which two were to be on wheels shod with iron; 4 brass port-pieces with two chambers a-piece; 28 forged iron port-pieces with two chambers a-piece; 625 round iron shot for demi-culverins; 175 round shot for sakers; 14 cross-barred shot for shakers; 50 cross-barred shot for demi-culverins; 480 stone shot for port-pieces; 3 lasts of common corn powder and 3 coils of breeching rope.

The Earl of Warwick also got orders to make identical issues to Kent, Sussex, Southampton, Dorset, Devon and Cornwall consisting of '2 sakers, 2 minions and 2 cast-iron falcons; in all 36 pieces well mounted on iron-shod wheeled carriages furnished with ladles, sponges, rammers and other necessities incident for travel and service, together with 36 spare axle-trees; 36 spare wheels shod with iron; 720 shot or bullets' as well as powder, lead and match.

Then in March 1588 the Queen informed the Lord Mayor and Corporation of London that the kingdom had to be mobilised, and for the City this meant furnishing 10,000 men equipped with arms and armour. The Privy Council repeated the order on 10 March, asking the Lord Mayor to have the men ready within the City; 6,000 were to be enrolled and the rest to undergo training forthwith. Further action was taken on 12 April when Sir John Norris and others were ordered to make anti-invasion plans with the lord lieutenants of the coastal counties. Secrecy was to be observed and a pioneer corps was to be assembled with scythes, bill-hooks and pitch-forks to strengthen defences.

Wisely the Privy Council required returns to be sent in of all able-bodied men, both trained and untrained, armed and unarmed, so that a true picture of the strength of the emergency force could be estimated. The footsoldiers were now listed under the headings of corselets, bows, bills, calivers and muskets, according to their equipment, and the cavalry under similar headings of lances, light-horse and petronels. Returns from London showed that the total number of fit men, aged 17–60, came to 17,083. It was decided to make up four regiments of 1,500 men each from this list.

Local authorities and individuals, according to their income, were required to supply men and equipment. A combination of nobles and gentlemen offered to supply 3,058 horse and foot, while Gloucester sent 300 infantry and 25 light horse, for example. Together with Tewkesbury, the city also supplied a ship and a pinnace for the fleet. In Mary I's reign a man worth £1,000 or more a year had to produce 16 horses, 40 pikes, 60 suits of light armour, 20 halberds, 20 arquebuses, 50 iron helmets and 30 sets of bows and arrows. If a wife had a gown with velvet on it or a silk petticoat, her husband was assessed as worth 100 marks (£70) and had to supply a horse. The clergy were not exempt. The Bishop of Winchester volunteered to raise a company of infantry and one of cavalry on behalf of his diocese. But the Privy Council complained to the Archbishop of Canterbury that many clergy were slow to equip the light cavalry expected of them. He was told to

VI

Arthur Ld Grey, Sr Francis
Knolles, Sr Iohn Norris,
Sr Richard Bingham, Sr Rog
Williams & others in a Councell
of War, consulting how y^e land
Seruice should be Ordered

VII

The Army of 20000 Sout-
diers laid along y^e Southern
Coast of England.

King

The Army appointed to
guard the Queenes persson &
consisting of 24000 Foot, and 2000
Horse, where of the Lord
Hunsdon was Generall

King

The Army of 1000 horse, and
22000 Foot, which y^e Earle of
Leicester comanded when hee
Pitched his Tents att Tilbury

Six of diamonds depicts a planning meeting between senior officers. 'Black' John Norris was in charge of the veteran mercenaries in Devon and Cornwall. Seven of diamonds refers to the deployment of troops. King of diamonds deals with the Queen's protection. Lord Hunsdon was the Lord Chamberlain. King of hearts shows the arrival of the Earl of Leicester's forces at Tilbury.

raise part of the queen's bodyguard, which he did by an appeal to his clergy which resulted in 560 cavalrymen. In all the clergy pledged 4,444 men. The training and placing of men in the right positions went on apace. On 2 April, four thousand were brought to London from inland counties for training.

Spy de Vega reported on 27 May that,

> the 6,000 men raised in London meet for drill twice a week. They are certainly very good troops seeing that they are recruits, and are well-armed. They are commanded by merchants as are also the ships contributed by London and other ports . . . The troops are dividied into 40 companies of 150 each . . . In London they are drawing 50 men from each parish at the cost of the city to send on board the ships; 4,000, they say, being obtained in this way. They give each man of them a blue coat, whilst those who remain here receive red ones.

Officers wore black velvet. Walsingham offered the London bands corselets from Norfolk, but they wanted to buy their own from Mr Hopkins in the Minories. They were prepared to pay him at the rate of 3s. if he would work through the night for them.

The Earl of Essex was put in charge of 13,062 infantry and 300 horse, with the promise of 4,000 more to come. The queen herself was to be defended by 2,000 men. By July it was considered 14,000 men would be needed. London parishes were told to supply 50 men each to produce 4,000 for the navy. The need to station 3,000 troops on the Isle of Wight was appreciated.

To keep lord lieutenants on their toes, the Privy Council informed them on 15 June that the Armada was already in the Bay of Biscay, and that consequently invasion was now a real possibility. All commanding officers were to remain in their shires and make sure that their men could turn out at an hour's notice. As a further security measure provost-marshals were appointed to round up vagabonds and other suspicious characters to prevent any possible acts of sabotage.

An early warning system, which operated almost at the speed of light, was the beacon system. This signal system, which was centred on the Isle of Wight, was capable of sending three different messages. There were groups of three beacons at each end of the island. The firing of a single beacon in either group warned the coastal defences to be on the alert. It was not repeated to other stations. But if two were lit, all the beacon stations in Hampshire, Wiltshire, Dorsetshire and Sussex were to fire one of their two beacons to alert troops in those counties. If all three were lit on the Isle, all the two-beacon stations of the four counties were to light theirs to alert the stations in Oxfordshire, Berkshire, Gloucestershire and Somersetshire. Their fires would in turn be seen by counties further inland. To ensure that the system was not misused a magistrate had to authorise the lighting of any beacon. The parish accounts of Launceston, near Drake's birthplace, record: 'Paid to Jasper Bedlime to warn the parish that they should be ready at an hour's warning, 11*d*.' However the normal rate was 8*d*. a day, with the insistance that no watcher was allowed to keep a dog with him lest it distract him. Moreover no seats were to be fitted in any weather-protection huts that might be erected for fear the occupants would fall asleep. On the Isle of Wight the drill to be followed when the alarm was given, was for one watcher to rush off to ring the church bells, while the other alerted the nearest magistrate. Soldiers would then be ferried across to the island in thirty-seven boats which were capable of taking 1,186 men at a crossing.

On 27 June the Privy Council instructed the lord lieutenants to divide their men into two groups, a striking force and a defence force. The former was to garrison sea-coast defences to repel invasion, while the latter should join the special force allocated to protect the queen herself. The resulting two armies were to be known as 'The Army drawn up to engage the enemy' and 'The Army formed to protect her Majesty's person'. To ensure that there were no arguments about who was in command, the Earl of Leicester was appointed as the 'Lieutenant-General of her Majesty's Forces in the South parts'. This put him in charge of 23,000 foot, 2,765 horse and 4,892 pioneers. Of course forces were still left in their own counties.

On 23 July the Privy Council informed the lord lieutenants that a landing was expected in Essex, and that the Earl of Leicester had gone there. This necessitated some troop concentrations at Brentford and Stratford-by-Bow for the defence of the Thames estuary. This meant assembling a total of 1,049 horse and 11,000 foot there, in addition to 6,000 men from Kent assembled at Sandwich. The latter, based largely at Dover, were raw recruits and they deserted in large numbers when news came that the Armada had been sighted off Calais. This move was certainly backed up by the fact that they had not been paid.

Tilbury was the site of the army assigned to defend the Thames estuary. By July 10,000 troops had arrived there. But when they were joined by Essex's 4,000, the

. A. MAP of the BEACONS in KENT, as they where appointed by the Lᵈ Lieut of the County, in the Year 1588, when the descent of the Spaniards was expected

A Scale of Miles

Map of Kent showing the position of the beacons. The lines indicate how signals could be passed on.

Earl of Leicester complained bitterly that they had not brought their own beer and bread. He said he was more 'cook, caterer and huntsman' than captain-general. A royal proclamation fixed food, horse-meat and lodging prices within a 20 mile radius of the camp. For example, 'a fat pig, the best in the market – 14*d.* [6½p]; a couple of chickens – 8*d.* [3p]; a dozen pigeons – 18*d.* [7½p]; a full quart of good single ale or beer – ½*d.* [¼p]', while a soldier's supper, which was to include on the menu boiled beef, mutton, veal or lamb, was 3*d.* [1p]. A night's lodging on a feather bed was fixed at 1*d.* [½p].

The defences for Tilbury, where the Privy Council expected the invasion to be targeted, were not begun until as late as 3 August. Between Gravesend and Tilbury Fort a boom was fixed at a cost of £2,087. It consisted of an anchored string of barges, reinforced by ships' masts as stakes. However, it broke under its own weight at the first flood tide.

In August the Lord Chamberlain, Lord Hunsdon, was appointed Lieutenant-General of the 'Army to protect her Majesty's person'. Sir Henry Cromwell's horse wore straw-coloured uniforms, while those of Huntingdon's infantry were 'light popinjay green' and the Earl of Essex's lancers', orange. Hearing of the establishment of this army, the gout-ridden Earl of Shrewsbury hastened to assure the queen that though he was 'lame in body yet lusty in heart', he hoped he could strike a blow for her still. He reminded her that three years earlier she had freed him from the two she-devils he hated most, Mary, Queen of Scots, and his wife. Documents still existing today give conflicting accounts as to exactly how many men formed this army. The nearest figures seem to be 4,081 horse and 41,381 foot, so that both armies put together numbered 5,130 horse and 58,381 foot. A grant of £20,000 was made to cover the upkeep of both armies.

Would these measures have proved effective? Spanish orders were clear. They were to land at Margate and take London by storm, hopefully seizing the queen and her ministers there. It was believed that Catholics in the north and west, as well as in Ireland, would rise up and aid them. There was an alternative plan to cope with the absence of any such uprising, or if London could not be taken, which involved the Duke of Parma forcing Elizabeth to make concessions. Thus while the English forces were finally concentrated at Tilbury in Essex, the Armada army prepared to invade at Margate in Kent. It is strange that the Privy Council had not seriously considered the possibility of invasion there, for the Romans, Saxons and Danes had all landed at this point in the past.

Devon's defences: part of an engraving by J. Pine, after H. Gravelot, showing the defences of Cornwall and Devon.

Sir Walter Ralegh, writing a mere twenty-five years after the Armada sailed, was convinced that the English were 'of no such force as to encounter an Armie like unto that, wherewith it was intended that the prince of Parma should have landed in England'. This is not surprising considering the Spanish army in the Low Countries was a highly professional one which had been on active service since 1572. An assault force of 17,000 Spaniards, Italians, Burgundians, Germans, Walloons and English Catholic exiles, was awaiting the arrival of Medina Sidonia's ships. The mixture of nationalities did not mean they were a motley crowd; far from it, they were in fact the cream of the most formidable European army of their day. That much was admitted by Sir Roger Williams, when he wrote from his four years' experience of them in the Netherlands, 'To speake troth, no Armie that ever I saw, passes that of the Duke de Parma for discipline and good order'. Not a particularly encouraging statement to come from the third in command of the army at Tilbury. His fears were echoed by the Earl of Leicester himself when he informed Lord Burghley that they were 'ye best soldyers at this day in Christendom'. An eye-witness commented that they were 'powerful men, well-armed and of martial aspect, highly trained and always ready to obey and fight'. They were led by experienced officers who had risen from the ranks and so held the respect of their men.

With regard to the troops on board the Armada itself, they were essentially Spanish in composition. Five heavy infantry brigades (*tercios*) were each commanded by a colonel (*maestro de campo*). Thirty-two companies of light troops were divided into platoons of 100 each.

Such a frightening assessment of the odds against the English rudimentary army gathered to await the arrival of this force must be offset by the weaknesses this invading army also contained. While it was true that it contained fine soldiers of long experience, this could not be said of all its members. Furthermore, the duke would not be so foolish as to leave any of his best men behind to keep the Dutch under control. The winter of 1587–8 had also taken its toll, for, housed in temporary lodgings in cold conditions and short of food, following the devastation of the land from the bitter fighting, it had had its effect on the army. The facts speak for themselves on this point. The 2,662-strong regiment of Don Antonio de Zuniga, assembled for the 'Enterprise of England' in July 1587, was down to 1,500 by the following April. In a similar way, the 9,017 extremely well-equipped Italians who had marched to the Netherlands in the summer of 1587 to join in the invasion had, within six months of arriving there, been reduced to a mere 3,615. Death, disease and desertion had accounted for the remainder.

At first sight, Parma also seemed to lack sufficient siege artillery. Had he had it, the flyboats and barges would have been scarcely capable of transporting it across the Channel for him. This seeming deficiency was offset by Philip having ensured that the Armada carried some forty-eight 50-pounder siege guns. Moreover these guns were carried by ships with derricks capable of unloading them into large lighters. Had these guns been landed they would have made short work of the town and castle walls of England, which left much to be desired, dating back as they did to medieval times. Rochester Castle's walls, for example, were completely decayed. The only strongly defended sites were those Henry VIII had seen to, namely the Sandown, Deal, Walmer, Sandgate and Camber forts and a further five along the Thames estuary. But these only had thin circular walls and the Spanish siege train could have tackled anything short of wide moats round solid quadrilateral bastions such as Upnor Castle, which defended Chatham dockyard, alone possessed. Margate, where the Armada would have landed, had no defence system at all, which suggested Philip knew England's defences only too well. No doubt he had had ample personal opportunity to take stock of them when he was consort to Mary I.

In contrast the west country seems to have been well fortified to judge from a contemporary map in the Cottonian MSS, which suggests an almost continuous defence line from Land's End, as well as west of Falmouth to Plymouth and Dodman Point.

From a financial point of view Parma's army had all it needed, and would have received adequate funds to hold England once the invasion had been effected. Consequently, had the army got ashore, they could have covered the eighty miles from Margate to London in about a week, judging by the speed with which they had invaded other lands in the past. There would have been no problem about food supplies as the Kent farmers would have just finished harvesting at that time. London's medieval walls would have presented little problem to them. After all, they had captured Antwerp, with its far better defences, in 1585.

Parma would have been well aware of the importance of the morale and leadership of forces defending home towns. The strength of a town's fortifications could come second to the determination, or lack of it, of a town's garrison. Besides the train bands, they would be garrisoned by 4,000 troops, withdrawn from the

Netherlands because of their recent experience in battle. Provided, that is, they could be really trusted. For fresh in the memory was the fact that as recently as January 1587, Captain Roland York and Sir William Stanley, with their 700 men, had defected to Spain when they betrayed their defence of Deventer and Zutphen. The quartermaster-general to the 4,000 was Roland's brother. Moreover, not only were there not enough defenders, but they were not stationed at the area targeted by the Spanish for their landing. The English commander in Kent admitted that the Isle of Thanet, a prime Spanish target, though this was unknown to him, was virtually undefended. The reason he gave was alarming enough, for he reported that the local officer in charge was absent from his place of duty. Furthermore it was no good assuring the public that the Isle of Wight was well defended, if the enemy had no intention of landing there.

This raises the question of why were England's defences so disorganised, given all the activity stemming from the orders given by the Privy Council. Part of the answer must lie in the fact that the Earl of Leicester, as commander-in-chief, had no power to issue orders to troops outside Essex before 2 August. This drawback was added to by the fact that while he was elsewhere arguments over the necessary strategy to pursue had occurred between Sir John Norris, in charge of defence precautions in the south-east, and the local commander in Kent, Sir Thomas Scott. With the Armada sailing steadily up the Channel to Calais, Sir Thomas was still arguing his case for spreading out his men along the beaches in contrast to Sir John's argument that it would be better to concentrate forces at Canterbury, while leaving a mere token force on the beaches. While Sir Thomas argued for preventing a landing being secured, Sir John pointed out that this was wishful thinking and that a stand further inland was the solution. On 18 July the government accepted Scott's view, giving an order on the same day for forces in Kent to move to the beaches. But this did not mean the order was a final one.

Behind this argument lay the fact that the country simply could not afford to perfect defence plans earlier because, on the one hand overseas bankers were convinced the Spaniards would capture England, and on the other a trade recession meant that loans could not be raised at home. Thus if Parma had managed to land, probably on 8 August, he would have been met by a motley collection of men who lacked clear orders. Having swept those aside, he would have found the towns he approached poorly fortified and thus London within reach.

But an invaded country can fight beyond all expectation as resistance to Nazi

Germany showed in the Second World War. Patriotism, reinforced by religion in the form of Protestantism, might give Parma's men more than they bargained for. Anti-Spanish feeling had been built up over some time. Not only was Philip's Spain linked with all that Mary I had stood for, but pamphlets produced within the previous ten years had given vivid accounts of Spanish invasion brutality elsewhere. The *Spoyle of Antwerp*, written by George Gascoyne in 1576, had been followed by *Destruction of the Indies* by Bartholome de Las Casas in 1583. Both gave frightening descriptions designed to infuriate readers. The problem was that they might create a feeling of fear which could overcome patriotism when put to the test.

Exactly one hundred years later when William arrived to make the 1688 Revolution 'Glorious', the ordinary people offered no resistance as they saw him as a saviour. The unanswered question in August 1588 was whether fear would lead to the 'man in the street' standing aside and accepting a return to Catholicism, or would he resist in the name of patriotism, his queen and his 'new religion'? No wonder Elizabeth defied her security advisers and did a 'walkabout' among her troops at Tilbury, dined with her officers and gave her forces a rousing speech, as we shall see. She knew that she must ensure that patriotism, focused on herself, must conquer their fear in the hour of crisis.

Whereas the prime object of the Armada was the capture of the whole country, it must not be forgotten that there was a fall-back plan which involved getting three concessions from Elizabeth, namely toleration for Catholics in England, an end to her support for the Dutch Republic and payment of a war-indemnity. If Parma's forces had managed to capture and hold Kent, Elizabeth would probably have agreed terms, at least covering the first two points. This in turn would have led to a collapse of Dutch resistance, another gain for Philip. Opinion in the Netherlands was sharply divided over whether a negotiated peace with Spain was a necessity or not. At least it would seem likely that a temporary capture of Kent would have been well within Parma's grasp had his forces landed.

Given the weakness of England's land defences, it is all the more important to discover whether her navy could have prevented them ever being put to the test.

CHAPTER FIVE

The English Navy

England's main defence against invasion was undoubtedly her navy. It had to be, if an effective invasion was to be prevented. In addition to being a statutory service, with headquarters and queen's ships, it was reinforced by the conscription of ships during a crisis. Consequently on 5 October 1587 the Privy Council informed the Vice-Admirals that the Queen's Navy was to be made ready for sea and to be reinforced by other ships and men. They were to put an embargo on all ships in harbour until it was known if they would be needed in the coming struggle. The royal fleet on its own consisted of thirty-six ships and pinnaces, 4,296 sailors, 555 gunners and 1,481 soldiers.

For some months Lord Howard of Effingham, the 'Admiral with the Lion on his Crest', had been using his ship, the *White Bear*, as his headquarters to put the navy on a war footing. She was docked at Queenborough in the Lower Thames, where some of the queen's ships were being fitted out; the remainder were being attended to at Chatham on the Medway. By December the War Council was meeting almost daily and Howard was forced to travel regularly up to Court. It was in that month that he received his commission to command the fleet. The instructions he received were clear. He was to order Sir Francis Drake to patrol between the Irish coast and the Scilly Isles or Ushant to prevent any landing in Ireland or in the south-west. He was not to overlook Scotland in his patrols. He himself was to patrol the other end of the Channel to ensure no invasion was launched from the Low Countries. Anticipating that Drake might find the task too big with the ships he had, the queen also told Howard to combine the fleets if need be, or strengthen Drake's at the expense of his own. At this time Drake commanded 31 ships with a complement of 2,820, while Howard had 17 ships with 3,820 men. The difference in the manpower figures was due to Drake's ships being of a smaller tonnage than Howard's.

Lord Howard of Effingham with the Armada in the background.

Then in early January the queen heard that Philip was disbanding his fleet and she seized the opportunity of this false information to pay off half the men on board. Naturally Howard was horrified and he wrote to Walsingham, 'They know that we are like bears tied to stakes, and they may come as dogs to offend us, and we cannot go to hurt them . . . .If her Majesty would have spent but a 1,000 crowns to have had some intelligence [of the rumoured disbanding of the Armada], it would have saved her twenty times as much.' He went on to warn Walsingham that England must not overlook the danger of Parma attacking Scotland.

The cutback left him with only sixteen royal ships and 2,000 men, and some 20 armed merchantmen. His other commanders were not much better off. Sir Henry Palmer had nine ships and pinnaces with 800 men for the Narrow Seas, while

Drake still had to gather his squadron together – three ships were at Portsmouth and three at Queenborough. But the queen had been persuaded by Sir James Croft, Comptroller of the Household, not only that wars were costly, but that England was not even technically at war with Spain. Her Council, on the other hand, urged her not to be deceived by news from Spain. They argued that Spain would attack as soon as it was realised that she had relaxed her guard. However, to Howard's dismay, she returned to the negotiating table.

Throughout the spring, Howard was convinced that 'Scotland is the mark which they shoot at to offend us'. He saw James VI and the kings of France and Spain as a 'Trinity that I mean never to trust to be saved by'. He wrote to Walsingham, 'We have to choose either a dishonourable and uncertain peace, or to put on virtuous and valiant minds, to make a way through with such a settled war as may bring forth and command a quiet peace'. This was nothing less than the manifesto of a 'war party'. It was clear that he wanted the negotiations abandoned and decisive steps taken to secure Scotland and send the fleet off to hinder the Armada's preparations. When Elizabeth refused to let Drake go out on such a mission, Howard wrote to Walsingham in March, 'the stay that is made of Sir Francis Drake going out I am afraid will breed grave peril'.

That month he switched his flag to the new *Ark Royal* and took his fleet over to Flushing to prevent any enemy move to attack Scotland. As time passed he wrote again and again to urge stronger policies and greater preparations. He suggested that so keen a force of men should get special treatment, such as an advance of pay for clothing as well as six weeks' pay for the time of partial demobilisation. All the time he showed a marked interest in the fighting man's welfare, recognising that a healthy man is better than a sick one. The problem was that the supply system of those days was not up to coping with such a large force on stand-by for so long. It was customary to victual ships for only a month at a time when serving in the Channel. Not only did this leave more room for ammunition, but it meant that the food was fresher. Howard's fear was that the Armada would arrive just at the end of such a month's supplies, so leaving the fleet in a vulnerable position. In April he got agreement for the fleet to be victualled until virtually the end of May, only to find that calculations indicated that the Armada might well arrive just three days before those rations were used up. 'Then we have 3 days' victuals. If it be fit to be so, it passeth my reason', he wrote in some despair. In the end his complaints did result in some ships being loaded up for three months at a time.

On 13 May 1588 the queen ordered him to hand over his command of the Narrow Seas and take command of a new squadron further west. This followed a re-arrangement of the available ships, which was made possible because of the commissioning of many more on emergency basis. The total force available amounted to 187 ships and 15,410 men. It was divided into three squadrons. Lord Henry Seymour was told to watch for any move by Parma in the Netherlands, while Drake covered the western end of the Channel. This left Howard in the middle of the Channel to move to the aid of either of the other squadrons as the need arose. Drake, supremely confident in his own ability and suspicious of any other's, had been reluctant to accept his role at first, as he wanted to be allowed to sail to Spain itself.

Aware of this, Howard took great pains not to upset Drake's pride. He carefully avoided giving him any direct instructions about how to handle his ships and men, though after an accident in Portsmouth harbour during gunnery practice in which one man was killed and another wounded, he wrote to Walsingham, 'If you would write a word or two unto him [Drake] to spare his powder, it would do well'. Down at Plymouth, he wrote again to Walsingham to suggest that a word of praise would not be amiss with Drake. 'Sir, I must not omit to let you know how lovingly and kindly Sir Francis Drake beareth himself; and also how dutifully to her Majesty's service and unto me, being in the place I am in; which I pray you he may receive thanks for, by some private letter from you.'

Howard was careful to consult Drake and other senior officers on all strategic matters. In June, when he selected his War Council, Drake's was the first name on the list. Noticeably, the list included 29-year-old Lord Thomas Howard, Howard's cousin, and 25-year-old Lord Sheffield, his nephew. Both were given their first commands of ships at this time, and it is clear that they were not on the Council so much to give advice as to learn their task. Howard gave his eldest son, William, command of the Lord Admiral's own galleon, the *White Lion*, and his son-in-law, Sir Robert Southwell, the *Elizabeth Jonas*, one of the queen's biggest ships. His secretary was his brother-in-law, Sir Edward Hoby, and his sister's stepson, Lord Henry Seymour, commanded one of the three squadrons.

There are no records of his Council's meetings, but it seems likely he took their advice on the whole. The fact that he held such meetings, when his commission gave him full authority to take decisions, says something for his willingness to listen to others. He was not a headstrong man, although his personal vanity was

Sir John Hawkins, Treasurer of the Navy and designer of 'race-built' ships.

considerable. Certainly he had no illusions about knowing 'all the answers' as Drake claimed to do. So he was capable of accepting the opinion of experts and listening seriously to informed opinion.

It was the fact that Sir Francis Drake and John Hawkins had examined the whole method of fighting at sea that was to count so strongly in England's favour. They had seen the need for ships which would be truly 'sailor's weapons' rather than mere floating islands for troops to fight 'land' battles upon. Instead of following the established tactic of coming alongside the enemy and using grappling irons, followed by hand-to-hand fighting, they saw the possibility of fighting across open water. Such warfare would mean that troops on board would be largely superfluous, and the high fore- and aft-castles quite unnecessary. It was these 'castles' which were to catch contrary wind so much with the Armada, so adding to their problems of tacking and reeling. Hawkins' 'race-built' ship, lacking such superstructure, presented no such problems. The word 'race' here comes from 'raze', referring to the *razing* of the castles, not *racing*.

Not only were Hawkins' ships lower throughout, their length to width ratio was significantly higher too, so that they cut through the water far faster. It also meant they could sail a course two points to windward, which was some four points better than the Armada as a whole. The contrast in the dimensions of two English ships of the time, the 'high-charged' (castled) *Elizabeth Jonas* with that of the 'race-built' *Golden Lion* shows this. The former was 100 ft. long, 40 ft. wide, 18 ft. in depth and 986 tons, while the latter was 102 ft. long, 32 ft. wide, 14 ft. in depth and 614 tons. It should not be overlooked that the English and Spanish

A 'high-charged' ship, probably the *White Bear*. Engraving by C. J. Visscher.

A 'race-built' ship, probably the *Ark Royal*. Engraving by C. J. Visscher.

methods of measuring tonnage were not the same. An English ship of 800 tons was much the same as a Spanish 1,000 ton ship. Thus it is a myth to suggest that English ships were smaller than Spanish ones.

Although the evidence is difficult to come by, there is sufficient to show that during the sixteenth century English ship-building underwent significant changes. Contemporary pictures only give a slight clue as to what happened, but they do show that high superstructures and low waists did disappear; sails were flatter and main masts moved slightly forward. The really important change was in hull shape. The anonymous author of *A Treatise on Shipbuilding* (1620–25), stated that with the average ship, 'the depth must never be greater than half the breadth nor less [than] one-third, and the length never less than double nor more than treble the breadth'. William Borough, who successively held the posts of Clerk of Ships, Surveyor of Ships and Comptroller of the Navy between 1580 and 1598, agreed with the Treatise on this point, but argued that for warships, 'the best proportions of the breadth to the depth is as 7 to 3, of the breadth to the length of 9 to 25'.

The development of the navy in Elizabeth's reign is best divided into four stages. The first, lasting from 1558 to 1569, saw her inheriting a navy strengthened by the construction work insisted on by Philip of Spain when he was married to Mary I. But it also saw a period of neglect following the fall of Le Havre in 1563. The *Elizabeth Jonas* was built at this time. The second period, from 1570 to 1579, saw stern superstructures being substantially reduced in height, and a lesser reduction in that of forecastles. Deck structures still continued to overhang bows, however. The development of a new hull shape was continued from its beginnings in the first stage. Ships were made deeper, probably because of increased Atlantic trade and the need for more cargo space. At this time a new building programme was needed and put into action. It led straight into the rebuilding programme of the third period, 1580–85. This began when John Hawkins, Treasurer of the Navy since 1577, took over the care and building of ships too. Cash shortages meant that he had to be content with a repair and rebuilding programme to start with. Ships with high superstructures had them reduced, for example.

Finally, the period 1586 to 1587 witnessed Hawkins' direction of a new building programme. The *Vanguard* and the *Rainbow* showed a marked improvement with their greatly reduced depths in relation to their lengths. At the same time, Robert Chapman improved on their proportions when he built the 540 ton *Ark Royal*, with its keel to beam ratio of 2.78 and depth to beam ratio of 0.417. Overall, the Elizabethan ship designers had begun by lengthening and deepening the shallow, short vessels they had inherited, until they reached the dimensions of the *Ark Royal*. Her keel/beam proportions are noticeably nearer those of the Treatise mentioned above, though the depth/beam ones are somewhat deeper, probably to enable the ship to carry sufficient stores for lengthy voyaging.

The resulting fleet consisted of about 140 ships, but by no means all of them were 'race-built'. In fact the majority were armed cargo ships. However, the running battles up the Channel were soon to show that the advantage lay with the quicker, more mobile English ships.

Gun Sizes and Capabilities

Gun sizes	Calibre	Weight of shot	Point-blank range	Random range
	(in.)	(lb.)	(paces)	(paces)
Cannon	7¼/8	50/60	340	2,000
Demi-cannon	6¼	30/32	340	1,700
Cannon perier	8	24	320	1,600
Culverin	5	17/18	400	2,500
Demi-culverin	4¼	9	400	2,500
Saker	3½	5	340	1,700
Minion	3¼	4	320	1,600

Comparison of the two Fleets

Gun sizes	Whole English Fleet	Whole Spanish Fleet	Queen's ships	Galleons/ galleasses
Cannon & demi-cannon	55	163	55	163
Cannon perier	43	326	38	196
Culverin	153	165	130	165
Demi-culverin	344	137	200	47
Saker	662	144	220	27
Minion	715	189	40	132

Tables such as these show how the English preferred lighter guns for their new tactics, while the Spaniards kept to the traditional heavier ones for close-in fighting. But no such tables can be really accurate, for 'range' depends on the quality of the gunpowder available and 'windage', which is the gap between the inside of the barrel and the outside of the shot. As every gun and almost every shot could vary, the 'windage' could be as high as half an inch. Furthermore 'a pace' was not clearly defined, and varied from 5 ft. (1.5 m) to half that. Thus a culverin's range could work out at 2½ miles or 1¼ miles. An examination of the 'random range' distances shows that the English were safe beyond 2,000 paces, but unable to score against their enemy if they went over 2,500 paces away. The Spaniards were to discover, as we shall see in due course, that their shot and powder were below standard, which resulted in ineffectual fire against their enemies.

As it turned out both sides really failed as artillerists, the English because of the lightness of their guns and the Spaniards due to the quality of their guns and ammunition, but also because of their ship designs. Potentially the heavier Spanish guns were much more effective as they could smash the hulls of their opponents, whereas the English ones could only make holes in what their cannon-balls passed through. Until the Armada reached Calais the shooting was indecisive on both sides. But things changed then as both sides were short of shot, which meant that the English had the advantage of being able to get more from home. They then moved in closer to the enemy ships, no longer fearing them, so that their light-weight guns could at last prove effective. In other words, the English guns could only have an effect when they were within effective firing range of the Spanish guns.

By the time the Armada was actually under way the English navy had been re-divided once again into two fleets. Lord Henry Seymour was in charge of some 40 ships guarding the Thames and the Straits of Dover, while Lord Howard in the *Ark Royal* had about 100 ships and 10,000 men at Plymouth. Drake was Howard's Vice-Admiral and sailed in his 500-ton *Revenge*, while Hawkins was Rear-Admiral in the *Victory*, with Martin Frobisher in the *Triumph* and George Beeston in the *Dreadnought* completing the leadership.

They were not without their problems. There was a chronic ammunition and food shortage, which was no one's fault since a fleet of that size had never been kept on active service for so long – since May in fact. The shore supply services simply did not exist to service them. The rearrangement of available craft so that both Drake and Howard were at Plymouth had meant that Marmaduke Darell, who was responsible for victuals, had to supply food for twice as many men. He now saw to 18,000 in 200 ships along the south coast. He managed to purchase a cargo of rice from a Hamburg merchantman, but he had to continually scour the Devon countryside for further supplies. On board five or six men were ordered to make do with the rations for four. The beer brewed at Sandwich turned out to be undrinkably sour, a serious point given the need for each man to have a gallon of beer to offset the saltiness of his diet.

The L:d Hen:Seymor wth 40
English and Dutch Ships
keeping the Coast of the Netherlands to hinder y Prince of
Parma's coming forth.

The L:d Admirall Howard
ranking his whole Fleet into
4 Squadrons y 1st he ruled
himselfe, Drake y 2d Hawkins
y 3d and Forbisher y 4th

King ♣

The English Fleet whereof
the L:d Charles Howard
was L:d Admiall & St Fran:
Drake vice Admirall.

Queen ♠

The first Squadron ruled by
y L:d Admirall Howard

Eight and ace of diamonds; king of clubs, queen of spades, and on page 94, ten and nine of clubs.
The English fleet ready to oppose the Armada.

The 3ᵈ Squadron ruled
by Hawkins.

The 4ᵗʰ Squadron ruled
by Forbisher.

In fact Howard felt the Armada was pursuing some dark plot to delay to the point when the English ran out of food and would be obliged to stand their fleet down. Little did he know the Armada faced similar shortages to its own. On top of the shortages problem, there was that of the queen's unpredictability. She had found in the past that this role had its strengths since it left enemies confused. She had an inbred dread of war and clung to hopes of arranging peace through the Duke of Parma. Unknown to her, or her negotiators, Philip had ordered Parma to mislead her on the possibilities of obtaining peace.

The problem went deeper, however, as neither she nor her council really understood naval strategy or tactics, and certainly not the new ones advocated by Drake and Hawkins. They must be forgiven for this lack of appreciation as naval strategy could hardly have been said to exist before. It originated with Drake and stemmed from the fact that he assumed he could be at sea regardless of weather conditions. This, in turn, meant that planning could have a greater freedom than hitherto thought possible. It followed that Drake was restless to use attack as the best method of defence by means of cruising off the enemy ports. He wrote to the queen in March, 'With 50 sail of shipping we shall do more good upon their own coast that a great many more will do here at home'. He was summoned to Court to explain his ideas in May.

Although Howard began by opposing him, Drake presented his case so effectively that both he and the queen were convinced. Indeed in June Howard wrote to Walsingham to say that he, Hawkins, Drake, Frobisher and others were convinced 'that the surest way to meet with the Spanish fleet is upon their own [coast], or in any harbour of their own, and there to defeat them . . . I [am] verily persuaded they mean [nothing] else but to linger it out upon their own coast, until they understand we have spent our victuals here; and therefore we must be busy [with] them before we suffer ourselves to be brought to that extremity'. In urging preventive aggression, Howard was even in favour of taking the Portuguese Pretender Don Antonio with them in the hope that his arrival in Portugal would trigger off a national uprising. In this he was being over optimistic as Antonio's popularity was no more likely to start such a revolt than Cardinal Allen's was to start a Catholic uprising in England as Philip hoped for.

The plan proposed by Drake was acted upon, once the wind was favourable, which was not for some weeks. On the way out they had to battle against a gale for a week, and by the time it had died down, they learnt that the Armada had left Lisbon. Howard, seeing the danger of it getting up the Channel before he could return to secure Plymouth, decided they had no alternative but to put about at once. Perhaps it was as well, for when they got back to Plymouth they read the queen's latest dispatch to the effect that she had changed her mind and they were not to go after the enemy, but 'ply up and down'. Ironically the queen's refusal to allow Howard to exercise her instructions to him, which gave him 'full power and authority to lead and command' all her subjects in her fleet and army at sea, and her refusal to allow a real blow to be made against the Armada before it left dock, led in the end to her admirals becoming the heroes of the fight up the Channel which was soon to begin.

When Howard saw her latest dispatch, he wrote back an angry, indeed sarcastic, letter. In clear and simple terms he spelt out the arguments for her again. In due course she replied, saying that she agreed with him – provided his Council supported him. Food arrived too! At this very moment an Irish barque, which had been held by the Spaniards for a while, reported some of the Armada ships had been at the Scilly Islands, but were not returning to Spain. Drake was convinced the Armada was badly damaged by the gales and in Corunna or Vigo. On 4 July, when the wind was finally in their favour, Howard and Drake set out again with some 90 ships. But ten days of gales trapped them between Ushant and the Scillies, again convincing Howard the Armada would outmanoeuvre them. Drake wrote his condemnation of this viewpoint and sent it across to Howard. A Council meeting was held on 17 July to settle whether it should be assumed the Armada had sailed or not. Drake insisted they should go on, declaring the enemy could not have sailed. He won the day and they set sail for the Bay of Biscay. But the wind let them down when they were 60 miles short of the Spanish coast. With the problem of a growing food shortage, they had no alternative but to turn back on 20 July, the very day the Armada's Council decided to set sail from Corunna.

CHAPTER SIX

Up the Channel!

From 22 July the Duke of Medina Sidonia had been making regular entries in his *Journal of the Enterprise of England*, which he was eventually to send to the king. Then at 4 p.m. on Friday afternoon, 29 July, a sailor in the crow's nest of his ship had shouted that land was in sight. That evening as they neared the Lizard, the duke wrote, 'I hoisted at the main the banner bearing the image of Christ crucified with the Virgin on one side of Him and Mary Magdalen to the other. I ordered three shots to be fired, as a signal to every man to make his prayer'.

That same evening, Captain Thomas Fleming, in the barque *Golden Hind*, arrived in haste to say he had spotted the Armada near the Scilly Isles. Drake promptly paid William Page £5 to take the news to the queen. The story that he was playing bowls at the time and replied, 'We have time enough to finish the game and beat the Spaniards too', does not have much evidence to support it. That no one should know the score of the most famous game of bowls ever played seems curious, but more obvious is the extraordinary absence of any card depicting the scene among the fifty-two cards in the *Spanish Armada* pack produced sometime after the defeat of the Armada. Nor is the game mentioned in Ubaldino's second edition of *Discourse Concerninge the Spanish Fleete Invadinge Englande*, which Drake himself had commissioned. Even if the game had occurred, it was probably played with the old-style larger bowls in a different way from the modern game. The first documentary evidence of the story did not appear until it was mentioned in 1624 in an anti-Spanish propaganda pamphlet called *Vox Populi*, which was fictitious in content. There was no mention of Drake's actual words until 1736, when in a life of Ralegh William Oldys wrote, 'The tradition goes that Drake would needs see the game up, but was soon prevailed on to go and play out the rubbers with the Spaniards'. Admittedly the former evidence is within the lifespan of some of those present in 1588 and the event would have been typical of Drake, but 'not-proven' will have to be the verdict unless further evidence comes to light. In any case the

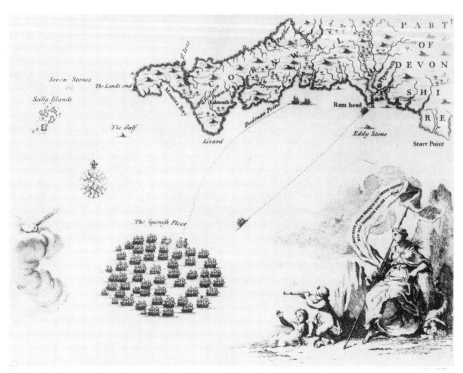

Chart 1 from Ubaldino's *Expeditionis Hispanorum*, 1588, showing the Armada off the Lizard, with the *Disdain* making her challenge (see pages 104–5).

tide may well have been low and nothing could be done until the water rose.

Be that as it may, while the English admirals considered what best to do, it is worth pausing to examine how the Armada had finally arrived at the Lizard. Until a few years before it sailed, safe navigation had been restricted to inshore pilotage called 'caping', that is, following the coast from cape to cape, using navigation books called *rutters*. These books covered the route the Armada was to take, as it was a regular trade route. But they gave distances only in *kennings*, the distance at which a sailor could be expected to recognise, or *ken*, the coast. The Straits of Dover were given as one ken, while the west end of the Channel was five kens. In 1584–5 Janszoon Wagenhaer published the first atlas of sea charts of western and northern Europe in two volumes. A Latin edition appeared in 1586 and an English one, entitled *The Mariner's Mirror*, was commissioned by Lord Howard in October 1588.

It would be reasonable to presume that the Armada pilots had the Latin edition, if not a Spanish version. Each chart in the atlas had its rutter, giving courses and distances in leagues. Leagues could be a problem as while Spanish ones were 3½ nautical miles, Dutch ones were 4 miles and English ones, 3 miles. Anyone consulting the atlas today must remember that the compass variation at that time was 1½ points, or 17 degrees, more easterly than those given in modern charts.

Even with the atlas, pilots were wise to follow either the European or English side of the Channel. The Armada chose the English side simply because Philip had told them, 'You must keep away from the French and Flemish coasts because of the shoals and banks'. He must have had the shoals *beyond* Calais in mind as there were none west of that port. This order was to account for many of the Armada's problems in the following days as it meant they were close to the English shore from which resistance would come. Moreover, if the wind turned southerly, the merchantmen, unable to sail at right angles to the wind, would get swept right inshore.

So it is not surprising to read of the duke's fears on the night of 27 July when the Armada was hit by yet another gale. 'The waves mounted to the skies, some broke clean over the ship, and the whole of the stern gallery of Diego Flores' flagship was carried away . . . It was the most cruel night ever seen.' A regular sailor, Pedro Calderon, did not consider the storm to be so severe. He noted in his diary, 'A strong wind, and the armada kept its course'. Still, it was necessary to send pinnaces looking for forty ships which had strayed. Within two days all but four of them were found.

One incident that emerged from the gale was the false tale told by Welshman David Gwynne. He was a convict-oarsman, who claimed that his captain on the *Bezaña* panicked and asked him what he should do as David was a seaman. David said he took charge, ordered the sails to be taken in and the ship rowed to France. Then, when he thought the time was right, he signalled to the other oarsmen to kill all the Spaniards on board with home-made stilettos. It was customary for oarsmen to make toothpicks from odd bits of swords, etc., when they had the opportunity. As a result, David claimed they captured the ship and another before reaching Bayonne. Ashore he led 460 men to La Rochelle and was received by King Henry of Navarre. Eventually he reached England to be congratulated by the queen.

The truth was rather different. David was actually on the *Diana* which, he said, sank. There was no mutiny and his ship was wrecked as it landed at Bayonne.

Plymouth Haven from a chart drawn in the reign of Henry VIII preserved in the British Museum.

David simply ran off with the rest of the crew. In England people believed his mutiny story and he became a hero until the truth came out, when he was sent to Ireland as a translator to deal with Spaniards taken from galleons wrecked on their return journey.

The main outcome of the storm was that the pilots' 'dead reckoning' calculations were thrown out and they were uncertain where they were. By Friday, 29 July, the lead recorded 56 fathoms and they reckoned they were at 50 degrees N. If so, this would put them on the Lizard's latitude. The happy-go-lucky atmosphere, which the earlier good weather had put them all in, had by now given way to one of quiet excitement. They must be near England and so within enemy waters. Now that there was no turning back they were remarkably cheerful. The miseries they had endured might soon end in victory and glory.

The same day the duke sent a coded message to the king expressing his astonishment at the lack of news from the Duke of Parma.

> Without information from him I can only proceed slowly to the Isle of Wight, and go no further until he informs me of the state of his forces. All along the coast of Flanders there is no harbour to shelter our ships, and if I took the armada there from the Isle of Wight it might be driven on the shoals, where it would certainly be lost . . . I have decided to stay off the Isle of Wight until I know what the duke is doing, as the plan is that the moment I arrive he should come out with his fleet, without making me wait a minute. The whole success of the enterprise depends on this . . .

It was not surprising that the duke was a worried man. He had not heard from Parma since he received a letter dated 22 March. If the king knew more than he did, he had not bothered to tell him. By telling the king he intended to stop off the Isle of Wight, the duke was disobeying orders. Hopefully the king would take the hint that Parma must be made to communicate with the Armada and, above all, be ready when it reached him.

That night, or early the following morning, the duke held a council meeting, but its minutes do not survive today. Clearly it was to make final battle decisions. It seems likely that Alonzo Martinez de Leyva (or Leiva), Captain-General of the Milanese Cavalry, argued for an attack on Plymouth. The duke pointed out that not only was that against the king's orders, but the entrance was too narrow and

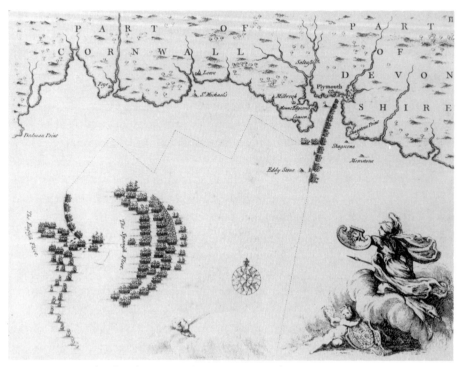

Chart 2. The Armada off Dodman Point. The English *warped* out, using capstans to pull on anchors dropped ahead by rowing boats.

well defended to make it feasible. The rest agreed. It is possible that a landing at Wembury Bay or Whitesand Bay from which to make an attack on Plymouth from the landward side was discussed. If so, it is probable that the duke argued that garrisoning Plymouth would leave their forces seriously depleted.

Meanwhile the English fleet had taken action. 'Upon Saturday, we turned out very hardly, the wind being at south west.' Although this suggests the need for hard tacking, the modern compass direction would make the wind WSW and so not such a problem. If they had timed it rightly with the tide, they should have managed to get the fleet out in under three hours. At all accounts, by 3 p.m. they had managed to get 54 ships near the Eddystone Rock, a distance of thirteen miles from Plymouth.

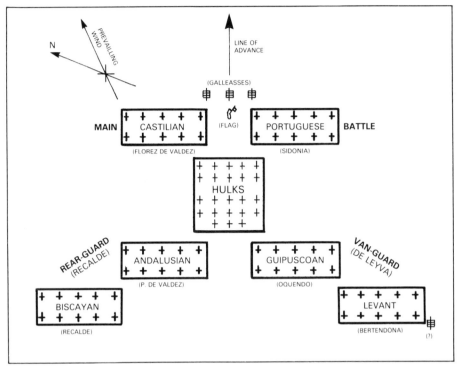

The Armada formation used army terminology. It was the military custom for the van-guard to take up the right-hand position, and the rear-guard to take up the left, when battle commenced. This layout explains why the accounts refer to the van-guard taking part in all the 'rear-guard' actions. It is not certain precisely where the galleasses were.

Between the squally showers of rain the duke spotted the English pursuers and noted in his diary, 'A number of ships, but as the weather was thick and rainy, they could not be counted'. Someone in the English fleet wrote that he could see the Spaniards 'to the westward as far as Fowey'. It was now essential for both fleets to position themselves in such a way that they could take advantage of the wind. Howard's tactic was to take in all sail for a while in the hope that the Armada would pass ahead of him. However, during the night he changed his mind and sailed further out to sea. Meanwhile the duke had ordered his fleet to close up ready for battle.

At dawn the English were shaken to see just how big the Armada was, while for their part the Spaniards were upset to see that their enemies were to windward of them. More horrifying was the sight of eleven English ships tacking upwind to join the rest at what seemed to the Spaniards incredible speed and manoeuvrability. Clearly the English were in a position to attack where and when they pleased. The fact that the best Spanish ships were in the front of the Armada's formation was now a distinct disadvantage as the attack was going to come from the rear.

The formation used by the Armada as it sailed up the Channel has given rise to much discussion. According to a contemporary historian, William Camden, who was no seaman, it was in the form of a 'half-moon', and this is endorsed in the charts compiled shortly afterwards, as well as in the House of Lords' tapestries of the event commissioned by Howard himself. From a naval point of view the formation would have been pointless and difficult to keep to. The historian, David Howarth, has written that the formation was more like that of a bird, the main body of the urcas and merchantmen being in the middle, with the duke's squadron of Portuguese galleons and four galleasses ahead. That would leave Don Pedro de Valdes' squadron astern, with on either side a mixed 'wing' of galleons and other ships in echelon formation. The whole would be some four miles across. Its lines would be *abreast* as the idea of *line ahead* had not been considered, although it would have served better for broadside firing. It must be remembered that the formation was primarily a *defensive*, not *offensive* one. As such it was undoubtedly very strong. As Howard found, the ships were so close together – officially they were meant to be 50 paces apart – that it was impossible to sail between them without running the risk of being boarded from both sides. Under these circumstances it is not surprising that neither side could really do much, given the tactics they wanted to follow. The English could only use their 'across water'

The five of diamonds' *Defiance* was in fact the *Disdain* which delivered Howard's challenge.

cannonade technique against the outer ships, while the Armada could not board them as they were so nimble.

The *Relation of Proceedings* is the nearest thing to an official English report of what followed. Probably by Howard, it was translated into Italian by Petruccio Ubaldino with R. Adam's drawings. Ubaldino did a version called *Discourse Concerninge the Spanish Fleete Invadinge Englande* for Drake. But the accounts muddle leeward with windward, and east with west! The Spanish accounts are more detailed and differ from Petruccio's. In fact what the duke wrote disagrees with Purser Calderon's version. Calderon said seven ships were involved and some had to be ordered back into line when they took flight. The duke recorded that 'My flagship became so closely engaged that we had to attack the enemy in force; whereupon they retired . . .'

Howard began the battle in true 'heraldic' fashion by sending Captain James Bradbury in the 80 ton barque, aptly named *Disdain*, to fire a 'challenge' shot across what he assumed was the Armada's flagship (see chart 1 page 98). In fact she was the *Rata Sancta Maria Encoronada*. The barque then slipped easily away as the *Rata's* shots fell short. The Lord Admiral of England then ordered the standards and pennants to be hoisted and the gunports opened as he led his fleet into action.

Howard in the *Ark Royal* led his line of ships into the enemy's vanguard, dodging around them as they struggled, and failed, to close in on him. Little damage was done on either side. Meanwhile Recalde's powerful galleon, *San Juan de Portugal*, which led the rearguard, became the centre of an attack by Drake, Frobisher and Hawkins. For an hour or two Recalde withstood the onslaught of seven ships at a range of some 300 yards (274 m) aided only by the *El Gran Grin*. Her rigging was damaged and one Spanish officer lost a leg. It is not clear why other ships did not come to his aid, but it may be because they panicked or that Recalde did not signal properly to them, or even that he disobeyed instructions when he turned to face his attackers. If he had indeed disobeyed it may well have been because he believed the only way to regain the advantage the English had of the wind was to precipitate a general mêlée. One must not forget that he expected the enemy ships to come in and attempt to put grappling irons aboard his ship, just as he wanted to do with theirs. It was their new tactics which caught him out. In the end some of the 'Apostles', including *San Martin* and *San Mateo*, rescued him.

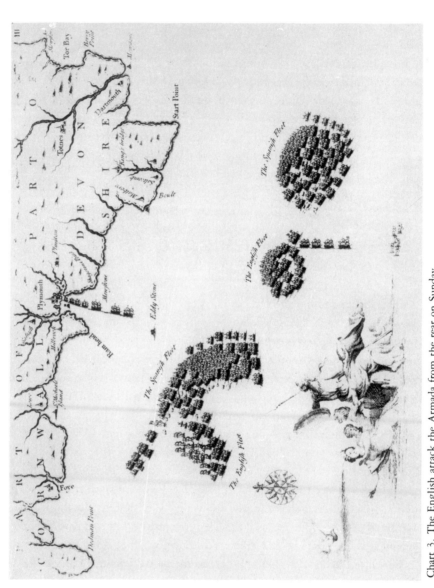

Chart 3. The English attack the Armada from the rear on Sunday.

The four of diamonds records the attack on Recalde's ship. Nine of hearts shows the 'Apostles', a group of warships in the Armada.

The verdict on the first skirmish between the two fleets was given by their commanders. The duke commented, 'The English ships being very fast and well handled, so that they could do as they like with them'. Howard paid the Spaniards a compliment when he wrote, 'We durst not adventure to put in among them, their fleet being so strong'. He added a postcript to Walsingham, 'Sir, for the love of God and our country, let us have with some speed some great shot sent us of all bigness, for this service will continue long; and some powder with it'.

By the end of the afternoon the fight was over. The duke signalled to his fleet to reform. In the confused attempt to do so, the *Santa Catalina* rammed the *Nuestra Señora del Rosario*, 1,150 ton flagship of the Andalusian squadron with its crew of 420, wrenching off her spritsail yard and bowsprit. Before she had time to shorten sail, a strong gust of wind brought down her mizzen mast and her mainyard. The duke responded to her call for help, but as he swung his ship round, the *San Salvador* seemed to go up in a huge explosion.

The *San Salvador* was the ship of the Vice-Admiral of the Guipuscoan squadron

The explosion on the *San Salvador* from an engraving by J. Pine after C. Lempriere

and the paymaster-general, Juan de la Herta, and so it contained a large proportion of the Armada's finances. The whole powder magazine must have gone up, probably accidentally, blowing away the stern and leaving the two upper decks of her poop in ruins. The wounded howled as the fire burnt them horribly. The ship carried 64 sailors and 319 troops and Calderon claimed that over 200 were killed or had jumped overboard and been drowned. Subsequently stories arose of sabotage by a gunner – French, English, Dutch or German according to which version you read – who had been flogged by Captain Priego. One version has a German gunner revenging himself on the captain for seducing his wife who seems to have been on board.

The rescue operation was led by two pinnaces which tugged her into the wind so that the flames would not blow forward. Rescuers climbed aboard to do what they could. The swell increased as the wind continued to squall, so making the task of moving around the decks, slippery with blood, all the more difficult. Arms and legs lay around and a charred head rolled from side to side across the deck. The wounded were said to give off a 'regular rattle' as they were taken off to two hospital ships. There is mention of limbs falling off as men were picked up. When the fire was under control two galleasses towed the ship over to the hulks to 'transfer the coffers without delay onto a seaworthy ship'.

That evening Lord Howard sent Lord Thomas Howard and Hawkins in a small skiff to board her. They found a 'very pitiful sight, the deck of the ship fallen down, the steerage broken, the stern blown out, and about fifty poor creatures burnt with powder in most miserable sort. The stink of the ship was so unsavoury, and the sight within board so ugly, that the Lord Thomas Howard and Sir John Hawkins shortly departed', recorded the *Relation of Proceedings*. The next day she was towed by the *Golden Hind* into Weymouth, where the mayor made an inventory, listing 53 barrels of wine, 3 of beef, and 1 of beans. On board he found 12 dead and, still alive, 10 Spaniards, 4 Germans, 2 French and a German woman. So it is just possible that the story involving a German gunner's wife was true.

At the same time the fate of the *Rosario* was on the duke's mind. She was trailing behind with only her foresail and main topgallants in use. Then a gust of wind carried away her mainmast which was no longer supported due to the damage her rigging had suffered earlier on. The duke wrote later that he ordered the whole fleet to heave to and wait until he had a hawser aboard her, but an officer on the *San Marcos* maintained that no one went to her rescue as 'there was a hard wind blowing, a heavy swell, and the English were hard behind. We abandoned her at vespers, following a signal shot from the Duke'. This is supported by one of the duke's own men, Jorge Manrique, who recorded that 'the Armada carried on its way leaving her astern in full view of the enemy'.

The stricken ship's captain, Don Pedro de Valdes, subsequently wrote to the king to say that

> Unable to make the necessary repairs, I sent someone to inform the Duke and fired . . . four shots to signal our distress . . . The Duke was close enough to see quite clearly what sort of difficulties I was in and to come to my aid . . . but he did nothing of the sort! He seemed to have forgotten that we were servants of Your Majesty and in his command! He . . . sailed on leaving me in distress, and the enemy only a quarter of a league astern of me.

In all probability the duke had intended to go to his aid, but his Chief of Staff, Diego Flores, had persuaded him that with night coming on and the weather worsening it would have been foolhardy to do so. He might imperil the whole fleet if it was to scatter as a result of delaying for one ship. However the duke did send his personal *patache* over to the *Rosario* to take off the king's treasure it carried. Valdes bluntly told the *patache*'s officer that if he had to risk his own life and that of his crew, the treasure could be risked too. He refused to hand it over. Even if the duke was right in abandoning the ship to her fate, the Castilians felt he had forfeited his honour in so doing. Not one squadron commander would speak to Diego Flores after this event. Diego Flores was known to bitterly hate his cousin Don Pedro, so that the ship's abandonment was seen by some as part of a personal vendetta.

That night the merchantman *Margaret and John* came upon the *Rosario* in a seemingly deserted state. The sea was too rough for them to board her, but they opened fire on her, only to be fired at in response. Sometime during the night

The Galleon of Don Pedro taken Prisoner by S.r Francis Drake, and sent to Dartmouth.

Three of diamonds records Don Pedro's surrender.

Drake in the *Revenge* who had been ordered to lead the English fleet with his stern lantern, extinguished it and slipped away to starboard to go in search of the stricken ship. This action was to lead ten days later to an outburst from Frobisher, who raved, 'Like a coward he [Drake] kept by her all night, because he would have the spoil. He thinketh to cozen us of our shares of fifteen thousand ducats; but we will have our shares, or I will make him spend the best blood in his belly'. Perhaps this is not surprising, for Drake's excuse that he had sighted suspicious ships to seaward and had gone to investigate, only to discover they were German cargo ships, makes for doubtful reading.

At dawn Drake called on the *Rosario* to fight or surrender. Surprisingly she surrendered in spite of the fact that she was one of the strongest and most heavily armed ships – she had 46 guns – in the Armada. But no attempt had been made to repair her following the battle. Perhaps Don Pedro was furious at being abandoned; certainly he subsequently wrote as much to the king as we have already seen. But he went on to falsely claim that he had defended himself all night. In fact he had fired but two shots. What he wrote subsequently landed Diego Flores in prison. Don Pedro came aboard Drake's ship with forty of his officers and gentlemen before his ship was escorted to Torbay, and then on to Dartmouth, by Captain Whiddon's *Roebuck*, on Drake's orders. When she docked the local people grabbed what booty they could before magistrates stopped them. Whiddon took ten of the thirteen good cannons from her, while Drake must have added some 55,000 gold ducats to his booty, to say nothing of the possible ransom of a senior officer and sundry nobility. Frobisher went so far as to challenge Drake's right to claim prize-money for the *Rosario*, let alone ransoms for her officers. Nevertheless Drake bought a seventy-one year lease on Herbery, a fine London house, and obtained £3000 for Don Pedro. The Spaniard had to remain his prisoner for some years until the sum was paid. When he left, he was given a farewell banquet by the Lord Mayor of London before being exchanged for Edward Wynter who had been captured by the Spanish.

The rest of the crew had to be maintained by the local inhabitants at the rate of 2*d*. a day. This resulted in Sir George Carey complaining that a fellow member of the gentry, Sir John Gilberte, was using those stationed nearby to do his gardening for him, while putting 226 others in the bridewell sixteen miles from Carey's house, so that they were unable to be of service to him. Carey was also suspicious of what Gilberte had done with 'all the wine I left with him'.

CHAPTER SEVEN

The Channel Chase

The night following the skirmish the Duke of Medina Sidonia wrote to Parma begging him to send pilots who knew the Flanders coast and to answer all his earlier queries. Interestingly he did not say he intended to wait near the Isle of Wight until he knew Parma's true position. Juan Gil, in charge of the pinnace which conveyed the message, may well have flown both Spanish and English flags during the course of his mission, since it is said that he told passing Rye fishermen he was sailing to alert Seymour's fleet of the approach of the Armada. True to form, Parma did not reply.

Medina Sidonia's next concern was the fact that his fleet's formation was too vulnerable, and the rearguard too weak. The problems involved in sending reinforcements from the vanguard to the rearguard had been obvious in the first day's fighting. As Robert Sténuit recently put it, the duke changed his 'quarter moon into a plum, with the hulks as the kernel'. The rearguard and the vanguard were linked up to form a single rear aided by the galleasses and four galleons. This meant that a total of forty of the best ships protected the rear.

But an improved formation would be wasted if it was not held together by firm discipline. Again the duke showed his leadership qualities by taking steps to tighten matters. He summoned all *sargentos mayores* (sergeant-majors) who were in charge of discipline and told them to take written orders to all ships stating each one's station. These officials were ordered to hang any captain whose ship disobeyed. He ordered gallows to be fixed to the yardarms of several *pataches* and a *capitano de campo* (military attorney or provost marshal) and hangman were posted to each of them. At first sight this seemed to be a highly unusual and ruthless order, but when it is remembered that not only were sea-captains regarded as subordinate to army officers, but that some of them were German, Italian or Portuguese, the order has reasonable justification. Ten days later twenty captains were to face the death sentence charges as we shall see.

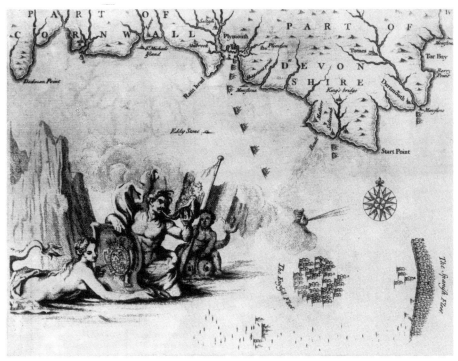

Chart 4. The Armada passes Start Point. Bottom centre, the *Rosario* is attacked.

No fighting took place on the Monday as the Armada crossed Lyme Bay followed by Howard with a mere three ships. All the rest of the English fleet was in disarray following the disappearance of Drake's guiding lantern during the previous night. Supply ships brought food, beer, cannon-balls and powder ('mixed with a certain amount of sawdust, for they had had to scrape the bottom of the barrels') out to them. This action only served to emphasise the advantage the English had over the Spaniards in being near to their supply source.

On the morning of Tuesday, 2 August, the NE wind came to the aid of the Armada in what was to prove the biggest battle yet, off Portland Bill. Even Sir George Carey, governor of the Isle of Wight, was aware of it as he sat listening in Carisbrooke Castle. Interestingly he wrote, 'The shot continued so thick together that it might rather have been judged a skirmish with small shot on land than a fight with great shot at sea'.

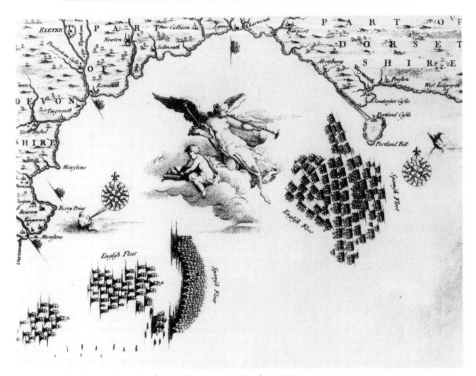

Chart 5. The fight off Portland Bill, Dorset on Tuesday, 2 August.

In fact most of the shooting was at long range, with the result that few were hurt. Surprisingly there was no proper organisation in the English fleet in contrast to the regimented formation of the Spaniards. It was the English custom for junior captains to simply attach their ships to the leaders they favoured most, be it Howard, Hawkins, Drake or Frobisher. The weakness of such freedom of choice was beginning to be appreciated by the end of the day, however.

The English also realised it was too risky to get really close to the enemy, and that in turn this meant it was no good using their demi-culverins at 'random range'. Sakers and minions were of even less use. Such shot could only cut rigging or pierce the 'castle' superstructures of the Spanish ships, and do nothing to hole their thick hulls.

The outcome was to prove disappointing for the Spaniards for, starting with the wind in their favour, they were unable to grapple with any enemy ship. Apart

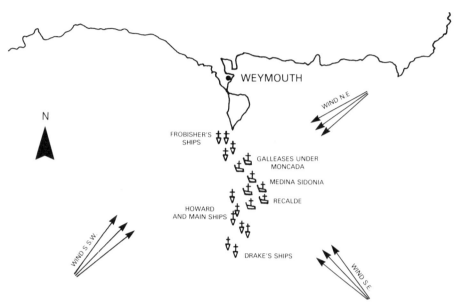

Wind N.E. at first Spanish to windward. Their attempt to corner Frobisher failed. Wind changed through S.E. to S.S.W. English attacked in three squadrons

The fight of Portland, Tuesday, 2 August.

from a brief fire on one English ship and the chance sinking of a very small ship, the *Pleasure*, they could claim no achievements. But that is not to say that they did not try. The Levant squadron had done its best to pick out Howard's flagship, while the galleasses forced Frobisher to take evasive action.

Frobisher's *Triumph* was the biggest ship in the English fleet, and probably in the enemy's as well, but it was a 'high-charged' one and so comparatively slow in handling. Supported by five armed merchantmen, he was under the lee of Portland Bill when the action began at dawn. It is possible he had stationed himself there in order to tempt the enemy onto the Shambles, a long shallow bank two miles east of the Bill. The tidal race there, which could touch four knots, would draw them on. Medina Sidonia spotted this small group of ships and persuaded the haughty Don Hugo de Moncada, who was in charge of the four galleasses, to attack them. The duke would have been unable to see the effect of the tidal race.

Frobisher, realising his shot would have little effect on the enemy hulls, concentrated his fire amidst their oarsmen. This forced them to stop rowing and use sails alone, thus surrendering their freedom of movement advantage.

During the morning the wind changed direction several times, so that what had started as a land breeze ended as a sea one. Drake, ever alert to such likelihoods, had drawn 50 ships away with him further out to sea. Then, when the sea breeze took hold, he led them down on the Armada in the *Revenge*. Medina Sidonia acted at once, recalling his galleasses and concentrating his forces against the approaching force. Not only did this give Frobisher a chance to recover, but it enabled Howard's ships to pick off any scattered Spaniards. It appears that Howard invented a rudimentary 'line of battle' manoeuvre, which was subsequently to be developed and used as the chief naval tactic down to the Battle of Jutland. This involved approaching the enemy in 'line ahead', with eight of his ships following him into the attack. Thus the duke found his ship attacked by one ship after another as they sailed by.

The tactic was not so successful as it might have been on this first attempt at using it. The *San Martin* fired 'over 80 shots from one side only, and did great damage to the enemy. The latter shot at the duke at least 500 balls, some of which struck his hull and others his rigging, carrying away his flagstaff and one of the stays of his mainmast'. This was not much of an achievement for the expenditure of 500 cannon-balls, although it did include the duke losing fifty men; but whether they were all on his ship or from the Armada as a whole is not clear.

By 5 p.m. the fight which had begun at dawn was over. The Armada reformed and continued up the Channel, and to that extent it must be conceded that they had not lost the day. They were upset at failing to catch and board a single English ship, even with the wind in their favour. Did this mean that they would be unable to clear the sea for Parma's crossing? It seemed uncommonly like it. Perhaps the greatest frustration was that felt by the soldiers on board their ships, for they had stood to arms all day and been given no chance to scramble aboard the enemy ships.

But the English too felt frustrated. They had not stopped the Armada's progress. Were they powerless to do so? Medina Sidonia estimated that more than 4,000 shot had been fired by both sides at the rate of a shot every ten seconds. If so, most of it had clearly been wasted, whoever fired it.

On Wednesday, 3 August, the action was resumed. De Leyva's rearguard were involved in a skirmish which forced Recalde and the galleasses to join in. One

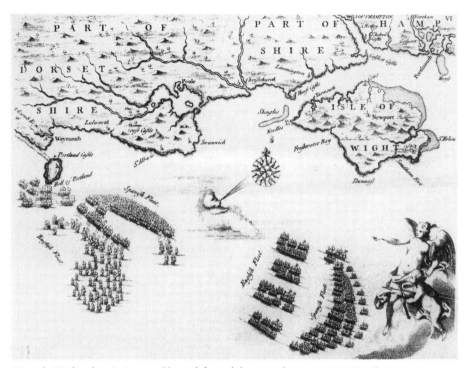

Chart 6. Wednesday, 3 August. Howard formed four squadrons near the Isle of Wight.

galleass took the *El Gran Grifon*, the urcas' flagship, in tow after she had become separated and set upon. She had been hit 70 times and had suffered 70 casualties, but no Englishmen had boarded her as her bloodstained decks were crowded with some 200 Spanish troops itching to play their role in the fight. Some gunners found their guns overheating and wrapped them in sheets soaked in water and vinegar in an effort to cool them. But it was the English shortage of powder and shot which brought things to an early close. Historian Michael Lewis has calculated that whereas the Armada had an overall average of some 80 shots per gun (with the galleasses having as high as 134 per gun), the English average was nearer 20–30. Still, the duke reckoned a further 5,000 shots had been fired. While his hospital hulks coped with a further seventy wounded, some sixty bodies were unceremoniously thrown overboard. To finish the day's work, the duke wrote to the king, 'I intend to take the Isle of Wight and occupy the port. This will be my base when we join forces'.

The action off the Isle of Wight on Thursday, 4 August, from an engraving by John Pine after the tapestry which hung in the House of Lords until destroyed by fire in 1834. Notice the troops on board the Spanish ships as well as the different designs of ships.

Howard was not only concerned about the shortage of his ammunition. He had to do something about the lack of organisation in his fleet, for without some improvement on that front, too many of his ships, especially the temporarily armed merchantmen, would use their remaining resources to little effect. He decided to adopt the squadron organisation as the solution. There were to be four squadrons, under himself, Drake, Hawkins and Frobisher. If nothing else it should go some way to bringing about an ammunition economy. Hopefully it would also ensure a higher degree of co-ordination in any manoeuvres that were necessary. That this was necessary had already been made clear by Drake's action on the night he was told to lead the fleet by his stern lantern, and then again on the Tuesday, first when Frobisher and his small group had drawn the firepower of the galleasses upon him, and secondly when Drake detached some 50 ships and sailed out to sea before turning to attack. Howard had certainly not ordered any of these actions. For that matter, how had Drake collected his fifty? It seems likely that they had simply joined in on their own initiative, assuming that wherever Drake went there was sure to be some tangible success. It must not be forgotten that sending messages by flag-signalling was virtually non-existent. Everything depended upon mere shouting if close enough, the dispatch of messenger boats, or the firing of signal guns by a pre-arranged code. Finally there was the problem of integrating the growing number of 'volunteer' ships with their motley array of weaponry which were joining the fleet daily. Thus each ship was assigned to a specific squadron to whose commander allegiance was to be given.

Howard's urgent call for ammunition brought a positive response. Use the enemy's! The Mayor of Weymouth contacted his opposite number at Lyme Regis, and, through him, the deputy lieutenants of Devon, who were in Torbay, on the Wednesday. By 9 p.m. they had taken steps to off-load the *Nuestra*'s stock. Two days later they reported that 1,600 shot and 88 barrels of powder had been dispatched to Howard. On the following Sunday the queen's council at Richmond heard of the *San Salvador*'s presence at Weymouth and ordered the mayor to send

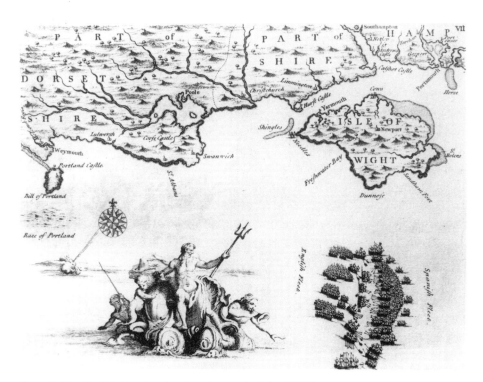

Chart 7. The English harrying the Armada past the Isle of Wight.

its powder to Dover. In fact Captain Fleming of the *Golden Hind* had already off-loaded 140 barrels of powder, 2,000 shot and 1 ton of match. Portsmouth hastened to send all the powder and shot in town as soon as the Armada had passed by. Powder and shot was also sent to the coast from the Tower of London, and the queen ordered the best musketeers in Kent to assemble along the shore in case Howard had need of them.

On Thursday, 4 August, the Spaniards sighted the Isle of Wight. It was the feast day of St Domingo de Guzman, a saint whom Medina Sidonia was wont to invoke. Surely a most propitious day for a real achievement. At dawn they were twelve miles from Spithead, and so not far from Portsmouth itself. The tide would be right for an attack between 7 a.m. and midday, and the Armada stood a good chance of carrying out the significant strategic move of occupying the Solent and the Isle of Wight. But, instead of the south wind needed, there was a calm. Not only did this mean that the Spaniards could get nowhere, it also deprived the English of their manoeuvrability. Indeed, the previous evening Howard's council had decided on the novel plan of a night attack. 'Six merchantships out of every squadron should set upon the Spanish fleet in sundry places, at one instant, in the night time, to keep the enemy working.' The calm had prevented its execution.

Howard was so frustrated on Thursday morning that he ordered rowing boats to tow some of his main ships after two Spanish ships, the galleon *San Luis* and the urca *Santa Aña*, which were lagging behind. When three galleasses emerged, one of them also towing De Leyva's great carrack, Howard claimed he had succeeded in inflicting 'much damage' on them. In fact little was done, beyond the *Girona* losing her poop lantern and the *San Lorenzo* her figureheads; though the *Zuniga*'s hull was holed at water level causing a bad list. Essentially the 'damage' was among the oarsmen, who with four pulling and three pushing to each oar, were an easy target. If one oar stopped due to the loss of one or two oarsmen, a chain reaction of clashes between oars could rapidly develop.

The accounts of what happened that day are confused. At one point it seemed as if the duke's ship was in position for the classic 'grapple-and-board' tactic. The *Triumph*, which the Spaniards mistook for the Armada's flagship due to its size, was within reach. Marksmen were sent aloft on the rigging of the *San Martin*, boarding parties stood to arms and grappling hooks poised ready. But for some reason the duke hesitated and the opportunity was missed. Many Spaniards mouthed oaths at this failure to act. De Leyva bellowed across to the *San Martin* a torrent of abuse, of which a printable extract was, 'God's body, His Majesty has given us a man to command us at sea, who looks as if he wouldn't know how to walk on dry land!' Oquendo added to this, 'Go on then, chickens! Get to your fishing nets, and go fish for tuna if you don't want to fight!' The reference to tuna was a neat one, as the duke's family had long held the monopoly on tuna-fishing rights. Oquendo finished off by shouting to the flagship's soldiers to throw Diego Flores, the duke's adviser, overboard there and then. Though the duke subsequently reported this incident to the king, nothing was ever done.

Later the Duke of Medina Sidonia wrote to Parma that the enemy had kept their distance, so making boarding impossible. To the king, he pointed out that, 'This time we felt quite sure we would succeed in boarding, the only way we can win a victory'. Finally, in his diary he noted that, 'They came closer than they had done on previous days, firing their heaviest guns from the lowest deck, cut the trice of our mainmast and killed some of our soldiers'. Perhaps this was the first day calm enough for the lowest gunports to be opened.

If so, this may explain why in earlier skirmishes only the lighter guns on the higher decks had been used. No one can have forgotten the fate of the *Mary Rose* which had sunk only ten miles away in 1545 when water entered her gunports.

By midday the wind had changed to SW and any prospect of the Armada taking Portsmouth or the Isle of Wight was gone. In fact, if it had done so, it might well have found itself trapped and open to fire-ship attack. Medina Sidonia and his council resolved to head on up the Channel, regardless of whether Parma was ready or not. No mention was made to the king of the failure to take the Isle of Wight, although Medina Sidonia had been all for doing so not long before. It was better that failure should simply not be mentioned.

The six of clubs wrongly shows Howard performing the knighting ceremony on land.

Wagenhaer's *Atlas of the English Channel* from the Isle of Wight to Dover. Notice the land profiles at the top.

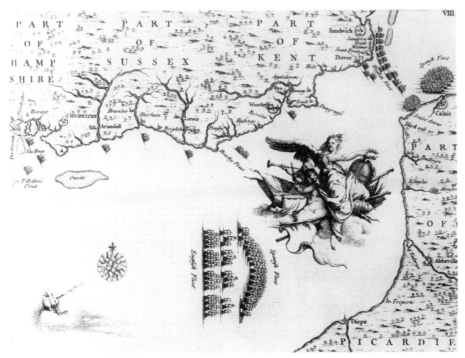

Chart 8. The two fleets off Calais on Saturday, 6 August. Seymour's ships coming to help.

On Friday morning Howard took advantage of the calm to mark Thursday's battle as if it had been a victory. He knighted Hawkins, Frobisher, Thomas Howard, Lord Sheffield, George Beeston and Roger Townsend on the deck of the *Ark Royal* – three sailors and three soldiers.

The sea was so calm that the two fleets drifted slowly along only two miles apart. No doubt carpenters and other craftsmen were put to work to carry out repairs necessitated by several days of fighting. The duke wrote to Parma asking him to send forty or fifty of his fast ships full of soldiers to help fight the English. He also asked for powder and a variety of cannon-balls, to say nothing of food. The request for fast ships showed that the duke was still under the misapprehension that Parma had them to send. In fact Parma had none ready for sea.

By Saturday morning the English fleet had got some replacements for their ammunition shortages from barques coming out from Sussex harbours. They had also caught the Armada up. At 10 a.m. the Armada sighted the French coast and by 4 p.m. they were near Calais, which was a French port and not held by Parma. This last point posed a major problem. What exactly was Medina Sidonia to do? He still had no clue as to Parma's true position or resources. He called a council meeting to assess the situation.

Until now Dunkirk had been the destination they had been aiming for. But the pilots informed the council that it was impossible to get the Armada in there. They were quite correct in telling them that there was no shelter for such a fleet on the Flemish coast. Today artificial breakwaters have been erected at five ports, which in those days were only shallow creeks. Moreover, Parma only held Dunkirk and Nieuport, while the French had Calais and Gravelines and the English, Ostend.

Wagenhaer's atlas marks the sandbanks as liable to shift, but that was not really so. However, it was correct in saying those at Calais were a serious threat, while those at Dunkirk extended as far as 12 miles off shore. The fact that Parma had sent no local pilots made the task of approaching the latter impossible, as there were no buoys marking the entrance channel in those days. That the Armada might have to heave to as far as 12 miles from Dunkirk was something no one had realised before. Although some on the council argued Calais was unreachable by Parma's craft, Medina Sidonia decided that there was no alternative but to anchor 4 miles off Calais. The enemy did so too, a mere 'culverin shot' away. By evening Lord Henry Seymour's and Sir William Wynter's squadrons had joined them. The Armada was almost surrounded by some 230 ships.

Up until now the Armada's seamanship, discipline and fighting spirit had been unquestionably good. It had kept to its planned formation and done its best not to abandon any ships caught up in the fighting. For nine days it had sailed up the Channel, forcing the English to use up their shot to little effect. Four sharp skirmishes had left it still intact and ready for a further fight. But now the crucial moment had come. The link-up between fleet and army had to be done effectively or all would be lost. The full implication of the Spanish not having a deep-water port was now clear for all to see. Parma's ability to act promptly was vital if the 'Enterprise' was not to become a total disaster. Yet his barges could not leave their ports while the 130 Dutch shallow-draught flyboats, commanded by Justin of Nassau, patrolled outside them; and the Armada's ships could not get close enough to tackle the flyboats because of the shallow waters. Consequently Medina

Sidonia's requests to Parma to bring his troops out in their barges were impossible to fulfil, for such a move would mean their inevitable destruction at the hands of the Dutch. Thus Medina Sidonia's position was now a hopeless one. He was in an exposed position and the English had him covered to windward.

Parma's role in the events which followed can only be understood by glancing back over the previous months. In February 1588, Elizabeth had sent emissaries to him to negotiate peace. They had been doing so ever since. Philip had told Parma to make sure the negotiations dragged on, prolonging them with every excuse he could find. This meant that the duke had been deliberately deceiving the emissaries all along. Philip had told him to demand an apology for Drake's attack on Cadiz. Then,

> when you have got this, you are to act as if you were completely deceived by it, and pretend to believe anything they tell you; you will then renew the negotiations, name commissioners, and propose a meeting on neutral territory . . . It is the best way to take them in, so that the peace commissioners may meet. But to you only, I declare that my intention is that these negotiations shall never lead to any result, whatever conditions the English may offer. On the contrary, the only object is to deceive them, and to cool them in their preparations for defence, by making them believe such preparations will not be necessary.

He went on to say that if Parma had to get out of the negotiations, he was to do so with 'great honour by taking umbrage about some point of religion, or the other outrageous proposals they are likely to make . . . Thus you will proceed, now yielding on one point, and now insisting on another, but directing all to the same object – to gain time while preparations for the invasion are completed'.

Parma did so for six months. He had no difficulty, as the queen believed him to be an honest man. Furthermore, her commissioners were not astute men. The five included Sir James Croft, who was in his dotage, and two learned doctors, who wasted time making lengthy Latin speeches which were both boring and off the point. The first meeting was held near Ostend in May. Parma disguised himself as a servant to one of his own commissioners so as to enter Ostend to assess its defences. The English demanded sight of Parma's written commission to negotiate. The fact that he had not got this commission did not deter him from saying they could see it. Hurriedly he wrote for one which, when it did eventually arrive, was written in French, together with a note stating 'on no account to be used for anything but show'. Consequently, negotiations were still continuing when the Armada arrived off Calais, when Parma wrote that they ended with the recall of the commissioners by the queen. 'My efforts to persuade them to continue the negotiations, notwithstanding the presence of the armada, were unavailing.'

All along he had received Medina Sidonia's letters, which had arrived between 2 and 7 August, but he only answered the first when the Armada reached Calais. Interestingly he had them all copied on 7 August and sent to Philip, together with a letter to say that there was no need to comment on them. He even claimed that he had hastened to deal with the requests in them for pilots and ammunition as far as 'our poverty here permits'. On 10 August he wrote to say the sea was too rough for either to be sent out to the Armada!

Parma pointed out that when the duke had asked for help, he had ordered the embarkation to begin on 5 August. In fact he was personally 40 miles away in Bruges at the time. Parma wrote,

To judge from what the duke says, it would appear that he still expects me to come out and join him with our boats, but it must be perfectly clear that this is not feasible. Most of our boats are built only for rivers, and they cannot weather the least sea . . . as for fighting as well, it is obvious they cannot do it, however good the troops in them may be. This was the principal reason why Your Majesty decided to risk sending the armada, as in your great prudence you saw the enterprise could not be carried out in any other way.

On 7 August he wrote to the king, 'No one regrets this situation more than I do, from the very beginning I have regretted it.' The next day Parma hammered

The seven of clubs records Medina Sidonia's impatience with Parma.

home the same points once more, adding that it was the king's plan that the Duke of Medina Sidonia should clear the seas and it was the duke who should be blamed if this had not been done. This raises a vital point for, unbelievable though it seems, Parma argued that he had never heard of the Armada's plan to pick his men up at Dunkirk and escort them across the Channel. Moreover he claimed that he had not understood from the duke's letters that it was impossible to 'clear the sea'. One is tempted to surmise that this was wilful misunderstanding on Parma's part. It is beyond belief that he could have failed to grasp the import of so many letters from Medina Sidonia.

Medina Sidonia's call on him to act quickly was pointless in Parma's opinion, for he could achieve nothing until the duke had cleared the Channel for him. Then fair weather would finally decide when embarkation of his troops was feasible. The misunderstandings which existed between the two dukes rest with the king for giving them each false information, or no information, about what the other was doing, or capable of doing. Parma had been led to believe the Armada would clear the Channel; Medina Sidonia had been deceived about the ability of Parma to bring his troops out in suitable craft. Had there been a deep-water port in Spanish hands the rendezvous could have taken place without difficulty. It was the need to meet at sea which proved impossible.

As soon as the Armada anchored off Calais, Medina Sidonia sent his secretary with an urgent message to Parma. 'I have constantly written to Your Excellency, and not only have I received no reply, but no acknowledgement of their receipt has reached me . . . the enemy's fleet being on my flank and able to bombard me, while I am not in a position to do him much harm'. He went on to press for at least the 40–50 fly boats he had requested earlier on.

A few hours later he sent Captain Heredia ashore to explain to the governor of Calais why he had anchored there. The captain found the governor, with his wife, sitting in a carriage on the seafront waiting to watch a spectacular battle which he was sure would take place. So friendly was the governor, that the duke sent officials ashore on the Sunday morning with 6,000 ducats to buy food. But Sunday was to see the arrival of most unwelcome news.

CHAPTER EIGHT

Fireships at Calais – Battle of Gravelines

At dawn on Sunday, 7 August, Captain Rodrigo Tello arrived back from Dunkirk, bringing not only a letter from Parma, but also his own up-to-date eye-witness report on the position of Parma's forces. The letter, written from Bruges, promised embarkation would be complete in six days, but what Tello had to say of his own visit to Dunkirk suggested otherwise. He had seen no sign of soldiers embarking on Saturday evening. Hurriedly the duke sent his secretary, Arceo, to check this. Later that day, Arceo wrote to say the carpenters were still at work and he reckoned it would be a fortnight before the boats could leave.

It is not known whether either of them was in a position to tell Medina Sidonia just what those boats were really like. He does not seem to have appreciated that they were no more than river barges, normally pulled by horses. While some were new and badly built, others were old and rotten. Some were uncaulked and sank when the loading did finally begin. In one sense it did not matter now, for it was clear that the Armada could not wait a fortnight. Nor could he fight the English fleet without further supplies of ammunition. Indeed the decision of what to do next might not matter either, if the English resolved to fight off Calais. All the duke could do was to write yet another letter to Parma begging him to help him find a port – for he would have to leave at the first sign of bad weather – and for local pilots on whom reaching such a port depended.

To safeguard himself, Parma wrote to the king on 8 August to the effect that Medina Sidonia's messengers were misled when they saw his 'boats unarmed and with no artillery on board, and the men not shipped'. They were simply wrong in telling the duke the ships were not ready.

The boats are, and have been for months, in proper order for the work they have to do, namely to take the men across. We have not as many seamen as we ought to have; but enough for the job. The boats are so small that the troops cannot be kept on board for long . . . Putting the men on board these low, small boats can be done in a very short time, and I am confident that in this respect there will be no shortcoming in Your Majesty's service.

In fact Parma had still not been to Dunkirk or Nieuport to see the situation for himself, whereas both the duke's messengers had. Parma had trusted his subordinates too much, it seems. Although the boat-builders had been imported from the Baltic and Italy for the task, he had had to rely on captured Dutch labour for the manual work. Could there have been sabotage? Certainly, good timbers had been intermixed with rotten ones. At an embarkation exercise several had left their troops standing neck-high in the water when they promptly sank! An anonymous letter was to find its way to the king, pointing out, 'There has been very bad management with the Flemish ships. They cannot be ready for another fortnight because of the neglect of the commissaries, whose only care has been to steal everything they could. The ships are short of sailors, because the sailors have been neglected and dreadfully ill-treated'.

Parma's neglect is out of character for a man of his great energy. It is amazing that he had river barges built instead of sailing ones. He does not seem to have considered whether a horse-drawn boat can be rowed across a sea. Indeed no orders had been given to train the troops in oarsmanship. One explanation of this seeming failure on his part could be that he had decided in his own mind that the 'Enterprise' was never going to succeed, and that the peace negotiations could be successful if handled genuinely. There are signs that he thought negotiation could achieve more than invasion, as early as March, when he wrote to the king, 'The conquest of England would have been difficult if the country had been taken by surprise. Now they are strong and armed; we are comparatively weak'.

He approached the whole problem in a much more detached way than his master for he did not tangle religion with politics in the same way. Furthermore he was more intelligent and had met Protestants who were loyal to their queen and country, unlike Philip, whose only contact with the English had been with disgruntled Catholics or swashbucklers like Drake. Parma was actually experiencing the running of a country which involved long term occupation in the face of

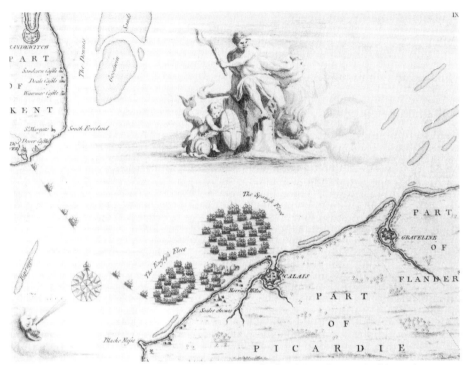

Chart 9. On Sunday, 7 August, the two fleets gathered off Calais as Seymour's ships arrive.

hostile inhabitants, so he could see the overwhelming difficulties of attempting a similar task in England. Invasion was futile if prolonged occupation was impossible.

It is also possible that he felt his family had not received the rewards they should have for loyalty to the crown in the past. He could point to royal blood in his family, which he felt should have entitled them to a kingdom, such as Portugal. If the enterprise to capture England was solely to add another kingdom to Philip's collection, with nothing for his own family, he would be far from content. He would have been fascinated to know that within the Armada there had been discussion as to whether he or Philip would be king of a captured England. The joke aboard was that it would take a civil war in Spain to resolve that problem!

Parma was now convinced that Philip was wrong in thinking the Armada was in God's cause and hence was bound to succeed. Peace negotiations were far more

Four of clubs shows the two fleets off Calais. Five of spades emphasises Parma's late arrival at Dunkirk.

likely to be successful. It followed that one way in which those negotiations could become meaningful would be to ensure that the invasion became an impossibility.

It is significant that he had no knowledge of the contents of a secret letter Medina Sidonia was carrying, for if he had, his desire for the peace negotiations to succeed would have been even greater. For the letter contained the king's minimum demands for peace to be concluded. They included freedom of worship in England, the forgiveness of Catholic exiles and a withdrawl of English troops from the Netherlands. He could have got two of the three points – the exception being that of the exiles. Moreover, Elizabeth would have rewarded him more generously for his pains than Philip.

Before returning to naval matters, we must follow Parma's movements over this crucial period. On the evening of Monday 8 August he rode to Nieuport and then on to Dunkirk. He was to claim at Nieuport that 16,000 troops had already embarked but had found the weather too inclement for sailing. The number amounts to that of the entire forces at his disposal and so is immediately suspect.

At 9 a.m. on the Tuesday morning he claimed to have witnessed his troops on the quayside ready to embark by the end of the day. He omitted to record that he met the duke's Inspector-General of the Fleet, Don Jorge Manrique, there, and that he gave Parma his blunt opinion of his boats! It seems that Don Jorge thought his position gave him charge over Parma's boats and so was ordering his supplies officer about when the duke arrived. The result was a violent argument in which Parma nearly hit Don Jorge.

At the height of this quarrel a small boat arrived bringing a shivering, distraught and soaking Prince of Ascoli ashore. The Prince was Philip's illegitimate son. He brought the first news of a terrible battle fought the previous day, adding that the Armada had now disappeared to the north.

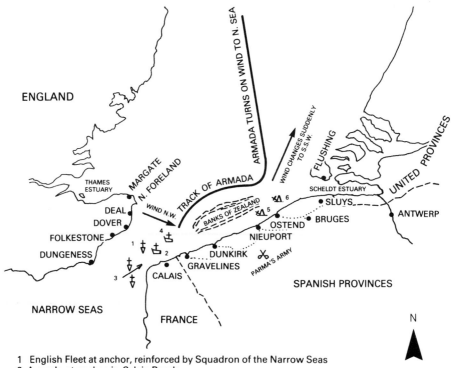

1 English Fleet at anchor, reinforced by Squadron of the Narrow Seas
2 Armada at anchor in Calais Roads
3 Fireships
4 Armada forming again after fireships, early on 8 August
5 *San Felipe* wrecked
6 *San Mateo* wrecked

The fireship attack on Sunday and the Battle of Gravelines on Monday.

Three and two of clubs show the fireships in action off Calais.

On the previous Saturday evening, the newly-arrived Sir William Wynter, Seymour's Rear-Admiral, raised the question of using fireships against the anchored Armada. The tide and wind were likely to prove favourable if the timing was right. No doubt he was not the only one who had thought this tactic a possibility. Indeed an order had been sent from London to Dover to prepare ships for that very purpose. But they would not be in place for some while to come. So, when Howard's council decided to use fireships when they met early on the Sunday morning, there was no alternative but to devise some 'home-made' ones. The call for captains to volunteer ships was not unheeded, for compensation for an old ship, especially if it was claimed that it was well-stored at the time, was worth the taking. Drake subsequently received £900 for his 200 ton *Thomas*, for example.

Eight ships were eventually chosen and these included five from Drake's squadron. None were less than 90 tons. They were filled with combustible materials and their cannon loaded. They were not unexpected, for in the Armada there were rumours that the Italian engineer Federigo Giambelli, inventor of the *hellburner* ship specially designed to blow up at the right moment, was in England at the time. It had not been forgotten that at the siege of Antwerp three years earlier, delayed-action ships had drifted on the Scheldt and killed a thousand Spaniards. In fact, he was not there to supervise the construction of his ships but to devise the boom which proved a failure across the Thames at Gravesend. However, fearing the worst, the duke gave orders to Captain Serrano to position eight pinnaces equipped with grappling irons to tow any approaching fireships clear of the main fleet.

By midnight on Sunday the fireships were ready and the tide was right. On the *San Martin* someone wrote, 'We waited because there was nothing else we could do. We had a great presentiment of evil from those fiendish people and their arts. So we continued anxiously on Sunday all day long'. Morale was low, and would

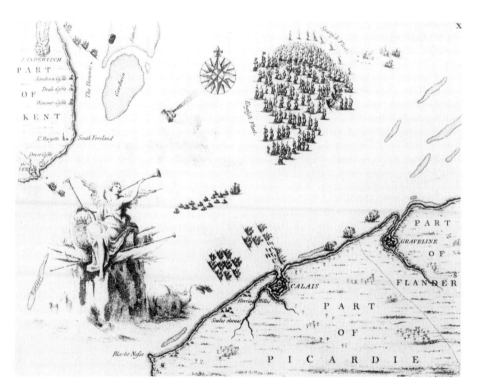

Chart 10. The Battle of Gravelines, Monday, 8 August. *San Lorenzo* attacked near Calais.

King and six of spades show the Battle of Gravelines.

have been lower still if the news about Parma's barges had been known throughout the fleet.

The duke's orders were that if the fireships got through to the fleet, they were to tie buoys onto their anchor cables and then cut the cables free. They would return on the morning tide to recover the anchors. In fact they never got a chance to recover them, when they were forced to carry out the buoying orders.

Just after midnight the signal for the fireships to sail was given. Off they went, accompanied by other boats which would take their skeleton crews off when the fires were lit. They must have been a dramatic and terrifying sight to behold when they burst into flame. Fire and smoke poured out of their gunports and the flames raced up their rigging and set their mainsails alight. The Spaniards, expecting purpose-built *hellburners*, were surprised to see that the English were using such large vessels. One or two pinnaces managed to get their grappling irons aboard them, but to no avail as the flames simply burnt the ropes through.

One after another the Spanish skilfully buoyed their anchors and cut them free.

The attack on the 'Capitana' *San Lorenzo* galleass of Calais, 8 August. An engraving by J. Pine after C. Lempriere

A mere five minutes after the fireships had got past the pinnace line, the Armada's sails were unfurling and the ships got under way. But in the dark and hurry there were collisions. The *San Lorenzo*, the galleasses' flagship, was badly damaged when her rudder became entangled with another's anchor cable. No fireship exploded, and they finally fizzled out. Indeed none set fire to any Spanish ship as the fleet had managed to move clear of them. But they had scattered the enemy and, as time was to show, deprived them of their vital anchors and cables.

At dawn on the Monday, the duke found his fleet more scattered than he had dared to hope. They were stretched from Calais to Gravelines some ten miles away. Beside the flagship were only two galleons and eight *pataches*. As the duke moved to unite his fleet the English struck, with Drake and Seymour going straight in on the attack.

It was the start of what can only be described as a gigantic free-for-all, commencing at 7 a.m., reaching its peak two hours later, and dying out by 4 p.m.

The 2ᵈ Fight betweene ỹ Englisħ and Spanisħ Fleetes being the 23 of Iune 1549. wherein onely Cock an Englisħman being wᵗ his litle Veſſell in ỹ midſt of ỹ Enemies died valiently. but ỹ Spaniards much worſted.

Two of diamonds shows the action around the galleass. William Coxe, alias Cock, took part in the attack and was killed later that day. The date on the card is wrong.

Although some 260 ships were present off Gravelines that day, such were the problems of warfare which depended on wind and current, that only some forty English and thirty Spanish ships were directly engaged. The tide carried the battle some five miles in each direction as the day wore on, first ebbing towards Calais, then flooding towards Dunkirk. The SW wind of the previous night turned in the morning to WNW and in the afternoon to NW.

It was immediately apparent that the galleass *San Lorenzo*, with its damaged rudder, was an obvious target. She was doing her best to row to Calais to get under the protection of its fort, when Howard's whole squadron swung round to chase her (see pages 134–5). If Drake had let the fleet down when he chased Recalde's ship, Howard was now behaving disgracefully for an admiral of a fleet about to enter a major battle.

The galleass, with her 300 soldiers and 450 oarsmen, and a store of gold and silver, managed to beach herself in shallower water than the galleons could cope with. Promptly Howard sent fifteen long boats manned with volunteers to finish her off. A musketry fight ensued in which many were killed. It was only stopped when Don Hugo de Moncada, the squadron's leader, died when a ball blew both his eyes out. Immediately the galley slaves jumped overboard to swim ashore. They were promptly followed by Italian artillerymen and sailors. Undaunted by the loss of some fifty of their number, 200 English pursuers clambered aboard to ransack the ship, stealing from her chapel as well as her cabins. Some 22,000 to 50,000 gold ducats are mentioned in different accounts, as well as candlesticks, plate, crystal, gold chains and insignia. None of the booty was ever declared, for officially 'there was no treasure on board at all, other than a very few things': so wrote Captain Richard Thomson, one of the pillagers.

The governor of Calais sent his cousin and other gentlemen to congratulate the English victors, saying they accepted that the English had the right to the booty, but the governor regarded the ship and her guns as his. It was pointed out that if they tried to tow her away, the fort's guns would prevent them! But at that point, wrote Thomson, 'some of our rude men . . . fell to spoiling the Frenchmen, taking away their rings and jewels'. This led to the fort opening fire, which resulted in the deaths of some twenty pillagers, either directly or by drowning as they rushed to escape the fire. The galleass was destined to rot away in the course of time. This incident meant that the whole of Howard's squadron had missed the opening of the battle.

Consequently it fell to Drake to lead the main attack of the day. His squadron followed him in line astern. First his *Revenge*, then the rest, bombarded the *San Martin* at close quarters. His squadron was followed by those of Hawkins, Frobisher and Seymour. Finally, Howard brought four of his galleons to join in, while four Spanish galleons came to their admiral's aid. In the heat of the engagement Medina Sidonia climbed the rigging to get a better view of the situation. His ship received 107 direct hits; 'enough to bring down a mountain', commented Alonzo Vanegas. Twelve of her crew were killed and 120 wounded. Later that day her two divers had to stop the leaks with lead plates, tow (coarse hemp) and pitch while her pumps just kept the incoming water in check.

What is really significant in this attack, and in others during the day, is that the English shots were actually piercing the enemy's hulls. The *San Felipe* was the first to suffer as seventeen ships closed in on her. With her rudder gone, foremast broken and hull holed, she lost 200 men. Still she struggled on, as an Englishman, standing on the maintop of his ship with sword and buckler, shouted, 'You are good soldiers. Surrender on fair terms'. The Spaniards' reply was to shoot him as he climbed down the rigging. Subsequently most of the stricken ship's crew was removed by an urca, leaving her to drift until she finally sank. The *Maria Juan* sank suddenly, taking 275 men with her, after repeated distress signals had brought her little aid. The speed of her sinking confirmed the effectiveness of the English cannonade. The *San Juan de Sicilia* and the *Nuestra Señora de Begoña* also suffered severely. Indeed the *San Juan* and the *San Mateo* were so awash with blood that they left red wakes behind them in the sea. In all some 800 Spaniards were wounded and 600 killed, while on the English side not a ship was lost and no more than twenty men killed.

The battle ended with a sudden squall of wind and heavy rain sweeping down upon it. No one on the English side quite realised what a victory they had gained. Certainly they did not appreciate that the action would prove to be the final major one of the year. Perhaps this was because they only reckoned on having knocked out two galleons, not realising that a dozen more were near to sinking. As Howard put it, when he wrote to Walsingham, 'Their force is wonderful great and strong; yet we pluck their feathers by little and little.'

But why had the English shooting proved so much more effective on this Monday than it had earlier in the chase? It seems clear that they had realised the need to sail closer to their enemy so as to fire at point-blank range: a mere 100 yards. If so, this poses the question of why the Spaniards did not take similar advantage of the shorter range. In fact they did what they could. Drake's ship had her upperwork pierced. According to Ubaldino's narrative, Drake's own cabin was

twice pierced by shot and there was an occasion on which two gentlemen, who towards evening had retired to rest a little after the battle, and one of them lying upon the bed, when it was broken to pieces under him by a saker ball, without his taking the least hurt. And shortly afewards the Earl of Northumberland, who had come to fight as a volunteer, and Sir Charles Blount, were resting on the same bed when it was again hit by a ball of a demi-culverin which passed through the cabin from one side to the other without doing any harm other than scrape the foot, taking off the toes of one who was there with them.

But piercing the upperwork of a ship is nothing compared to piercing its hull, and the English hulls remained intact. Suspicions as to why the Spanish fire had less effect than the English had to await the confirmation of modern archaeologists before they could be substantiated. Analysis has shown that whereas the cannons used by the Armada, which were cast in Italy, the Netherlands, and even England, held firm, the majority of iron shot was made in Spain or Portugal within a few weeks. The fact that Spain had no worthwhile gun-making industry did not deter her from producing her own shot. Today it can be proved that this shot was very badly made. Its iron was full of impurities; too much carbon and ferric oxide having been used. All the shot found and examined by archaeologists had concentric rings showing, which indicated that during the process the iron had been *quenched* while still red hot. This method has the effect of making the iron very brittle. Although the Spanish shot industry was not so knowledgeable as the English one, the chief reason for such quenching must have been the speedier production of shot that it made possible. A check of the Spanish records shows that Medina Sidonia wrote to Philip to say the allowance of 30 shots per gun was inadequate. The outcome was a sharp increase in production involving some 350–400 tons of shot, which is about 53,790 more cannon-balls; a staggering achievement in the available time.

The fact that England had developed a sound gun-making industry and Spain had not was due to the former possessing a commercially-minded middle class which the latter lacked. Spain used the wealth of the Indies to purchase guns from abroad, while the contrasting poverty of the English monarchy forced the navy onto local production. Although no gunsmiths knew it at the time, English iron ore contained what has been called the 'Greys', masses of tiny fossilised sea shells, which provided the 'flux' necessary for the effective purification of the ore. It seems likely that the Spanish cast iron was very brittle because it lacked the flux to remove the slag in the ore. The poor quality of their cast iron can also been found in the quality of their anchors. The Dutch saying, 'As meagre as a Spanish anchor', confirms this. Furthermore, archaeologists have subsequently found several guns which burst when fired, as well as snapped anchors.

It has also been discovered that all the Spanish powder was the black fine-grained ('fine-corned'), musket variety, which produces a higher and quicker pressure in the gun than the coarser 'serpentine' powder used by the English. This meant that when the gun was fired there was a sharper and harder explosion, which affected both the ball and the gun. The result was that cannon-balls often broke into small pieces, either at the moment of firing or when they hit their target. The English, with their inferior powder, had a reduced muzzle velocity but a surer chance of delivering their cannon-balls intact.

Consequently, victory that day depended more upon the inadequacies of Spanish powder and shot than it did on English heroism. In fact Professor Michael Lewis, the expert on gunnery of the period, has argued that both sides failed as 'artillerists'. He concluded that the Spanish failure was due more to their ships' lack of manoeuverability than to the quality of their guns. The English, however, failed to get sufficiently close to the enemy to make their lightweight firepower effective until they did so at Gravelines. They then came within the *Spaniards'* effective firing range and so achieved results. The fact that they escaped the potentially far more damaging effect of the Spanish heavy guns on this occasion was due to the latter's shortage of ammunition. In ideal conditions the heavier guns would have been far more damaging to their target as their shot could 'smash', whereas the lighter shot of the English guns could only make holes. For Lewis it was the sailing ability of the English ships which really tipped the balance against the Armada – plus the fact that further supplies of ammunition were nearer to hand for the English.

CHAPTER NINE

The North Sea and Home

'Not a man among us slept that night,' recalled Fray de la Torre. 'All we could do was wait for the moment when we would be hurled into the shoals.' He was referring to the Zeeland Banks on which the surf was breaking. But, after this rough night, the dawn of Tuesday brought a slight moderation in the wind. Although the English bore down upon the duke again, they drew off without attacking due to lack of ammunition, perhaps fearing the banks as the Spaniards did. The Spanish leadsmen were shouting out six, then five fathoms. In desperation the duke's officers crowded round him, calling on him to take to a pinnace to save himself and the Holy Banner from certain capture.

Captain Alonzo Vanegas of the *San Martin* wrote afterwards,

The duke was advised that if he wanted to escape with his life he would have to surrender. It was impossible to avoid being driven aground. He replied he trusted in God and His Blessed Mother to bring him to a port of safety . . . People appealed to his conscience not to allow so many souls to be lost by shipwreck, but he would not listen to such advise . . . He summoned the pilots . . . [and] . . . discussed with them whether it would be possible to reach Hamburg or the Norwegian coast, or to attack some other harbour to save part of the fleet. They all replied that they would make every effort, but were doubtful of success unless God helped them with a miracle, and shifted the wind so that they could get out to the open sea . . . It seemed to everyone that we could neither save the ships nor reform the fleet to renew the attack on the enemy. We were expecting to perish any moment. The duke was not convinced by these opinions, which showed such lack of courage.

It is worth mentioning that the duke's ship had the only available Flemish pilot aboard her. Not that he was of much encouragement as he only prophesied doom, presumably because he could not see any obvious landmarks when questioned. Wagenhaer's charts and rutter did not show that most of the sandbanks in the area were long and very narrow, running parallel to the shore with deep-water channels between them. As they were then sailing parallel to the shore themselves, it is possible that they were fortunately following one such channel.

The duke and his officers said their confessions and prepared to die. 'It was the most awful day in the world. Everyone was in utter despair and stood waiting for death,' commented someone. But then the wind suddenly changed and out to sea they went. None had run aground! Surely a miracle had occurred. The duke explained, 'We were saved by the wind which shifted by God's mercy to the south west'.

Taking a tally of the Armada, the duke noted that eight ships were lost and all the others damaged and taking in water. Nearly all were short of shot and many of the crews were decimated by sickness, wounds or death. De Leyva voiced his opinion on the situation facing his ship. 'I have now no more than thirty cannon ball, my ship is riddled with small shot, and pierced in several places. She is taking in water badly. But I do not consider any of this sufficient reason not to do my duty. I am not in favour of entering the North Sea'.

But the question of where they should go had to be faced. The duke asked his council whether they should go back down the Channel or home via the North Sea and Scotland. Recalde suggested cruising in the vicinity for a few days and then returning to Calais if the wind turned favourable. De Leyva wanted to try for Norway to get fresh supplies. The duke pointed out the danger of leaving Spain herself defenceless if they did not return by winter. They finally decided to return to the Channel as soon as the wind permitted. 'And if not, to go back to Spain via the North Sea.' In fact the question proved pointless, as the NE wind they needed did not materialise. The strong SW wind which persisted meant the North Sea was the only route they could take. True to form the duke wrote to his king, 'The armada was so completely crippled and scattered that it seemed my first duty to Your Majesty was to save it, even at the risk of a very long voyage in high latitudes'. He calculated the journey would amount to some 750 leagues. This works out at 2,625 nautical miles, a good calculation.

Meanwhile the English fleet was taking stock of its position. Seymour and Wynter were angry with Howard for sending them off to guard the Straits in case Parma should attempt to cross them. In fact they had little grounds for complaint

The Spaniards Consulting — and at laft refolving to return into Spain by the north Ocean many of their Shipps being difabled

Ten of spades recalls the decision to return by the North Sea.

since they had disobeyed their queen's instructions to guard the Straits when they came across to join in the previous day's battle. In his turn Howard was annoyed with a bureaucratic demand from the Queen's Council to send in precise returns of the number and tonnage of the ships with him, detailing their manpower, victuals and ammunition, including where the powder and shot had come from. Furthermore the Council wanted to know why none of the Spanish ships had been boarded. Not surprisingly he refused to answer. Indeed it is difficult to see how he could have done under the circumstances. He wrote urgently for more food and ammunition, as 'we know not whither we may be driven to follow the Spanish fleet'. He added, 'Their force is wonderful great and strong; and yet we pluck their feathers little and little'.

Drake too wrote of the Battle of Gravelines, 'God hath given us so good a day in forcing the enemy so far to leeward as I hope to God the Prince of Parma and the Duke of Medina Sidonia shall not shake hands this few days, and whensoever they shall meet, I believe neither of them will greatly rejoice of this day's service'. He too was concerned about the English fleet's ability to follow up their success. He added, 'There must be great care taken to send us munition and victual withersoever the enemy goeth'. Neither he, nor Howard, could know that there would be no further battle to face. Nevertheless the English fleet was resolved to pursue the Armada come what may. As Howard wrote to Walsingham, 'Notwithstanding that our powder and shot was well near all spent, we set on a brag countenance and gave them chase, as though we had wanted nothing'.

On that day the Armada passed the Dogger Bank. On the previous day, Wednesday, the English were catching up on its rearguard, when the duke took action. He slowed the rest to protect his rear by ordering all to shorten sail. The *San Pedro* and the urca, *Santa Barbara*, failed to carry out this order so that they sailed several miles ahead of the rest. Promptly their captains were ordered back to the flagship to be hung. Captain Francisco de Cuellar of the *San Pedro* protested furiously, saying that one of his officers had sailed on without his permission on the grounds that he wanted to make time for the ship to heave to for repairs. She had holes which were still letting water in. Francisco claimed that he had asked his 350 crew to hack him to pieces if he had not done his duty. Be that as it may, he had committed a technical offence forbidden in standing orders under threat of hanging, if nothing else.

Both captains were sent to the Judge Advocate General, Martin de Aranda, who was not in the same ship as the duke. He heard Francisco's defence and wrote to the duke to say he could not carry out the sentence without his superior's written order. The duke then annulled the sentence, but he did relieve Francisco of his command. No such plea was made for the other captain, Don Cristobal de Avila, whose ship had been further ahead than Francisco's. He was duly hung and his still hanging body paraded round the fleet as a warning to others. It seems eighteen other captains were under sentence of death for disobedience at the same time, but all were committed to the custody of the judge advocate general in the end.

Subsequently Francisco wrote that the hanging was not on the duke's orders, but on those of the Senior Army General, Bobadilla, who acted as prosecutor and as judge of both of them. In fact the duke does not seem to have heard of Cristobal's hanging until after it had been carried out. There is a possibility that Cristobal had not done all he should at the Battle of Gravelines. Certainly there seems to have been a lot of recrimination going on in the Armada, which is hardly surprising seeing that they were now on the retreat. There was a widespread feeling of shame and disappointment. The army officers felt frustrated that the failure of the sea captains to grapple with the enemy ships had deprived them of their recognised role in naval warfare. The Armada had been defeated without even trying to use its soldiers in battle; there could hardly be anything more humiliating for generals or troops, to say nothing of gentlemen volunteers.

The duke, for his part, realised the fault lay with the design of his ships, rather than in any weaknesses on the part of either his sailors or his soldiers. Too many of the Armada's ships were built for Mediterranean, not Atlantic, use. Consequently their rigging was too light and they were overmasted for the turbulent seas they had to face. The 'castles' added to the merchantmen, together with their heavy guns, only served to emphasise their weakness for northern waters. As they went on hulls began to flex and break up. Planks became loose, caulking worked its way out as ships 'spewed their oakum'. This, in turn, led to trenails – the wooden pegs which hold planks to their frames – loosening, followed by the iron bolts holding plank ends in place. These facts were to become only too obvious as the ships struggled, and lost, the battle to round Scotland and Ireland. Of this more anon.

With the arguments raging in his fleet the weary duke, exhausted by recent events, retreated to his cabin for the rest he so desperately needed. It was while he was resting that Bobadilla was able to deal with the two recalcitrant captains in his superior's name. Interestingly, the duke's diary and letters make no mention of these two captains.

Although the English fleet came close to them several times on the following day, the Spanish rearguard kept it at bay. It followed the Armada for four days as far as 55 degrees north, which is in line with Newcastle. As the Armada showed no signs of attacking Scotland, Howard decided to enter the Firth of Forth to obtain what food and water he could, and alert the King of Scotland. He left a pinnace and caravel to check that the enemy rounded the Orkneys and Shetlands, while turning the rest of his fleet round. Of the return journey from Scotland, Sir Thomas Heneage wrote that he had heard 'they [were] driven to such extremity for lack of meat, as it is reported (I wot not how truly) that my Lord Admiral was driven to eat beans, and some to drink their own water'.

On Thursday 18 August the English fleet came in to Harwich and Margate Roads, having abandoned the chase six days earlier. No supply ships had reached them since they left Calais, so they were acutely short of ammunition, food and especially beer. As soon as they docked, Howard wrote to Burghley for money for his men and for £1,000 of clothing,

> for else, in a very short time, I look to see most of the mariners go naked . . . Sickness and mortality begins wonderfully to grow amongst us, and it is a most pitiful sight to see, here at Margate, how the men, having no place to receive them into here, die in the streets. I am driven myself, of force, to come a-land, to see them bestowed in some lodging; and the best I can get is barns and outhouses; and the relief is small that I can provide for them here. It would grieve any man's heart to see them that have served so valiantly to die so miserably.

On that very day the queen left London in her royal barge to encourage her troops at the Tilbury Camp. False reports had been circulating in the south of England that there had been a battle off Scotland on August 13, involving the loss of fifteen English galleons and the capture of Drake. A report to this effect had reached Mendoza in Paris. Another report maintained that Drake had been wounded in the leg by a cannon-ball. Clearly the queen's presence among her troops was needed to boost their morale.

The rumours maintained that Drake had tried to board the *San Martin* and been injured and captured in the process. The story probably arose as a result of the English fleet being scattered by a north-easterly wind on the Tuesday after it abandoned the chase. It had then taken shelter for the next two days wherever it could in the Thames estuary. Thus at any one place, only a few galleons appeared to have survived the chase. Naturally, broadsheet printers would not miss the chance of relaying any rumour that was newsworthy. Whereas hitherto Protestant and Catholic publications were broadly in agreement as to facts, though not propaganda, it is noticeable that some Protestant ones got quite carried away as to what had happened to Drake in the imaginery North Sea battle. Howard himself spent the following weeks pressing Walsingham to ensure that the navy was kept on a war footing, for 'they [Spaniards] dare not return with this dishonour and shame to their King, and overthrow of their Pope's credit. Sir, sure bind, sure find. A Kingdom is a great wager. Sir, you know security is dangerous; and God had not been our best friend, we should have found it so'.

The Catholic news-sheets differed on details as to whether Drake had been killed or simply wounded. What wounds he had suffered

Knave of spades shows Jesuits hanging in England. In all twenty-one priests and ten laymen were executed in 1588, four as the Armada sailed up the Channel and the rest from 7 September onwards.

varied too. It was even claimed that he had fled from the battle in a small boat, never to be seen again! Mendoza sent the story that he had been captured on to his king and lit the bonfire he had built at the embassy for celebrating the Armada's victory. Of course the news of Drake's supposed capture spread rapidly across Europe. Count Olivarez rushed round to the Vatican to call on the pope to hand over the promised million and have a *Te Deum* sung at St Peter's. Sixtus promised to act, once the veracity of Mendoza's report could be proved. Once again the pope was more than a match for Olivarez.

Meanwhile the queen had come from St James's Palace in the royal barge preceded by silver trumpeters. When she arrived at 'Camp Royal', which was two miles from the Thames on a hill at West Tilbury, she found it clean and resplendent with its ditches dug and its palisades at last in place. Two weeks earlier the scene had been a far more modest one with scarcely a camp to see. Victuallers had not responded to the calls of town criers in the market places, and the brewing arrangements had been chaotic. In fact, the Earl of Leicester's

Queen of hearts and the queen of clubs. Elizabeth at the Tilbury Camp. Notice the choice of numbers and suits for these two cards. The latter is the first picture of a royal walkabout.

commission as Captain-General had not arrived — simply because it had not yet been signed. Nevertheless, by the time the Queen arrived he had worked wonders. As historian Garrett Mattingly put it, 'For the moment Tilbury combined the glamour of a military spectacle with the innocent cheerfulness of a country fair'.

On her 'walkabout' only four men and two boys escorted the Queen, at her own request. Before her walked the Earl of Ormonde ceremonially carrying the Sword of State. Elizabeth was dressed in white velvet with a silver cuirass embossed with a mythological design, and carried a silver truncheon chased in gold. She wore pearls and diamonds in her red wig and, when she smiled, her black teeth were evident. She rode around on a white gelding with a 'back like a barn door'.

That night she stayed at a nearby manor house before returning the next day. A march-past and cavalry exercises made up the day, together with dinner in her general's tent. She took the opportunity to deliver a speech which is worthy of quotation, at least in part.

My loving people, we have been persuaded by some that are careful of our safety, to take heed how we commit ourselves to armed multitudes for fear of treachery; but I assure you I do not desire to live to distrust my faithful and loving people. Let tyrants fear! I have always so behaved myself, that, under God, I have placed my chiefest strength and safeguard in the loyal hearts and good will of my subjects; and, therefore, I am come amongst you, as you see, at this time, not for my recreation or disport, but being resolved, in the midst and heat of the battle, to live, or die amongst you all, to lay down for my God, for my kingdom, and for my people, my honour and my blood, even in the dust. I know I have the body but of a weak and feeble woman, but I have the heart and stomach of a king, and of a king of England too; and think it foul scorn that Parma, or Spain, or any prince of Europe, should dare to invade the borders of my realm; to which, rather than any dishonour shall grow by me, I myself will take up arms, I myself will be your general, judge, and rewarder of every one of your virtues in the field . . . . In the meantime, my captain-general shall be in my stead, than whom never prince commanded a more noble or worthy subject . . .

In the two days she spent with her troops more reliable news began to arrive about her fleet. The all-important fact that no ship had been lost, and none seriously damaged either, was reassuring to some extent. But the Armada was not destroyed, and Howard's message that 'All the world never saw such a force as theirs' left the feeling that the crisis was not yet over. Drake reported that he was still not convinced that the Armada would not try again. In fact the other reports from those who had been present at Gravelines were more pessimistic, expressing the feeling that an opportunity had been missed. One such report, which reached Walsingham at Tilbury, was of a blunt nature from Henry Whyte. 'Your Honour may see how our parsimony at home hath bereaved us of the famousest victory that ever our navy might have had at sea.' Consequently the country was kept on the alert and the camp at Tilbury maintained. Another camp nearer London was also created regardless of the expense.

On 1 September, at a time when many ships had not enough fit men to weigh the anchors, Howard reconstituted his War Council at Dover. It divided the fleet into two for revictualling purposes. One squadron was to be stationed at the Downs and the other at Margate. As Howard put it, when the news of the Armada came in, 'We shall be able, with the help of soldiers from the shore, for to be ready within a day for the service'. Later that day news that the Armada was returning reached the Council, and Howard wrote 'in greatest haste' for all the powder and shot he could get, as well as tar, pitch, fireworks and more ships. In fact the news was false, but that it was assumed to be accurate showed just how much respect for the Armada the War Council had.

Just as Spain eventually had to adjust to the return of a defeated Armada, so England had to cope with the return of sick and unpaid soldiers and sailors. The economic situation demanded an immediate disbanding of the army and a demobilisation of the navy. Howard was given the task of supervising this operation. He soon found himself distracted by an endless stream of demands which required him to check what had happened to the ammunition supplied to Lord Sussex for his (Howard's) use, and who had authorised its issue, for example.

Demobilisation presented many problems. The normal procedure, which the men hastened to demand, was that payment and discharge went together. Without money they would not accept discharge. Behind this dilemma lay the fact that the fiscal system of the day was intrinsically inefficient. Once the wages money was approved by the Queen's Council, it was delivered by Lord Treasurer's warrant to the Treasurer of the Navy. By custom he was then able to privately invest the money, or even speculate with it, to his own advantage until actual payment was demanded. On 19 August, Howard wrote that his 'poor men . . . cry out for money, and they know not where to be paid'. If there was no money, it seemed to him that the men must be kept on. But if that were done it would only increase the unpaid wage bill. Furthermore, food would have to be purchased for them and there was no money for that either.

Howard was desperate as there simply was not the cash available to pay them off. He showed his humanity by refusing to discharge anyone who had not been paid. He decided to keep the *Rosario's* money and plate, which he had been ordered to get from Drake, without permission and then use it to pay off as many men as he could. He went on to double the sum out of his own pocket. He wrote at the time,

> Therefore I had rather open the Queen's Majesty's purse something to relieve them, than they should be in that extremity; for we are to look to have more of these services; and if men should not be cared for better than to let them starve and die miserably, we should very hardly get men to serve. All I ask is that the Crown will put down as much as I have. God knows I am not rich, but I would rather have never a penny in the world than that they should lack.

He then pressed the Crown to pay as much as he had given; it is not known whether he was ever repaid for his generosity.

It is a significant comment on the economy of the country and the queen's household that the Lord Admiral of England should have to pay half of his men's wages at the end of the greatest threat the country had faced for many a year.

Just how urgent his action was can be gauged from the fact that half-naked seamen were dying in the streets of Dover and Rochester. The discharged men not only faced financial hardship, but faced disease too. It appears that something of a major epidemic had broken out. It had started aboard the *Elizabeth Jonas*, which suffered the loss of 200 of her 500 crew. The ship was cleaned and fumigated before a new crew was put aboard. The infection broke out again, worse than before, and soon spread to other ships. Probably it was some form of food poisoning involving rapid death from toxaemia. Such an epidemic was not

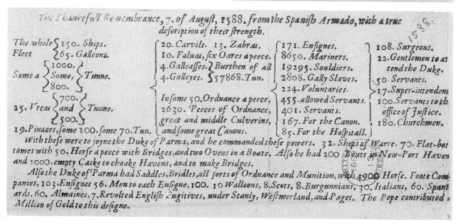

The service sheet of 'Thankefull Remembrance' details the threat faced, and showing left, England's defences at the ready, and right, sermon at St Paul's Cross to celebrate victory.

surprising, given the unhygienic conditions under which food was stored and prepared on board. Ovens and hearths were built of loosely spaced bricks, and were situated above the bilge with its soaking gravel ballast. A putrid atmosphere was thus inevitable which, with the humidity below decks, was bound to lead to growths developing on the food. Washing kitchen utensils in 'bad' water from contaminated harbours only added to the problem. In any case much of the food

Left, four of spades shows the Queen entering London in triumph. Right, three of spades shows the thanksgiving service in St Paul's Cathedral.

was putrid from the time it was brought aboard. There was no issue of water for personal washing, and many raw recruits failed to use the 'heads' of the ships (the external curving timbers on the forward sides of the stem) for toilet purposes.

On 26 August Howard wrote, 'The mariners have a conceit (and I think it is true, and so do all the Captains here) that sour drink hath been a great cause of this infection among us'. For the common sailor, the excitement and glory of victory was tinged with the reality of poverty and disease which faced him. Honour and riches were for officers, and particularly for national heroes.

Although the Armada had failed, many Englishmen grumbled about the high command failing to destroy the Spanish force utterly. Questions were raised as to why Howard had not come to close quarters with it. Had he been afraid? There was popular feeling that if Drake had been in charge things would have been different. As the hero of the year, he was praised for any victories there had been, although this overlooked his disobedience to orders and his 'privateering' while

(a)

(b)

(a) Obverse: The Pope, Philip II, the Emperor, bishops &c. with bandaged eyes and seated on a spiked floor, plotting against Elizabeth. Legend translates, 'It is hard to kick against the pricks', Acts 9 v 5. Reverse: The Spanish fleet driven against the rocks. 'Thou, God, art great and doest wondrous things; thou art God alone', Ps. 86 v 10. (b) Obverse: Philip II wearing the order of the Golden Fleece. Reverse: Globe released from bands held by two hands and attached to a yoke. 'Thus it was decreed by the fates.' (c) Obverse: Elizabeth I. 'No other circle in the whole world more rich.' Reverse: Bay-tree uninjured by lightning and winds, flourishing upon an island. 'Not even dangers Border of laurel leaves, which, like the bay-tree, had the virtue of being indestructible.

(c)

chasing the Armada up the Channel. The unfairness of this comparison of Drake and Howard was eventually to be set right by later historians.

Victory was duly celebrated. On the first occasion, 30 August, 'the Lord Mayor, Aldermen, and the Companies in their best liveries went to hear the Dean of St Paul's preach at the Cross'. Then on 18 September there 'were set upon the lower Battlements of the Church eleven Ensigns or Banners taken from the Spanish Fleet'. They were then carried to the Cross in Cheapside and the following day 'hanged on London Bridge'. A few days later Lord Howard was at court to receive the Queen's personal thanks. In reward he subsequently received a licence to export cloth and a pension of £200 a year.

On Sunday, 4 December,

the Queen, attended by her Privy Council, by the Nobility and other honourable Persons as well spiritual as temporal, in great number, the French Ambassador, the Judges, the Heralds and Trumpeters all on horseback, came in a chariot supported by four pillars and drawn by two white horses to St Paul's Church, where, alighting at the West Door, she fell on her knees, and audibly praised God for her own and the Nation's signal deliverance; and after a sermon suitable to the occasion, preached by Dr. Pierce, Bishop of Sarum, she exhorted the People in a most Royal and Christian manner, to a due Performance of the religious Duty of Thanksgiving, then going to the Bishop of London's Palace, where she dined, she returned in the same order as before, by Torchlight, to Somerset House.

Along Fleet Street, she heard a choir singing words she had written herself:

> 'He made the winds and waters rise
> To scatter all mine Enemies.'

The French ambassador had been tricked into attending by being told the celebrations were solely to mark the queen's thirtieth year on the throne!

Lord Howard decided to celebrate the victory by commissioning the Flemish artist Cornelius Vroom to do a set of tapestries for his house. Cornelius based them on engravings done by Augustine Ryther. Eventually Howard sold the tapestries to James I to meet his debts. They were then hung in the House of Lords. He also commissioned the Italian writer Petruccio Ubaldino, who lived in England, to translate his narrative of the whole event. When Drake read the account, he commissioned Petruccio to write a second version as the first did scant justice to his own role in the event. The 'Drake version' opens by showing how creditably Drake behaved when the Armada was sighted off Plymouth, arguing that he sailed out 'making a brave show of his skill and diligence'. It continues,

> Sir Francis Drake, out of respect to the rank and dignity of the office and in honour of the Lord Admiral, lowered his own admiral's flag to pay tribute to Lord Howard, from whose ship the Vice-Admiral's flag was taken down and sent as a gift to Drake, who was thus able to use it as his own from that moment.

Subsequently it refers to the two of them as being 'all of a company . . . [and Drake] always of one mind and thought with the senior admiral, although there were those who had thought, or maybe feared, a different outcome'.

Sailing to Disaster

Meanwhile the Armada was well on its way round the north of Scotland, skirting Ireland and heading for Spain. Many were not to see their homeland again, or only to do so after months of captivity. The northerly route was unknown to them; indeed, no large fleet had ever sailed that way before. The prevailing winds were against them, and Wagenhaer's charts only covered the east coast of Scotland, getting vaguer the further north they went. There were no sea charts of northern and western Ireland. Perhaps a few ships had a land map of Ireland. Recalde had been to the south-western tip of Ireland before, and this was to stand him in good stead.

In view of the uncertainty of the Irish coast it was decided to keep clear of the island altogether and apply ocean navigation techniques. The duke offered a Frenchman 2,000 ducats if he got them safely back to Spain. Orders were issued as they headed up the North Sea to the effect that

> The first course to be held is NNE, until you reach 61½ degrees. After that, you will take great care not to be driven on to the coast of Ireland, for fear of the harm that may come you there. Leaving the island and rounding the cape in 61½ degrees [which would be the northern point of Shetland] you will run WSW until you reach 58 degrees; then SW to the height of 53 degrees; then SSW, heading for Cape Finisterre, and so find your way to Corunna.

These directions would ensure that they passed some 30 miles north of the Shetlands and so miss Cape Wrath. The last part of the directions are incorrect, but this may be due to a translation mistake as the only copy of these directions still in existence is an English one found on one ship which reached Ireland. The impossibility of observing longitude correctly in those days meant that dead reckoning had to be used to judge the westerly distances. It was, however, a good route and in ideal conditions would have taken a month. Faced with shortages of food and water, sickness and low morale, it would be a far from ideal crossing. Starvation rations were imposed on everyone at once, consisting of ½ lb. biscuit, 1 pint of water and ½ pint of wine a day. Horses and mules were thrown overboard to save water. A passing merchant ship reported seeing the sea full of swimming animals.

Calderon came aboard the duke's ship to offer him a sack of rice for the wounded and sick. He had a number of 50 lb. sacks hidden on the urca *San Sebastian*, which he had listed as 'hospital delicacies', ready for sale to the needy. The duke persuaded him to make the same offer throughout the fleet. He did so, at a price agreed with their pursers.

On 15 August they captured three Scottish fishing boats and made use of their seamen as pilots. When freezing fog hit them two days later, Fray Bernardo de Gongora wrote, 'In latitude 62 degrees it is not warm. I am shivering, for I left my coat behind on Pedro de Valdez's ship when by a miracle I managed to escape'. The negroes succumbed to the cold quickest, followed by the Andalusians and the Sicilians. After a two-day storm, the weather turned better on 19 August. The wind turned to the NE, just what they needed. Soon Shetland was sighted and they sailed between it and the Orkneys at a speed of 2½-3 knots. They took the opportunity to buy all the dried fish the Scottish fishermen had, paying a good price for it. While the trading was in progress, the duke was making an assessment of the manpower of his fleet. He found there had been a sharp decrease since his last check a week earlier. Some 3,000 were sick and over 1,000 wounded, and this prompted him to write on 21 August to the Archbishop of Santiago and his fellow bishops in Galicia to prepare for receiving these unfortunate men.

The next day the wind turned to the south, forcing the fleet to turn at right angles to their intended course. Off Cape Wrath the seas pounded them to such an extent that many ships showed signs of breaking up. The Armada had reached the point when shipwrecks were to become a feature of its progress. A considerable amount of documentary and archaeological research has gone in to accounting for the wrecks, locating them and salvaging what remains of them. The archaeological techniques and finds will be dealt with separately in Chapter 14. The documentary evidence is difficult to handle as often it records the fact that people reported shipwrecks, but said they did not know the names or nationality of the ships concerned.

Certainly it was not surprising that shipwrecks now occurred. With one in five of those on board helpless for one reason or another, with the weather worsening and most on board not really knowing where they were, disaster was inevitable. With cloudy skies it was impossible to calculate latitudes. It was difficult to even keep together. Now the blunder of bringing 'Mediterranean' rather than 'Atlantic' ships as auxiliaries began to show itself. These ships had simply not got the hull strength needed, and seem to have had too many masts and too light rigging as well. The *San Juan de la Rosa* had lost her mainmast off Corunna. Her outer planking was only 3 in. thick and her keelson 10 × 8 in. Even her largest frames at their strongest point were only 12 × 8 in. Yet she was 945 Spanish tons and carried 233 troops, 64 sailors and 26 guns. Whenever she fired her 50 lb. cannon-balls from her 3 ton guns, the hull was wrenched. She hit a rock off Blasket Island on the SW of Ireland. Fifteen of the twenty-four 'Mediterraneans' were lost or wrecked, while eight out of the ten Mediterranean merchantmen of the Levant squadron were lost. Comparatively few galleons were wrecked or lost. In all it is likely that two or three ships were wrecked off Scotland, one off England and twenty-six off Ireland. On top of that number must be added those lost out at sea.

By Saturday 3 September, when the fleet was still around 58 degrees north, seventeen ships had parted company from it. They included Recalde in the *San Juan*, de Leyva's *Rata Encoronada*, several great ships, a number of hulks and two galleasses. That day the duke did his best to justify his actions to the king.

It has pleased God to ordain things otherwise than we had hoped. This enterprise was fervently commended to Him, so it must be that what has happened was the right thing for Him and for Your Majesty . . . The Armada was in such bad shape, that I considered the best way I could serve Your Majesty was by saving what was left of it, though it meant risking it in this long journey in such a latitude. Our best ships had no shot, and we had already seen how little could be expected of the rest. The Queen's fleet had shown itself vastly superior in battle, in tactics, in the range of its artillery, and in its manoeuvrability. So following the advice of the generals and of Your Majesty's appointed advisers, we set off on this course. We were driven to it also by the weather. The wind held first from the south then later from the south-west. Since the 21st we have had four nights of storms, and seventeen ships have disappeared out of sight, including De Leyva's and Recalde's as well as some other important ones . . . Today . . . we counted 95 ships.

The *El Gran Grifon*, the 38 gun 'admiral' of the hulks, 650 Spanish tons and built in Rostock, with a crew of 43 and 243 troops on board, began to split on the stormy night of 7 September. She had become separated from the main fleet. The next day some of her planks were a hand's width apart. For three days she ran NE, being unable to face the wind in her unstable state, and then the next three days it drove her towards Ireland. By 23 September the wind had forced her back towards Scotland. It was impossible to repair her for some time due to the bad weather. When the violence subsided for two days they were able to use ox-hides and planks to block the leaks, though these repairs were soon to prove only temporary. Three days later she was back in the vicinity of the Orkneys which she had passed six weeks earlier.

It was pitch black with occasional glimpses of the moon, when an unknown diarist aboard wrote,

> We were fit only to die, for the wind was so strong and the sea so wild that the waves mounted to the skies, knocking the ship about so that the men were all exhausted, and yet unable to keep down the water that leaked through our gaping seams. If we had not had the wind astern we could not have kept afloat at all . . . Truly our one thought was that our lives were ended, and each of us reconciled himself to God as well as he could, and prepared for the long journey of death . . . The poor soldiers too, who had worked incessantly at the pumps and buckets, lost heart and let the water rise . . . So we gave way to despair, and each one of us called upon the Virgin Mary to be our intermediary in so bitter a pass; and we looked towards the land with full eyes and hearts, as the reader may imagine . . . At the last, when we thought all hope was gone except through God and His holy Mother . . . we sighted an island ahead of us. It was Fair Isle, and we anchored in a sheltered spot we found, this day of our great peril, 27 September, 1588.

They were soon wedged in a rock cleft at Stroms Hellier ('Cave of the Tide-Race'). Clambering along the yard-arms, the crew jumped onto a 70 ft. high ledge. All three hundred were safe, together with their possessions, so that they far out-numbered the inhabitants of the 3-mile-long island. When the seventeen crofting families saw them coming, they thought the heavenly host and the Day of Judgement were upon them. (In Chapter 14 the finding of the ship's remains in 1970 will be examined.) The weather was too bad for the sailors to cross to the mainland of Shetland for a month. By then they had eaten all the sheep, cattle and ponies on the island, and paid for them. Wisely the islanders are said to have hidden their breeding stock. Some fifty Spaniards died there and are buried at 'Spainnarts Graves', a mass grave which sea erosion exposed on the south coast of the island at the turn of this century.

One survivor has left a vivid description of what they saw on the island.

We found the island peopled by seventeen households in huts, more like hovels than anything else. They are savage people, whose usual food is fish, without bread, except for a few barley-meal bannocks cooked over the embers of a fuel they use, which they make or extract from the earth and call turf. They have some cattle . . . but rarely eat meat . . . They are a very dirty people, neither Christians nor altogether heretics. It is true they confess that the doctrine that once a year is preached to them by people sent from another island, nine leagues off, is not good, but they say they dare not contradict it, which is a pity. Three hundred . . . of us landed on the island, but could save none of our provisions. From that day . . . we lost fifty of our men – most of them dying of hunger.

Robert Mentieth, a native of Orkney, wrote in 1633 of the mixed blessings the Spaniards brought with them,

. . . at first eating up all they could find, not only cattle, sheep, fishes and fowls, but also horses . . . the Islanders in the night carried off their beasts and victual to places in the isle where the Spaniards might not find them: the officers also strictly commanded the soldiers to take nothing but what they paid for, which they did very largely, so that the people were not great losers by them, having got a great many Spanish *reals* for the victuals they gave them . . . [after referring to the acute food shortage on the small island weakening the Spaniards, he went on] . . . and the rest were so weakened, that one or two of the islanders finding a few of them together could easily throw them over the cliffs, by which many of them died.

One tradition has it that the islanders killed a number of Spaniards by causing the heavy flagstone roof of a large turf hut to fall in on them. But such tales are denied by today's islanders. In fact the way in which the three hundred armed men were received into the community of the islanders is today remembered as one of friendship. Mentieth's version should be approached with some caution.

Eventually the survivors were taken to Shetland, and from thence to the mainland. The Revd James Melvill recalled being woken at daybreak on 6 December with the news that 'there is arrived within our harbour [Anstruther] a ship full of Spaniards'.

> Up I got with dilligence (noted Melvill in his diary) and assembling the honest men of the town, came to the Tolbooth; and after consultation taken to hear them, and what answer to make, there presents to us a very reverend man of big stature [Juan Gomez de Medina], of grave and stout countenance, grey-haired and very humble like, who, after muckles and very low courtesy, bowing down with his face near the ground, and twitching my shoe with his hand, began his harangue in the Spanish tongue.

There followed something of a theological argument on Catholicism versus Calvinism before the townsfolk could be prevailed upon to allow them ashore. The local laird thereupon entertained the officers. Eventually the crew reached Edinburgh. The Catholics in the capital fêted them on their arrival. They stayed there eight months, by which time a total of 600 had gathered from the different wrecks. On the tiny island of Kirkholm there remains a row of very small huts which may have been made by other shipwrecked Spaniards. Four hundred were fit enough to be shipped back to Spain via France.

Their presence posed a diplomatic problem to King James VI, who would one day be James I of England. His rather insecure throne relied upon the support of powerful Catholic leaders, but his future lay as successor to the unmarried and childless Protestant Elizabeth. Thomas Fowler, Walsingham's agent in the capital, reported 'Don John de Medina and divers captains of the Spaniards are going hence with great credit . . . on Sunday last I dined with Bothwell, where I found four Spanish captains whom he entertains'. He had good reason to report this incident for there was the possibility of a Catholic coup in Scotland led by the 5th Earl of

The Spanish Ships loft on the Coast of Scotland and 700 Souldiers and Marriners caft a Shoare.

The eight of spades records the landing of many Spaniards in Scotland.

Bothwell, nephew of Mary, Queen of Scots' husband. It seems that he intended to keep the Spaniards in Scotland, while he urged King Philip to send 4,000 more men for the revolution. He dispatched Gomez and his aides in a fly-boat to Spain for this purpose. In fact Philip did not respond and the rest of the refugees soon went home.

Scottish sea captains reckoned the cost of repatriating the Spaniards would be ten shillings a head, a sum which they could not muster. James was most reluctant to pay, and he even tried contacting Elizabeth to see if she would do so. He got no reply. Finally the Duke of Parma paid for four ships which sailed on 8 August, 1589. Safe conduct had had to be arranged lest foul weather force them into an English port.

Brief mention must be made of the much-debated 'Tobermory Galleon'. It was said that this ship became separated from the *El Gran Grifon* and finally anchored safely at Tobermory Bay. But her identity and whether she carried an immense treasure has led to many wild claims. It seems certain now that she was the *San Juan de Sicilia* (800 tons, 26 guns) in the Levantine squadron, commanded by Don Diego Tellez Henriquez. Possibly she carried her fair share of the equipment and weaponry needed on such massive enterprises, but certainly not the £30 million once claimed by would-be treasure hunters; unless, of course, the thirty million were virtually worthless *maravedis*, not pounds.

More interesting is the fact that Henriquez did a deal with the local laird, M'Lean of Dowart, a man who was a law unto himself. Henriquez's men served as the laird's strong-arm retainers in return for board and keep. When Walsingham heard of this, he sent John Smollett there. Smollett wormed his way onto the *San Juan* and 'cast in the powder-room a piece of lint, and so departed. Within a short time after, the lint took fire', killing everyone on board, including Henriquez. The ship sank and remains there to this day.

One isolated urca, the *San Pedro el Mayor* (541 tons, 240 crew), ran onto the submerged Shippen Rock under Bolt Tail in Hope Cove, off Salcombe, South Devon. One unsubstantiated theory is that she was one of the two Armada hospital ships. Most of her crew got ashore. The local magistrate, George Cary of Cockington, fed them for 1½*d.* a day each. This was not so generous of him, as basic food would have cost him 4*d.* a head.

CHAPTER ELEVEN

Shipwrecked off Ireland — Part One

Looked at from the point of view of England, the landing of any Spanish troops on the Irish coast was a potential threat. Most Irishmen were Catholics and the English forces stationed on the island amounted to fewer than two thousand, many of whom were poorly trained and equipped with weaponry 'rotting for want of men to maintain them'. Shortages of powder and shot simply underlined the hopelessly inadequate resources needed to police 32,000 square miles of rugged countryside.

The seven of spades shows the ships cast ashore and the warning beacon alerting the defence forces.

On 22 September, Lord Deputy Sir William Fitzwilliam put it bluntly when he wrote, 'There are not 750 foot in bands in the whole realm. We cannot impress the few soldiers for the shoeing of their horses. We feel rather to be overrun by the Spaniards than otherwise'. Sir William was based in Dublin, while Sir Richard Bingham, Governor of Connaught, was in charge of the west side from Mayo to the River Shannon at Limerick.

The strategic position of Ireland had been reassessed by both the English and the Spanish in recent years. On the one hand it was on the main shipping routes for the Americas, while on the other its closeness to England and its accessibility to Spanish shipping made it an obvious stepping stone for an invader. In the north it was a dozen miles from Scotland; in the east, Wales was visible on a clear day. Trade winds would ease the passage of any Spanish invasion fleet. If they landed in the north west, they would find little resistance from the English, whose control there was negligible. Elizabeth was only too aware of the fact that she had not the money to pay for the full-time garrisoning needed. She had to be content with policing the ports and larger towns and relying on a good spy service. But the fact remained that much of the country was ideal for guerilla warfare.

With invasion a logistical possibility, it was more than likely to take place, given the economic and religious connections between Spain and Ireland. Trade in fish, hides, furs, timber, linen and wine were on a regular basis. The export of wine to Ireland was one of Spain's biggest trade enterprises. It made Galway a renowned wine centre, ensuring that the whole economy of that area depended upon it. Spanish fishing boats regularly visited the rich banks off the Irish coast, to the extent that Sir Henry Gilbert had counted 600 of them in 1572. Sir Richard Bingham admitted as much when he wrote in 1591-2,

> Galway being an open road, and a town inhabited by a people that do generally favour the Spanish nation and their religion, their merchants having intercourse and daily traffic with the Spaniards, there is a great likelihood that the enemy should as soon bend his force for that place as for any other city or town within this realm [i.e. Ireland]. And that town is the worst provided for, and furnished of means to defend the same of all the towns in Ireland, for there is not so much as a gunner there, a piece of artillery . . . mounted, or any munition for war.

Many Irish catholic clergy had fled to Spain over the years. At least five Irish bishops had gone there. But in spite of these economic and religious contacts, the people of both countries still knew relatively little about each other. Philip failed to exploit the contacts that did exist to set up an efficient spy service. When Myles Brewitt met Santa Cruz in a Spanish port in 1587 he told him that Ireland had never been quieter, and was weakly garrisoned and governed, and the people sympathetic to a Spanish invasion. Yet Philip was not tempted to make Ireland his prime target. Why? Perhaps he realised he would get the country automatically when he captured England, but more likely he appreciated the fact that the Irish only wanted to get rid of the English, and would not take kindly to another occupying force. Ultimately, though, it was the failure of the Irish chieftains to persuade the Spanish to come directly there which deprived the enemies of England of a successful exploitation of the situation. The feeble Papal invasion force of 800 Italians and Spaniards which landed at Smerwick in 1580 proved this, for it did not receive the help which had been promised. The Irish leaders were too individualistic to unite and provide the necessary forces for an uprising. The clan structure was good for guerilla warfare, but rent with rivalry which made a full-scale revolt impossible.

The spring of 1587 had seen the spread of invasion rumours. Then there were only 1,800 English troops there and their 'guns rusty and carriages rotting for want of men to maintain them, supplies of powder and shot deficient'. In June 1588 an anonymous tract (possibly by Sir William Herbert) warned Munster of just how dangerous invasion would be. 'I think it very necessary that the English force of horsemen and footmen here were in time looked into. I fear me they will be found very defective; that the garrisons also, the storehouses and the munition, were carefully viewed; I think they will be found but in bad plight'. At that time Limerick, the strongest English town, had only '4 demi-cannons, 1 culverin, and a demi-culverin, a minion, and a faulkon, all out of reparation' as they were 'lying on the ground' with their carriages 'broken and rotten'. Even the feathers of the available arrows had rotted due to moisture.

Sir John Perrott, who had given up the post of Lord Deputy just before the Armada's approach, analysed the position carefully when he addressed his Council in June. Leinster, he reported, 'stands in reasonable good terms for quietness, save for stealths and robberies which are sometimes committed', while of Munster he said, 'most of the doubtful men there are in hand, so as the state of that province is reasonably well assured, unless it be disturbed by some foreign attempt'. This proviso is significant, and clearly intended to be a warning. As for Connaught, he was in more doubt, 'for that they are men disposed to stir and disturbance, and ill affected to the state of the time'. He ended by bluntly stating that it was 'not meet to diminish any part of the forces of this realm, but rather to increase them'. In the four years he had been Lord Deputy, he had shown just how sensitive he was to every scrap of information which Irish merchants and his spies brought to him from Spain. In January 1586, he had written to Walsingham, 'the King of Spain threateneth much, and, as they say, prepareth great armies that ever he made, the most part of them to be for Ireland'. Two weeks later he wrote to say he had heard that 20,000 Spanish troops would invade Ireland. A further two weeks found him writing that 'the Irishry here do hearken greedily for the coming over of foreign forces, sending for one to another, whereof I have secret and certain intelligence by my spials [spies] . . . that part of this Spanish invasion is for this island'.

On 18 September Sir Richard Bingham wrote to Sir William Fitzwilliam of strange ships which had been sighted. 'Whether they be of the dispersed fleet which are fled from the supposed overthrow in the Narrow Seas, or new forces come from Spain directly, no man is able to advise otherwise than by guess, which doth rather show their coming from Spain . . . I look this night for my horses to be here, and upon receipt of further intelligence I will make towards the sea coast, either upwards to Thomond or downwards to Sligo'. He went on, 'I would wish . . . that we had some lasts of powder with lead and match in the store here, for it is the thing we shall greatly want if stirs arise, and being there, it is as safe as in any other place'. The next day Vice-President Sir Thomas Norris wrote, '140 sail were on the coasts'. This idea that they were part of a second invasion force was a sensible conclusion to draw from their point of view. But within a week of the first spotting, reports flooded in from Donegal to Kerry. The Sheriff of Clare reported that 'last night 2 ships were seen westward of Arran and it is thought that more sails were seen westward from these islands'. Sheriff George Bingham of Sligo confirmed that 'seven ships have arrived at Car-e-colle [Carrigaholt in Clare]' and four at Loop Head, Clare.

The entire coastline became alert with the result that frightened appeals for help came in as landings were reported. The exaggerated nature of these reports, and their contradictory nature, led to the assumption that large numbers of ships were in the area landing armed troops. It seemed that a direct challenge to English control of the island was under way. Indeed it seems to have been accepted as the truth for a while by those in authority there. Only after a few weeks did it become clear that they were from the same Armada Drake had chased up the Channel months earlier. On 20 September Fitzwilliam and his Council renewed their

Strange weapons taken from Spaniards. Ace of spades poses something of a mystery as the weapons do not look strange at all.

urgent request for help as they had 'neither men, money nor munition to answer there extraordinary services'. Nevertheless on 24 September Elizabeth had sent an order to Sir Richard Grenville:

> Where we have some occasion offered to us by reason of certain ships of the Spanish Armada that came about Scotland and are driven to sundry parts in the West of Ireland, to put in readiness some forces to be sent into Ireland, as further occasion shall be given us, which we mean to be shipped in the river of Severn, to pass from thence to Waterford or Cork, we have thought meet to make choice of you for this service following.
>
> We require you that upon the north coasts of Devon and Cornwall, towards Severn, you make stay of all shipping meet to transport soldiers to Waterford, and to give charge that the same ships be made ready with masters, mariners, and all other maritime provisions needful, so as upon the next warning given from us or from our Council they may be ready to receive our said soldiers, which shall be 300 out of Cornwall and Devon, and 400 out of Gloucestershire and Somersetshire. We have also some other further intention to use your service in Ireland with these ships aforesaid, whereof Sir Walter Rawley, knight, whom we have acquainted withal shall inform you, who also hath a disposition for our service to pass into Ireland, either with these forces or before that they shall depart.

She followed this by orders to the Lord-Lieutenants 'for putting men in readiness to march for Ireland within an hour's warning'. She was reluctant to actually order the force into action because of the cost involved. Her Privy Council was already faced with the cost of paying off the navy, as we have seen. Although Sir Henry Wallop, a Council member, wrote to Burghley on 26 September to say that there was 'no fear of any hurt by foreign invasion this year', on 31 October the Privy Council ordered the levying of troops to repair the castles of Beaumaris and Chester, as '1,500 Spaniards, whose ships have been cast away on the north of Ireland, have combined with the Irish'. Then on 8 November the Privy Council told Fitzwilliam to use delaying tactics and avoid battle until 2,000 men could be sent to him. They were never sent.

Gradually it became clear that the majority of landings were as a result of shipwreck, not calculated anchorings. But why? There must have been some

Spanish fishermen on board at least some of the ships, who knew the Irish waters. Several reasons account for the disasters, not least the fact that many of the ships were not designed for stormy waters and were on the point of breaking up. Their crews were exhausted from the revolting rations they had had to survive on for far too long. But there are other reasons too. Contemporary maps showed a major error on the outline of the west coast, as they omitted the westward bulge of Mayo, especially in the vicinity of Erris Peninsula. It suggests a gently curving coastline, devoid of the jagged realities of the area. In fact the land protruded some 40 miles further west than suggested. Thus any ships sighting land north of Erris, in the area of Donegal or Sligo, would follow it to the south and hit the sheer cliffs, heavy seas and strong currents of Erris. As they crossed the 50 mile wide Donegal Bay, out of sight of land, they would suddenly find themselves facing the cliffs of North Mayo. It would then be too late to alter course due to the constant strong west winds which were so bad for square-rigged ships to head west against. North of Eagle Island, beginning with Broadhaven Bay, the line of wrecks is clear. Some ten ships, perhaps as many as a half or a third of Armada wrecks around Ireland, suffered because of the Erris Peninsula.

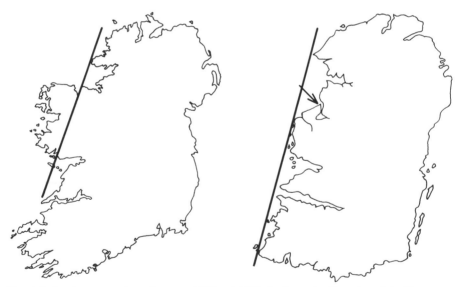

The right-hand map was drawn between 1577 and 1585. It shows the distortion of the Mayo coast when compared with the modern map on the left.

Another factor was that locally produced waves moved across the swell, so making it impossible for ships to keep heading into both simultaneously. They got into difficulties due to the local combinations of wind, waves, swell and currents. Even storms a thousand miles out to sea could start regular rollers sweeping across at considerable distances from each other, which would catch ships unawares. From the reports of the time, it is clear that exceptional weather conditions coincided with the arrival of the Armada off the Irish coast. Sir Richard Bingham wrote of 17–18 September, 'very stormy and foul weather . . . great floods'. The Mayor of Waterford and the Sheriff of Clare both commented on the extreme weather affecting the Armada.

The reception the Spaniards got depended a lot on who controlled the area where they landed. Often drowning Spaniards were left to their fate. Not only could few Irish swim, but there was a native taboo on rescuing the drowning. The sea-god Lir's ancient right to claim whom he wished was not to be tampered with. Destiny must be accepted, for anyone saving a drowning person would be claimed instead, or at least someone in his family would. This taboo was also held in the Orkneys and Shetlands. Edward Whyte, Bingham's righthand man, informed Walsingham that Don Pedro de Mendoza and 700 men had drowned off the 'Isle of Clear' and 'Dowdary Roe O'Maly has put 100 to the sword'. In other words, the numbers slaughtered when they staggered ashore must be offset by the numbers drowned. On Clare Island the local chieftain ordered the slaughter of some fifty or sixty of them. In one place it is said they were clubbed down as they waded ashore, then stripped of their possessions and left naked and cold. The Spaniards' clothes and jewels represented fabulous wealth to the peasantry of the coastlands, and it was this wealth, rather than bodies, that the Irish were after. True, Melaghlin McCabb, an Irishman in English pay, is said to have killed eighty with an axe, according to *The Calendar of State Papers (Ireland)*, but it should be noticed that he was taking English money. One way and another some 6,000 Spaniards died near or on Ireland. But further evidence must be examined before conclusions are arrived at.

The *La Trinidad Valencera* (1,100 ton Venetian merchantman, 42 guns, which set sail with 415 men, including 3 companies of troops, aboard), the fourth largest ship in the Armada, was originally named the *Balanzara* when she sailed as a merchantman. In 1587, when she was in Sicily, she had been seized on Medina

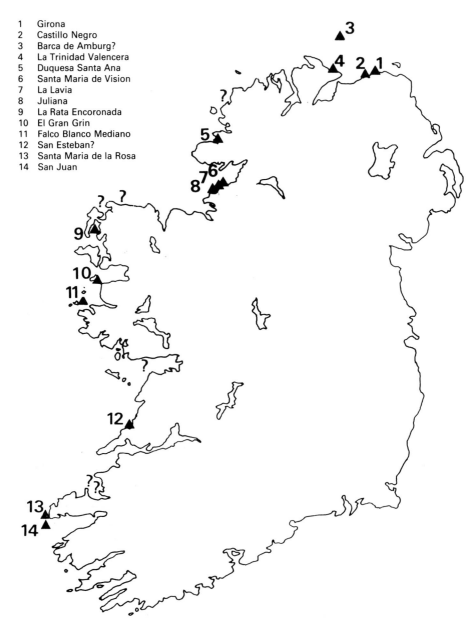

1   Girona
2   Castillo Negro
3   Barca de Amburg?
4   La Trinidad Valencera
5   Duquesa Santa Ana
6   Santa Maria de Vision
7   La Lavia
8   Juliana
9   La Rata Encoronada
10 El Gran Grin
11 Falco Blanco Mediano
12 San Esteban?
13 Santa Maria de la Rosa
14 San Juan

Armada wrecks off the coast of Ireland.

Sidonia's orders to carry war supplies to Spain. She subsequently reached Lisbon where she was commandeered for the Armada itself. When she sailed she had aboard 360 men, but this number was sharply increased when she picked up the crew of a sinking Armada ship. As the most powerful Levantine ship in the fleet, she carried the huge quantity of 125 quintals (5,750 kgs) of gunpowder. It is possible that she carried thirty-two, not forty-two guns as usually given.

She had been leaking for some days when she anchored 200 yards off shore in Glenagivney on 14 September. Her commander, *tercio-colonel* of the crack Regiment of Naples, Don Alonso de Luzon, and five others got ashore first in the ship's only boat, which itself was damaged. Cautiously advancing with rapiers at the ready, they were welcomed by four or five 'savages' of the O'Daherty clan. In minutes twenty appeared and made off with a bag containing 1,000 silver coins and a gold-embroidered cloak. However, within the next two days Don Alonso had managed to hire a local boat at a high price to get his remaining men ashore. During the process the *Trinidad*'s back broke and forty still on board were drowned. The wreck was found by the Inishowen Peninsula in 1971.

Those who did get ashore, some 350 in all, bought ponies to eat. The only escape route seemed to involve a march to the north east corner of Ireland and so across to Scotland. The way was barred by Lough Foyle, so that they were forced to walk along its western shore and cross the River Foyle at Derry, an English stronghold. Don Alonso made them march the 30 miles with drums beating and flags flying in some three or four days. They had heard that the Catholic bishop Cornelius of Down and Connor, who lived in a nearby castle, helped fugitives. As they approached the castle messages were exchanged, the bishop telling them to make a show of attacking the castle so as to deceive the English authorities into thinking he had to surrender to their force. When they arrived they found they had been tricked, as both cavalry and infantry awaited them. The shock misled them into thinking they were outnumbered, whereas in fact they were in a two to one majority, and far superior in training and experience to these lightly armed 140–150 Irish irregulars led by Richard and Henry Hovenden, both professional soldiers. The two sides halted, separated by a bog. Two days of skirmishes and shouted parleys followed. Don Alonso said that all they wanted was a ship to get them home, for which they would pay. Major John Kelly, an Irishman in English pay with the Hovendens, said that was impossible and they must surrender, adding the warning that 3,000 troops were on their way to cut their throats.

For two days Don Alonso de Luzon held out, but the starving state of his men left him little option but to agree in the end. He insisted that each man be allowed to keep his best suit. They laid down their arms, expecting to be treated as prisoners of war. But Kelly's men attacked them, took everything they possessed and left them naked. Those who resisted were killed. Afterwards Kelly maintained his men acted without his orders, which seems likely in view of their unruly nature. Alternatively, there may have been translation problems over the terms of the surrender.

What followed at daybreak the next day was far worse: with the Spanish officers and priests enclosed overnight in a square of Kelly's men, the rest attacked the naked troops with arquebuses on one side and cavalry on the other. 'They killed over 300 with lances and bullets. A hundred and fifty managed to escape across a bog, most of them wounded, and took refuge in the castle, where Bishop Cornelius rec'd them and sent a hundred or so by boat to Scotland', wrote one who survived. The most badly injured remained in the castle, where many of them died. The Hovendens' account of the massacre maintained that 'seeing that they were more than 600 men, we encamped at nightfall, at a distance of a musket shot, we not being more than 140. Towards midnight, we commenced skirmishing with them for about 2 hours, killing the *tiente de campo* and more than 200 men besides . . . without our having lost more than one man'.

Those who survived the massacre and eventually recovered were sent on to Scotland. On 23 October William Asheby, an English agent in Edinburgh, reported that '50 Spaniards, poor and miserable, [are] passing through this country, who were wrecked in a ship in the north of Ireland called *La Ballanzara*'. Only thirty-two eventually reached Le Havre.

After the massacre, the officers, gentlemen and priests, virtually naked, were marched 100 miles to Drogheda, an English headquarters. Before the march began the Hovendens wrote to Fitzwilliam begging 'you will be pleased to give orders that rations may be allowed them, as the prisoners are very weak and unable to march . . . that carts and horses be provided for their conveyance to Dublin. The chief of them [Don Alonso] has a certain air of majesty . . . among them'. They kept forty-two for ransom, but only two survived to be ransomed in the end. They were Don Alonso de Luzon and Don Rodrigo Lasso, and both were still prisoners in London in 1591. There remains the uncertainty to this day of whether the massacre was simply undertaken by unruly men, or whether it was ordered, perhaps by the Irish Earl of Tyrone, cousin of the Hovendens, who was in charge of the English forces in Ulster. Whether Kelly lied and deliberately misled Don Alonso, or whether misunderstandings based on translation problems were at the root of it all is impossible to say today.

The *Rata Sancta Maria Encoronada* (820 tons, 35 guns, Genoese carrack or 'Mediterranean' merchantman) managed to anchor in desolate Blacksod Bay, north of Achill Island, County Mayo. Although the Bay presented a low, rainswept coastline surrounded by the Great Bogs of Erris, it was the best emergency harbour on the west coast. The *Rata* should have aimed for Elly Bay within Blacksod Bay, but she went up an eastern arm of Blacksod Bay and entered a difficult tidal area, with a strong 3-knot ebb stream, and so was forced to anchor. Fifteen men got ashore in the *Rata's* only boat to look for water and food. Those on board saw them head for what was the biggest peat bog in Ireland, but then they vanished, captured by 'Devil's Hook', Richard Burke, the local chief. All day passed and still there was no sign of them. Swimmers were sent ashore supported by casks to retrieve the ship's boat. The *Rata* was extremely overcrowded with 335 troops and 84 sailors when it set out, to say nothing of sixty young gentlemen-volunteers who had attached themselves to Don Alonso Martinez de Leyva, Knight of Santiago, her commander. He had been designated Commander-in-Chief of the Armada's land forces and Medina Sidonia's replacement if the admiral should die during the voyage. With his thirty-six servants, he had established a glittering social circle aboard his ship, dining off gold and silver dishes. Others aboard had a dozen or so servants each. Consequently the 820 ton ship had some 600–700 aboard her. They all got ashore and took over a nearby castle, which must have been either Fahy or Doona castle. The *Rata* drifted until she hit the sandy bottom and her keel sank into the sand some 150 yards off shore. She was burnt as was the custom, and while she was still alight, Burke's men rifled her. Until sixty years ago she was still visible at low spring tides.

Subsequently the local sheriff, Gerald Comerford, put an armed guard on the half-burnt remains, and then wrote on 23 September to his superior, Bingham,

The Ship that is here aground is well stored of great pieces and other munition, wine and oil and many other things under water. Here are no boats able to come by them, neither is it possible to take anything of great value out of the same as yet . . . [Several individuals named by Comerford] took out of the wreck a boat full of treasure, cloth of gold, velvet, etc . . . I pray your Lordship that if they be taken they may be put up safe and not bailed . . . as we wish to charge them with disloyalty for they have disobeyed commandments given them in writing and beaten and wounded our people.

More important during the next week or two was, what would Don Alonso and his force do? Would the local Irish join them? The Lord Deputy was asked to send reinforcements to be ready.

Within two days of landing Don Alonso's men, including the Bishop of Killaloe who had been aboard, had marched round the whole 25 mile length of Blacksod Bay to join the 'Mediterranean' ship *Duquesa Santa Aña* (900 tons, 23 guns, Andalusian hulk with 280 soldiers and 77 crew), which had skilfully anchored in Elly Bay some days earlier. This brought the total muster to 1,000. As they were well armed and ably led, they were able to take over both Tiraun and Elly castles and make it impossible for Bingham's forces to capture them. In fact if they had come to an agreement with the local chiefs they could have taken the whole north west of Ireland.

They patched up the *Duquesa* and set sail for Scotland only to be driven back to Lough Erris, NW Donegal, by a great storm. The area is one of strong currents, dense fogs and high winds making the numerous rocks, islands and high cliffs an even greater problem. They got north round Rossan Point and anchored in 70 ft. of water, in a rocky bay now called Loughros More. This was a very unsafe anchorage due to the shallow sand covering the rock providing little grip for anchors. All got ashore, with the gentry clutching their jewel boxes. Subsequently two survivors said that a cable broke and the ship drifted ashore as sailors tried in vain to get a mooring line to a rock spur upwind. Another survivor, James Machary, said that 'Don Alonso before he came to land was hurt in the leg by the capstan of the ship in such sort as he was neither able to go, nor ride, neither during the nine days of his encamping, nor upon his remove, but was carried'. They fortified themselves with a ship's cannon in the ruined Kiltoorish Castle on O'Boyle Island in the lough. During the following week they emptied their ship of valuables, gold, silver and weapons. The area was controlled by the M'Sweeney clan who were positively warlike in their attitude towards the English. Consequently the Spaniards were warmly welcomed.

English spy reports, which daily confirmed the strength of the enemy, alarmed

The 1,400 ft high cliffs on Slieve League in Donegal where the *Duquesa Santa Aña* was nearly wrecked after leaving Killybegs.

the authorities. The Earl of Tyrone wrote to Fitzwilliam to say that there were '1,500 Spaniards in M'Sweeney ne Doe's country' and asked for 'munition and a commission of martial law', adding that he had provided 'a month's victuals for his company to go against the Spaniards'. On 20 October William Taaffe wrote that '2,000 Spaniards are camping at Forreside, within six miles of Strabane', and that he had had a report that they were 'going to aid Tirlough Lynagh O'Neill to make war on the Earl of Tyrone'. On the same day George Bingham's brother appealed to him, stressing that the enemy 'will be in Sligo in five days'. These reports reflect the fear of a mass march southwards, whereas in reality De Leyva did not want to join in any uprising, but simply leave Ireland. M'Sweeney had merely provided food.

The survivors of the *Duquesa* got ashore on the beach to the SE of Rosbeg and fortified themselves on O'Boyle Island in nearby Kiltoorish Lake. They marched to Killybegs and boarded the *Girona*.

Meanwhile M'Sweeney had told Don Alonso of three other Spanish ships in Killybegs harbour on the north shore of Donegal Bay, 20 miles to the south over the mountains. So the 1,000 Spaniards set off, with Don Alonso carried by four men in a litter.

In fact two of these ships had been wrecked, the sole survivor being the galleass, *Girona* (700–800 tons, 150 ft. long, 36 oars, a crew of 102/121, 244 oarsmen, 186/196 soldiers, 50 guns). Her crew were trying to patch her with planks from the other two ships, aided by M'Sweeney Bannagh's men and boats. The combined crews of the five ships probably mustered just over 1,500, the largest Spanish force then in Ireland, and she could not carry them all. The Irish among them were willing to stay in their homeland, while the sick and wounded were incapable of facing yet another voyage. This left them with 1,300 (800 to 1,800, according to different accounts) to take aboard. On 26 October they set sail, overloaded and with winter coming on, in what was now a fundamentally weakened ship. A spy, Henry Duce, reported their departure,

> . . . the said galley departed from the said harbour with as many of the Spaniards as she could carry . . . As it is judged they have left in one Brian M'Manus's house at the Killibegg's vicar of that place, one of the chief of their company, being very sore sick of the flux. They have likewise left with M'Sweeny an Irish Friar called James ne Dowrough, who first went into Spain with James Fitzmaurice . . . the Spaniards gave M'Sweeny, at their departure, twelve butts of sack wine, and to one Murrough Oge M'Murrough I Vayell, four butts. The M'Sweenys and their followers have gotten great store of the Spanish calivers and muskets.

The Spaniards set their course for Scotland, a 200 mile voyage which would take four days if the wind was right. Due to their weak rudder they dared not put on too much sail as they followed the coast with its dangerous rocks, reefs and swift currents. On the second day the wind shifted to the north, which was the worst possible as it pushed her towards the shore. Soon the wind reached gale force. By dawn on 28 October, she was closer to the shore and plunging in the heavy seas. By mid-morning, when she was close to the mouth of Lough Foyle with another 30 miles needed to clear Ireland, the rudder finally broke. The sea was too high to use the oars. She drifted on through the night only too near the sheer cliffs, until, just before midnight, she struck a reef at Lacada Point, near the Giant's Causeway on the coast of Antrim, which ripped her bottom open and probably turned her over. The aftercastle broke away and drifted eastwards, while the captain's cabin was ripped from the hull. Only nine survived; Don Alonso was not among them. The following January Mendoza wrote to Philip to report that 'A sailor passing by the spot where Don Alonso was lost with 1,300 men recognised many of the bodies strewn along the coast. He took 300 ducats out of the belt of one of them'.

In August 1589, the English authorities wrote to Sir George Carew, Master of the Ordnance, to hasten to Northern Ireland to retrieve what he could from the sea, presumably referring to the wreck of the *Girona*. He was then working on a wreck in Southern Ireland, where he reported that his diver, working at 30 ft.

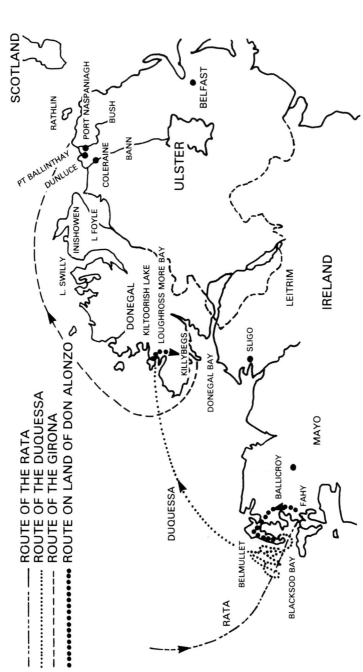

SCOTLAND

RATHLIN

PORT NASPANIAGH

PT BALLINTHAY

BUSH

DUNLUCE

BELFAST

COLERAINE

BANN

ULSTER

INISHOWEN

L SWILLY

L FOYLE

KILTOORISH LAKE

LOUGHROSS MORE BAY

DONEGAL

LEITRIM

KILLYBEGS

DONEGAL BAY

SLIGO

IRELAND

DUQUESSA

MAYO

BALLICROY

FAHY

BELMULLET

BLACKSOD BAY

RATA

ROUTE OF THE RATA
ROUTE OF THE DUQUESSA
ROUTE OF THE GIRONA
ROUTE ON LAND OF DON ALONZO

The three shipwrecks suffered by Don Alonzo de Leyva around the coast of Ireland.

down, 'was nearly drowned, but Irish aqua vitae hath such a virtue as I hope of his recovery'. In June he had raised guns from what was probably the *San Estéban*, off Doobeg, County Clare in 4½ fathoms. His ship, HMS *Popinjay*, took nearly a year to get to the *Girona* wreck, but by then two Spanish survivors and the locals had raised the guns and two chests of treasure. The guns were subsequently used to defend Dunluce Castle against English attack.

CHAPTER TWELVE

Shipwrecked off Ireland – Part Two

The *La Lavia* (728 tons, 25 guns), vice-flagship of the Levant squadron, anchored in the Streedagh Strand, about twelve miles north west of Sligo, when she found she could no longer cope with the southerly winds. It was a dangerously exposed anchorage but she stayed a mile off shore for four days, hoping for better weather. The surf made landing impossible. On the fifth day, 'there sprang up so great a storm on our beam, with a sea up to the heavens, so that the cables could not hold nor the sails serve us', wrote Don Francisco de Cuellar in a letter of October 1589, addressed to a friend, 'to amuse yourself somewhat after dinner'. 'We were driven ashore, all three ships [the other two were *San Juan* and *Santa Maria de Vison*] upon a beach covered with very find sand, shut in one side and the other by great rocks. Such a thing was never seen; for within the space of an hour all three ships were broken to pieces, so that there did not escape 300 men, and more than 1,000 were drowned, among them many persons of importance, such as captains, gentlemen and other officials'.

Don Diego Enriquez, the Camp Master, and other gentry, tried to get ashore in the ship's boat. He was the son of the Viceroy of Peru, who is referred to by de Cuellar as the 'hunchback', although *Spanish State Papers* do not allude to this. De Cuellar's description of what happened to him is vivid.

Fearing the very heavy sea that was washing over the highest part of the wrecks, he took his ship's boat that was on the deck, and he and the son of the Count of Villa France and two other Portuguese gentlemen, with above 16,000 ducats in jewels and crown pieces, hid themselves under the deck of this boat, and gave orders to close and caulk up the hatchway by which they had entered. Thereupon more than seventy men, who had remained alive, jumped from the ship to the boat. While she was making for the land so great a wave washed over her that she sank, and all on deck were swept away. Then she drifted along,

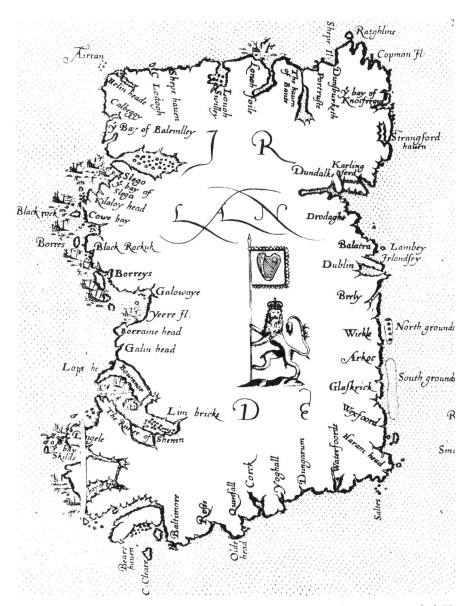

A contemporary map drawn by Robert Adams showing where the Armada ships were wrecked. The only one not marked is the *Girona*, the last to go down.

rolling in different directions with the waves until she was cast ashore, where she settled the wrong way up, and by these misfortunes the gentlemen who had placed themselves under the deck died within. More than a day and a half after she had grounded, some savages arrived who turned her up for the purpose of getting nails or pieces of iron; and breaking through the deck, they pulled out the dead men. Don Diego Enriquez expired in their hands and they stripped him and took away the jewels and money which the [dead men] had, casting the bodies aside without burying them.

Don Francisco de Cuellar was on board as he had been left in the custody of the judge advocate after the commuting of his death sentence earlier in the voyage. He had joined the Armada on a captain's pay of 25 escudos a month and the right to a servant, but without a command. At Corunna he was put in charge of the galleon *San Pedro* in the general switch round of commands carried out then.

Describing what happened to him in that hour of crisis, he wrote,

I placed myself on top of the poop deck of my ship and from thence I gazed upon the terrible sight. Many were drowning . . . others, casting themselves into the water, sank to the bottom without returning to the surface; others, on rafts, and barrels, and gentlemen on pieces of timber; others cried aloud inside the ships, calling upon God; captains threw their chains and crown pieces into the sea; the waves swept others away, washing them out of the ships . . . While I was looking . . . I did not know what to do, nor what means to adopt, as I did not know how to swim, and the waves and the storm were very great; on the other hand, the land and the shore were full of savages, who went about jumping and dancing with delight at our misfortunes; and when anyone of our people reached the beach 200 savages and other enemies fell upon him and stripped him of what he had on him until he was left in his naked skin.

Spotting a hatch-door, the size of a table,

I tried to place myself on it, but it sank with me to a depth of six times my height below the surface, and I swallowed so much water that I was nearly drowned. When I came up again, I called to the Judge Advocate and I managed to get him upon the hatchway with myself . . . [then] there came a huge wave breaking over us so that the Judge was unable to withstand it and the wave bore him away, and drowned him, [pulled down by the weight of the crown pieces he had sewn into his clothes] as he cried out, calling upon God . . . I could not aid him as the hatchway cover, being without weight at one end, began to turn over . . . and at that moment a piece of timber crushed my legs . . . four waves . . . cast me upon the shore where I emerged unable to stand, all covered with blood and very much injured.

He attributed the fact that he himself was not treated violently by the 'savages' as his 'legs and hands and linen trousers [were] covered with blood. I crawled on, little by little, meeting many Spaniards stripped to the skin, without any kind of clothing whatever, shivering with the cold, which was severe. I stopped for a night in a deserted place, and lay down in great pain in some rushes'. He was joined by a naked young man, but he soon died. Two Irishmen covered them with rushes during the night.

During the night the English garrison from Sligo arrived to join in the looting. Francisco's account seems to suggest that in the early hours he returned to the beach and saw 'six hundred . . . dead bodies cast up by the sea, and the ravens and wolves devoured them'. With the help of others, he quickly buried Don Diego's body in the sand, before moving inland again. However, he returns to the matter of seeing the bodies and burying Don Diego later on when he met two wounded Spaniards, and it is more likely that this was when he carried out this deed of mercy.

In the morning he dragged himself some way until in deserted Staad Abbey he found twelve comrades hanging from the window grills. The monks had fled to the woods.

I rushed outside and took a path through a large wood . . . I met with a rough savage woman, over eighty years old, who was driving five or six cows into the wood to hide them so that the English quartered in her village should not have them. When she saw me she stood still . . . and inquired [if I was a Spaniard]. I made signs that this was so . . . She began to lament and weep, indicating by signs that her house was nearby, but that I must not go there as the enemy, who had been cutting Spanish throats, were there. All this was terrible . . . news for me, alone as I was and suffering from my legs having been almost broken by a . . . timber.

He made for the shore and saw

> . . . two poor Spanish soldiers coming, as naked as the day they were born,
> crying aloud to God to help them. One of them had a deep wound in the head
> . . . I called to them from my hiding-place, and they . . . told me of the cruel
> murders . . . inflicted by the English on more than a hundred Spaniards they
> had taken prisoner. This was grievous news; but God gave me strength . . .

He then recounts the story of visiting the beach again and burying Don Diego in
the sand at the water's edge.

They went looking for food, 'such as biscuits thrown up by the sea'. Moving on
again, Francisco found the stony road was hard going

> . . . so that I could neither move nor put one foot in front of the other, for I was
> barefoot and in agonies of pain [from his wound] . . . My poor companions
> were quite naked and freezing with cold, which was very severe, and as they
> were more dead than alive and could give me no help, they went on ahead . . .

Finally he reached a wood, where two or three men and a girl stripped him of his
remaining clothes, gold chain and forty-five crown pieces, and one of them cut a
tendon in his leg. The girl, whom he describes as very beautiful, saved him from
further injury, and returned him his clothes, but took away his precious relics.
'She was a good a Christian as Mahommet', commented Francisco. Subsequently
she sent him some oatcake and milk, and dealt with his wounds. Following this
incident he set out to do some eighteen miles to reach a friendly village. On the
way he met a man who spoke to him in Latin, took him home and attended to his
wounds. He was the first person to whom he had not had to use sign-language.

The next day he was given a horse and a boy to guide him. But problems soon
faced him again as they had to hide when 150 English horsemen rode by. Then
they ran into forty 'Lutherans' who attacked him. He received six blows on the
back and arms before being left naked. Covering himself with bracken and some
old matting, he resumed his barefoot walk. It took him a week to reach the Dartry
or Dartraigh Mountains and a deserted village beside Lough Glenade. There he
found three naked Spaniards, all who remained of eleven who had staggered inland
together. Francisco encouraged them by saying that a short way away was Sir Brian

Benbulben, one of the Dartry Mountains.

O'Rourke's village where, to his knowledge, many Spaniards had taken refuge. So, after a supper of blackberries and watercress, they buried themselves deep in the straw for the night. Twenty-four hours later, 'wrapped in straw and hay against the bitter cold', they left their hiding-place. When they finally reached their destination, they found seventy starving Spaniards had overwhelmed the village. All Francisco could get was a bug-ridden old blanket. The next day twenty of them went to Sir Brian's house and begged for food. There they heard the glad news that a Spanish ship was offshore ready to pick them up. They set off immediately to reach her, but 'we met with many hindrances on the way, and it was a blessing that I never reached the haven where she was', for when she set sail two days later she was soon wrecked and two hundred drowned.

As he struggled along Francisco met a priest, dressed in lay clothes, who spoke to him in Latin and shared his food with him. The man pointed to M'Glannagh's castle some twenty miles away. But on the way there Francisco fell in with a blacksmith who lured him to a deserted valley [Glenade or Glencar Valley] and offered to teach him his trade. 'I did not know what to answer, and I did not try, in case he put me in the smithy fire. I worked with the bellows for more than a week, so as not to vex him and an accursed old woman he had for a wife'. Clearly Francisco no longer felt like a conquering invader, if he ever had done! Perhaps the couple thought they were doing him a favour. Fortunately the priest appeared again and succeeded in getting him to the island fortress of Rossclogher Castle, 100 yards from the southern shore of Loch Melvin.

The castle was owned by the fanatically anti-English chief of the MacClancy clan, called Dartry. This man was to help many Spaniards escape, feeding and clothing them, before sending them along an escape route. Here Francisco obtained sanctuary for three months along with ten other Spaniards. 'The wife of my master [Dartry] was beautiful in the extreme, and showed me great kindness.' He seems to have got on particularly well with her and the other ladies there, 'so much that no Spaniard was in greater favour with them'. They were forever pestering him to tell their fortunes. One can only surmise that he had got beyond the use of sign language by now. His comment that 'the savages liked us because they knew we had come against the heretics', is significant. He commented that 'these savages . . . live in huts made of straw . . . They do not eat oftener than once a day, and this is at night; and that which they usually eat is butter with oaten bread. They drink sour milk . . . They wear their hair down to their eyes . . . Most of the women are very beautiful, but badly dressed. They do not wear more than a chemise under a blanket and a linen cloth, much folded, over the head and tied in front'.

Eventually Dartry's spy network alerted him to the fact that Sir William Fitzwilliam was advancing through the countryside with 1,700 men to round up any Spaniards and punish those who harboured them. Sir William's policy was to kill every Spaniard as quickly as possible to prevent any alliance being built up with the Irish. The *State Papers* are full of reports of massacres of '140; 300; 1,100', and so on. He had left Dublin for Connaught and NW Ulster on 14 November as part of a 320 mile sweep which was to last seven weeks in all. He visited Streedagh Strand and saw the remains of the three ships, 'where, as I heard, lay not long before 1,200 or 1,300 of the dead bodies . . . there lay as great a store of the timber of the wrecked ships as there was in that place which myself had viewed

. . . besides cables, and other cordage . . . thereunto'. On 20 November Sir William reached Athlone and wrote to Burghley,

I at this present with HM's army am entered into it [his march] as far as Athlone; wherein, if either the deepness of winter, which yieldeth short days and long nights, foul ways, great waters, many stormy showers, want of horsemeat, hazard of spoiling, and loss both of horses and ponies, which have our carrieages, besides the report that there were not above 100 or thereabouts left of the ragged Spaniards would have persuaded me to stay, I should not have gone forwards. Every man has a liking to the journey. The Irish fearing my approach put the Spaniards away.

Midway through Sir William's march, Bingham wrote in protest to the queen, about 1,000 or so Spaniards

. . . who were put to the sword, amongst whom were officers and gentlemen of qualilty to the number of 50 . . . These gentlemen were spared till the Lord Deputy [Fizwilliam] sent me special direction to see them executed, as the rest were only reserving alive one Lewes de Cordova and his nephew until your Majesty's pleasure be known . . . My brother George . . . had one Don Graveillo de Swasso and another gentleman by licence . . . But the Lord Deputy . . . having further advertisements from the north of the state of things in those parts, took occasion to make a journey thither and make his way through this province [Connaught], and in his passing along caused both these two Spaniards, which my brother had, to be executed . . . reserving none but Don Lewes de Cordova and his nephew, whom I have here [at Athlone].

When Dartry heard of his approach, Francisco records what happened.

One Sunday after mass, the chief took us on one side, and with his hair over his eyes and in a furious rage, he told us that he could not stay any longer, but that he had decided to fly with all his clansmen, cattle and families, and that we must think what to do to save our lives. I replied begging him to calm down a little, saying we would give him our answer immediately. Then I went aside with the eight Spaniards who were with me . . . and told them to think carefully . . . and consider whether it would not be better to make an honourable end of it all, lest worse should befall . . .

They finally decided to stay. Armed with six muskets, six crossbows and stones, they prepared to hold the castle. By the end of November Sir William's force had failed to take the island castle as it was surrounded by a deep two mile by ten mile lake and a bog. Only clan members knew the twisting footpaths which lay beneath the surface of the bog water, so that any attackers needed boats to reach the castle. But boats the English did not have, nor artillery, so that their cavalry and infantry were virtually useless. For seventeen days they carried out a feeble siege and then retreated when heavy snow started to fall.

Dartry returned and 'offered us whatever he possessed. He wanted to give me his sister in marriage', wrote Francisco. He turned down the offer and asked for a boat to reach Scotland in. Dartry was reluctant to agree as he wanted the Spaniards to stay at the castle. When he made a feeble excuse about the roads being impassable, Francisco and four of the refugees decided to escape secretly. They marched for 20 miles up the north coast to Sorley Boy's Castle of Dunluce. It was hard going for Francisco as his old wound had opened up again. The other four had to leave him to limp along as best he could. Once again 'exceedingly beautiful girls' came to his rescue and he was kept in a mountain hut for a month until his wound was better. But one day two English soldiers arrived and challenged him as to whether he was a Spaniard. He admitted it, whereupon they told him to wait while they found a horse. Two of the 'exceedingly beautiful girls' promptly distracted the soldiers so enabling him to escape. Away in the mountains he reached Annagh Castle where Redmund, the retired Bishop of Derry lived. Disguised as a peasant, the bishop was scouring the area for Spaniards to ship to Scotland. He had twelve with him when Francisco arrived.

'He have gave us provisions for the voyage and said mass for us . . . He told me he intended to come to Spain as soon as possible after landing us in Scotland.' A final total of eighteen Spaniards set off on the two day voyage in a 'wretched boat'. After a stormy crossing they arrived to find the story that James VI was clothing and returning Spanish refugees to their homeland was far from true. 'For the King of Scotland is a nobody; he does not move a step, or eat a mouthful, that is not by order of the Queen of England.' After six months of begging and destitution, 'as naked as we had arrived from Ireland', he was one of two hundred and seventy to sail in one of the four ships arranged for by the Duke of Parma. His luck was soon put to the test again. Dutch fly-boats attacked them off Dunkirk and, in the ensuing wreck, he was one of only three to survive. He crawled ashore dressed simply in his shirt. Eventually he was able to pursue his journey to Spain successfully.

The first Galway wreck was the hulk *Falco Blanco Mediano* (300 tons, 16 guns, 103 men) lost somewhere in Connemara, perhaps on a reef near Inish Boffin. It is thought she had been trying to get through Bundouglas and Braadillaun, but hit the Freaghillaun rock. Most of her crew reached the shore and were looked after by the O'Flahertys for a while. They then went on some miles south of Clifden, where Murrough ne Doe was chieftain. Although he had been persuaded to support Elizabeth by the bestowal of a knighthood, Bingham had foolishly alienated him by murdering two of his sons and several grandchildren. This had prompted Sir Murrough to lead an uprising. But when defeated, he had had to surrender his titles and possessions. He had no alternative but to hand the Spaniards over to the English authorities at Galway. There they were joined by seventy others from another ship, as we shall see.

Other Galway wrecks resulted in the survivors being taken by Tadgh na Buile (literally, 'the furious') O'Flaherty, an old man who led a different branch of the O'Flaherty clan. Tradition has it that the ships were lured inshore by a fire lit for that purpose. It is said that only a boy survived from the smaller ship, and that bodies swept ashore were buried. The larger ship, the *Concepcion*, under Captain Juan Delcano, alias Juanes del Cano, was a Biscayan vessel of 418 tons, 18 guns and 225 men. In fact probably more survived and were taken by Tadgh to Galway.

The *El Gran Grin* (merchantman and vice-flagship of the Biscayan Squadron, 1,160 tons, 28 guns, 329 men) was lost on or near Clare Island in the mouth of Clew Bay, Mayo. The bay presents a treacherous and deceptive coastline with soaring cliffs. The area was virtually an independent republic under Grace O'Malley, a tall, towering, twice-married and bare-breasted person, who had once visited Elizabeth I. When the queen tried to win her support with the title of Countess, Grace had rejected it. Her clan had its own small fleet which dominated the whole Mayo coast and harassed English shipping. She was not on the island when the Spanish ship arrived, leaking badly and helpless in a gale. One theory is that the *El Gran Grin* struck the rocks close to the island's SW tip and sank. Over a hundred men got ashore in a pinnace; the rest died. O'Malley's people held them until Pedro de Mendoza led an escape attempt by trying to seize an O'Malley boat. In the fight, sixty-eight Spaniards were either slain or drowned, including Mendoza.

By 24 September, Bingham had already written to Fitzwilliam about capturing these Spaniards and the islands. On the other hand, George Wodloke, a merchant, had written to the Mayor of Waterford on 20 September to the effect that sixteen Spaniards had got ashore from a thousand-ton ship (*El Gran Grin?*) at 'Fynglasse' in Clew Bay 'with their chains of gold' on 16 September. The Earl of Ormonde owned the area and wrote to one of Bingham's sheriffs, telling him to make an inventory of the ship and lock the prisoners up in Galway or elsewhere. Significantly, he added that if the rumoured Duke of Medina Sidonia was there he was to be 'kept without irons and . . . to have my horse to ride on'. It seems sixteen Spaniards were then taken to Galway. By 10 October it was clear that this was not part of a Spanish invasion force, and Edward Whyte, Bingham's right-hand man, wrote to tell Walsingham that Don Pedro de Mendoza and 700 men were drowned off the 'Isle of Clear' and 'Dowdary Roe O'Maly has put 100 to the sword'. This amounted to the fact that the majority had drowned.

A long held theory is that the wrecks at Clare Island and 'Fynglasse' were the same; that is, the *El Gran Grin*, and that the ship was really wrecked at Fynglasse. The fact that a hundred Spaniards were on the island is explained by them abandoning their ship in a pinnace as she drifted eastwards. Both stories refer to a ship of about 1,000 tons and there were few of that size in the Armada. Possibly Bingham sent a boat to Clare Island for Mendoza, who was in fact dead by then, and so the three officers referred to in the accounts got to Galway. Alternatively, O'Malley brought them there. The historian Niall Fallon, however, is of the opinion that there were in fact two ships and so two wrecks, as Edward Whyte and Sir Geoffrey Genton, Secretary to the Irish Council, appear to confirm in their reports. Moreover, theirs is the best contemporary evidence available today. It is just possible that one of the two ships was the 834 ton *San Nicolas Prodaneli*, but just what did happen will never be known for sure.

The prisoners held at Galway were a problem for Bingham. Between 300 and 350 were in prison and Fitzwilliam had sent orders to 'apprehend and execute at Spaniards of what quality soever . . . torture may be used in prosecuting this enquiry'. So Bingham came to see the executions done 'with warrant and commission to put them all to the sword'. Three hundred were taken to St Augustine's monastery, now Fort Hill, outside the town and killed. The inhabitants made shrouds for them and buried them. There is a story that two Spaniards were hidden in the town and escaped to Europe. Today Spanish fishermen still come to kneel and pray at the Fort Hill Cemetery where a mass grave for thirty-seven is in one corner. Fifty others were set aside by Bingham for ransom purposes, in disobedience to Fitzwilliam's orders. In a temper Sir William denounced Bingham for this action, and so his subordinate had to execute most of them. Only Don Luis de Cordova and his nephew Gonzalo were spared, to be imprisoned in Athlone, before eventually being ransomed and returned to Spain. Bingham reported to the queen, 'thus was all the province quickly rid of those distressed enemies, and the service done and ended without any other forces that the garrison bands, or yet any extraordinary charge to Your Majesty'. Doubtless the queen must have been well pleased with this report, and gratified that she had made the right decision in not actually sending costly reinforcements from England.

The Blasket Islands, six islands near the end of the Dingle peninsula, which are separated from the mainland by a deep rocky and tide-swept sound, dangerous even in calm weather, were to be the centre of much drama. It began with the arrival there in mid-September of the *San Juan Bautista*, a galleon of 750 tons, 24 guns and 243 men, commanded by Marco de Aramburu. She was the vice-flagship of the Castile squadron, and, for her day, well designed for manoeuvrability. She had lost the rest of the fleet in the last week of August somewhere north-east of Rockall. Aramburu began a record of his voyage, entitled *An Account of what happened to Marcos de Aramburu, Controller and Paymaster of the galleons of Castile in the vice-flagship of those under his charge*, when she passed Rockall. On 12 September he referred to a 'stormy sea with heavy sky and rain . . . a most violent storm with a very wild sea and a great darkness on account of the heavy clouds'. Although Aramburu had ensured that regular soundings had been taken, the inaccuracy of his charts must have helped to mislead him as to where he was. Two days later, in driving rain, he caught glimpses of another ship. Then on the morning of 15 September, as the gale continued to blow from the west, two large islands of the Blasket group came in sight. The ship was now in deadly danger, hemmed in against the land by the wind on the starboard side and by the islands ahead; caught on the lee shore in a trap.

In desperation Aramburu turned the ship to the N or NE, trying to retrace the route he had taken. It was then that his ship fell in with Recalde's *San Juan de Portugal* (1,050 tons, 50 guns) and a *patache*. As Aramburu wrote subsequently, 'We turned towards him despairing and we ignorant of the coast, of any remedy, and saw that being able to double one of the islands, towards another stretch of land which he saw before him, he turned east.' Unlike Aramburu, Recalde knew just where they were as he had been there in 1580. The 62-year-old commander had been ill in his bunk for some time, leaving the piloting to a capable Scot. But now, on the day they needed him most, he had struggled on to the deck. He set course so as to enter the sound from the west, a wise decision which enabled them to aim for the northern tip of the Great Blasket, in spite of the rocks and reefs close at hand. They just got past the Great Blasket in a 40 ft. deep channel as wide 'as the length of a ship'. This enabled them to shelter behind this 5½ mile long, 961 ft. high island. It had needed great skill and timing to get through, and Recalde's ship's lead-sheathed keel must have scraped along the bottom.

Their problems were not over though, for there was no proper holding ground for their anchors, the sand covering the rocky bottom being too thin to provide a grip. Indeed Recalde had lost his heaviest anchor at Calais. Moreover the need for food and water was desperate so he sent eight seamen ashore to contact the local people. They were spotted by James Trant, an English official. His men seized them and took them to Dingle ten miles away. Two hundred infantry and fifty cavalry were then dispatched to prevent any attempt at a mass landing from the three ships. The Lord Deputy had given orders to his officers that any Spaniards were to be executed, no matter what their quality was. 'Torture may be used in prosecuting this enquiry', he wrote. Under interrogation it turned out that one of the eight was a Scotsman, captured by the *San Martin* off the Scottish coast and forced to act as a pilot. He now informed the English that the ships 'were destitute of victual, and in great extremity for want of knowledge'. What happened to him for giving this information is not known.

Another of them, Emanuel Fremoso, a Portuguese seaman, described life on board the *San Juan*.

He says that out of the ship there died 4 or 5 every day of hunger and thirst, and yet this ship was one of the best furnished for victuals . . . He says that there are 80 soldiers and 20 of the mariners sick . . . they do lie down and die daily, and the rest are very weak and the Captain [Recalde] very sad and weak . . . There is left in this flagship but 25 pipes of wine, and very little bread, and no water but what they brought out of Spain, which stinketh marvellously, and the flesh meat they cannot eat, the drought is so great . . . the admiral's purpose is with the first wind to pass away for Spain.

The last remark shows that Recalde had no intention of mounting an invasion of Ireland.

A fellow Portuguese, Emanuel Francisco, said the ship

. . . was many times shot through, and a shot in the mast, and the deck of the prow spoiled . . . He says the flagship's mast is so weak, by reason of the shot in it, as they dare not abide any storm, nor to bear such sails as otherwise they might do . . . and further, the best of that be in the Admiral's ship are scarce able to stand, and that if they tarry where they are anytime, they will all perish.

Meanwhile Recalde was taking stock of the ships' seaworthiness. He gave Aramburu, who still had a heavy anchor, two cables and a small broken anchor, receiving a bower anchor in exchange. Then, on 17 September, he sent fifty arquebusiers ashore to get supplies. 'They found only large rugged rocks against which the sea pounded', noted Aramburu, 'and ashore 100 arquebusiers were marching, bearing a white standard with a red cross. It was concluded that they were English'. Their conclusion was right. James Trant, a prosperous merchant of Dingle, was in charge of them. He subsequently wrote, 'We do not fear their landing here for they are in a most difficult road [anchorage], and themselves in a miserable state. We have 200 men watching upon the shore every day. We stand in no fear of them, for they are so much afraid of themselves.'

He was right. Recalde sent no more men ashore after his arquebusiers returned. Instead they did their best to take on water from a small spring on the cliff-top, using *San Juan de Portugal*'s longboat for the purpose. Each barrel had to be landed through the surf, rolled up the beach and heaved on to the cliff-top, then rolled back again when full. Aramburu had no ship's boat to get water with.

It was at dawn on 21 September that a terrible gale blew up without warning. Aramburu wrote,

On the 21st, in the morning, the west wind came with some terrible fury, but cloudless and with little rain. The flagship . . . drifted down on our ship, cast anchor and another cable, and having smashed our lantern and our mizzenmast tackle and rigging, the flagship secured herself. At mid-day the ship *Santa Maria de la Rosa* [also known as the *Nuestra Señora de la Rosa*] . . . came in by another entrance nearer land . . . She fired a shot on entering, as if seeking help . . . All her sails were in pieces except the foresail. She cast her single anchor, for she was not carrying more . . . she stayed there until two o'clock. Then the tide waned, and as it turned the ship began dragging on our two cables, and we dragged with her, and in an instant we could see that she was going down, trying to hoist the foresail. Then she sank with all on board, not a person being saved, a most extraordinary and terrifying thing. We were dragging on her still, to our own perdition.

She must have hit the Stromboli Reef, which was some 17 ft. below the surface, as she drew 18–20 ft. in depth.

But Our Lord had willed us, in case of such necessity, to put a new stock to an anchor which had only half a stock, which Juan Martinez had given us, with a cable. We dropped this anchor, and the ship turned her prow; and we hauled in the other anchor, finding only the stock with half the shank, for the rest was broken, and the cable chafed by the rocks over which we were lying . . . This same afternoon, at four o'clock, the ship *San Juan* of Fernando Horra came in with her mainmast gone, and on entering her foresail was blown to shreds. She let her anchor go and brought to.

The *San Juan de la Rosa* (945 tons, 26 guns), which had set sail with 233 troops and 64 sailors, was a 'Mediterranean' ship with a thin hull and had suffered from the strains of Atlantic weather and sea conditions. The following morning it was decided that as she could sail no further, her crew should be taken aboard the other ships. On shore, James Trant watched everything, reporting to the effect that

There are three great ships, the biggest of them is of 900 tons, and is Admiral of the whole fleet of Spain. The other two are great ships also. One of them has her main mast broken. They have two small barques. There came from the sea unto them yesterday a mighty great ship of 1,000 tons, wherein was Il Principa Dastula [Prince of Ascoli], base son of the King of Spain. The name of this ship was *Santa Maria de la Rosa*, and as soon as ever they cast anchor they drive upon a rock, and there, was cast away into the middle of the sea, with 500 tall men and the Prince, and no man saved but one, that brought us this news, who came naked upon a board.

In fact the prince was not on board at all. A mutilated and almost unreadable document dated 12 August was written by the prince himself to Philip II, detailing how he had changed ships and arrived at Dunkirk. He had written that, while anchored off Calais, the Duke of Medina Sidonia had ordered him to go with Captain Aramburu to the rear of the squadron. So that

. . . at daybreak I found myself in the midst of the enemy's ships, and our Armada too far away for us to reach it. Whilst I was in this position I saw a small pinnace in which were two majors who had been sent to carry orders through the Armada . . . I therefore went on board the pinnace with the intention of making for the galleon, and we clapped on all sail with that object. Both wind and tide were against us, and the enemy were engaged with our fleet, so that I was cut off and in the rear of both fleets. I decided to follow in the wake of the fleets, but I was so hotly pressed by the boats . . . that not a sailor could be induced to stir. Thus I remained all day until two o'clock next morning, when so violent a gale broke that I was obliged to run before it, I knew not whither, all that night without a pilot. In the morning I sighted Calais, but was too far to leeward to make it. I therefore determined to enter this port [Dunkirk] where I found the Duke of Parma, and gave him an account of my proceedings, begging leave to return to the Armada. This he refused to allow. I am very unhappy to be out of whatever events may happen to the Armada, but as God has ordained otherwise, it cannot be helped.

During prolonged interrogation at Dingle, a boy who survived the wreck of the *Santa Maria de la Rosa* by being swept on a plank to Slea Head, made his first statement to the effect that he was 'John Antony de Manona. An Italian. Son to Francisco de Manona pilot of the ship called *Santa Maria de la Rosa*, of 1,000 tons, castaway in the Sound of Bleskey'. In his second and third statements he said he

Slea Head.

was from Genoa and called Giovanni, so probably he was Giovanni of Genoa. He maintained that 'as soon as the ship broke against the rock, one of the Captains slew . . . {his} father, saying he did it by treason'. This may mean that the pilot had cut the anchor cable to try and save the ship. John went on under pressure to give precise details about 50 brass field guns, 25 brass and iron ship's guns as well as 15,000 silver ducats, more in gold in three chests. He named a considerable number of officers and 'gentlemen-adventurers' during his interrogations, but whether they were necessarily aboard his ship was quite another matter. Months later when King Philip was presented with a copy of his statement, he wrote against this list, 'He is wrong about most of these, perhaps he is so about the rest'.

Giovanni's statements were certainly detailed. Pressed for details about the prince, he said he was 'a slender made man of a reasonable stature of twenty-eight years of age, his hair of an acorn colour stroked upwards; of a high forehead; whitely faced with some little red on the cheeks. He was drowned in apparel of white satin for his doublet and breeches, after the Spanish fashion cut, with russet silk stockings'. The fact that the prince lived for years after 1588 belies the fact that he was on board on 21 September. Clearly Giovanni's interrogators were hoping for a good news-story out of the drowning of the king's illegitimate son. Some of the confusion involving the accuracy of his statements must lie with the interpreter, David Gwynne, a soldier of fortune, who had been a galley slave on the galley, *Diana*, as we saw earlier on. In October 1588 he was charged with 'manifest falsehood and perjury touching the embezzling of certain gold and coin received by him of the Spaniards', and with treasonable talk.

But to return to the four ships – Recalde's, Aramburu's, Fernando Horra's and an unidentified one – still in Blasket Sound. Horra's was another *San Juan Bautista*, a speedy, armed 'Atlantic' merchantman (*nao*) of 650 tons and 24 guns. It is known that in view of her very poor state (her mainmast was gone and the foresail in shreds) her troops were taken off on 22 September, and that Recalde intended to salvage her guns, but what followed then is obscure. Certainly she must have sunk there, probably scuttled. In fact there is considerable doubt as to whether there had been more than four ships there at various times. Niall Fallon suggests that there may have been six in all over the period.

Aramburu set sail on 24 September, writing that 'It pleased Our Lady, to whom we commended ourselves, that we should get out, sailing all that night to the west, so that by morning we found ourselves 8 leagues from land'. After a hard passage, he reached Santander on 14 October. He lived to fight the English again in 1591. Recalde left with the *San Juan* and the tenders on 27 September and reached Corunna. He was almost at death's door, and died four days later after writing a brief note to the king.

Back in September in Munster, SW Ireland, the Sheriff of Clare, Boetius Clancy, was faced with reports of Armada ships being sighted. Some years earlier the English authorities had concentrated on Munster as the land was not only the richest available for cattle breeding, but was also the most accessible. The Desmond clan had been crushed and younger sons of English gentry offered plantations at cheap rates. Now there was a fear that the Desmonds might seize the opportunity presented by a Spanish landing.

It was a particularly busy time for Nicholas Cahan, a sheriff's minor official in charge of the area south of Liscannor, as he had been in the south of Clare the previous week where seven ships were reported. These ships had anchored off Carngaholt. He got there just five days before the wrecks occurred at Clare. It appeared that the seven had anchored to take on water and food, and carry out repairs. When a ship's boat had brought some ashore, they had had a brief discussion with Cahan. Neither side was prepared to test the strength of the other at that time. The seven consisted of two 1,000 ton ships, two 400 ton and three small barques. Attempts to mend the largest ship, the *Annunciada* (700 ton merchantman, 24 guns, 275 crew) had failed, so that it was offered to the Irish as payment for aid. Cahan refused the offer. Fortunately for the Spaniards the wind improved and they were able to sail away, after setting fire to the abandoned ship. 'God be praised', wrote Cahan, 'those seven ships are gone, but one ship they have burned'.

He was at Doonby when he heard that on 20 September, 'God hath cast to the shore of Donbegy a great ship from St Sebastian's, wherein were 300 men all drowned but 3 score or thereabouts . . . Another great ship [is] cast in at I Breckane and lost; they had both men and munitions coming out of Flanders'. One of these ships was probably the *San Esteban* (736 tons, 26 guns, 274 men). Those who did survive were taken prisoner.

News then came that another ship, the *San Marcos*, 790 tons, 33 guns and some 450 men, had run aground near Tromra Castle, further up the coast. There were four survivors. Don Felipe de Cordoba, son of Don Diego de Cordoba, survived from one of the two ships. He appears to have joined some sixty Spaniards being held in Sheriff Clancy's castle at Spanish Point. Later they were taken to a hill, called the Hill of the Gallows, and hung before being buried in a common grave.

Boetius Clancy was also concerned about the galleass, *Zuniga* (50 guns, with a crew of 290 and additional adventurers, servants, medical staff and priests), which he reported to Bingham on 16 September. 'The said ship has 2 cock-boats, whereof one broke from the ship and landed, and it is not like our English cock-boats; it would carry 20 men at least, and it is painted red, with the red anchor with an earthern vessell like an oil "prock", and the small board which this bearer will deliver your worship was also therein found. What the vessel is I know not'. Under Captain Juan de Saavedra's command the galleass had passed between the Orkneys and Fair Isle with a damaged rudder. In vain he had tried to get help from both

Medina Sidonia and Recalde. In early September she was off Tralee Bay and then from 14–22 September, anchored off Liscannor, in no fit state to head for Spain. It was when she was taking on water and food that Bingham made his report.

The ship's purser was caught when bargaining for provisions. He told the Bishop of Kildare that the entire Armada was in flight and in a bad way 'for want of bread, flesh and water'. However she did manage to set sail for Spain, only to be driven up the English Channel until she reached Havre de Grace, near Calais, on 11 October. There, timber from the wrecked *San Lorenzo* was used to repair her and fifty-six survivors from that ship joined her. In April 1589, they set sail again, but were forced back to Havre by heavy seas. A mutiny followed, which was quelled. She became silted up in the sand, although there is a possibility that she eventually did get back to Spain.

On 3 November, Bingham wrote to Sir Henry Wallop to say that 'the Spaniards have departed, leaving but a few begging, sick men'. So the threat was over. English control of Munster and Connaught had ensured that hardly a Spaniard survived there. Only in Ulster, the last stronghold of the Irish clans, was there any need for anxiety. Two thousand Spaniards had landed there and obtained local aid. The turning point in the tense period was the sailing of the *Girona* with 1,300

The Cliffs of Moher, Co. Clare. The Galleass *Zuniga* was sighted close in, but escaped wrecking. Just to the south are Liscannor Bay and Doonbeg.

men from Killybegs. Sir William's march through a combination of rain, floods and snow in November and December had shown that only about a hundred 'most miserable, both in body and apparel, and few or none of them Spaniards' remained of those who had survived the shipwrecks.

Overall, few Irish had helped the Spaniards, although they had always maintained that they had been awaiting their coming for years. Interestingly it was only the clans with Scottish origins, the McDonnells of Antrim and the MacSweeneys of Tirconnell, who really offered help. Thus within a month or two Ireland was back to normal once again. Whether matters would have been different if the O'Neill and O'Donnell clans had been more resolute or de Leyva more determined will never be known. Perhaps Philip had made a basic mistake in not sending the Armada direct to Ireland in the first place.

Of the hundred, or perhaps fewer, Spaniards detained for ransom, sixty-one were transported to England. Their ransoms were not easily forthcoming. A further

Nine and two of spades. Many Spaniards suffered from shipwreck and capture.

thirty managed to escape as they were in transit from Dublin to Chester. Sir William Fitzwilliam hired the *Swallow*, belonging to Captain Christopher Carleill, Governor of Ulster, for the journey. Aboard this pinnace was a crew of eight and one of Carleill's cavalry officers. The thirty prisoners easily overpowered them and sailed the ship to Corunna. They were certainly back by the autumn of 1589 as the pinnace was seen there in August or September. Carleill petitioned the Privy Council for compensation for the loss of his ship, valuing it at £173 6*s*. 8*d*. In his petition he explained that the prisoners had captured the ship and sailed away. It is not known if he received any compensation or not.

CHAPTER THIRTEEN

Return to Spain

On the return journey to Spain the Duke of Medina Sidonia was confined to his bunk with a burning fever and dysentery. He slipped in and out of consciousness as his ship made slow progress home. When the *San Martin* finally anchored at Santander on 23 September, he was lowered into a pilot boat as he was too weak to sit upright. Fifty 'gentlemen all apparelled in black like mourners accompanied him' ashore. In fact nearly all the senior officers aboard were unfit for duty. Recalde and Oquendo were to die in mid-October.

The duke tried to cope with day-to-day administration and make reports about the state of the ships and the half-clothed, unpaid and poorly-fed crews. Just how ill he was can be seen from the muddled way he wrote about these problems at this time. With nowhere to house them ashore, many men were left dying aboard their ships. Half his crew were to die in all. Forty had died in battle, but a further one hundred and eighty of sickness. Some sixty-six ships arrived at Spanish ports about this time, all with the same problems of disease and exhaustion. One ship even ran aground in Laredo Harbour as there were not enough fit men left to haul down the sails and lower the anchor.

Overall out of the 30,000 men who had sailed, some 20,000 were to die. Probably 1,500 died in battle, 6,000 in ship-wrecks, 1,000 were killed, judicially

Knave of diamonds shows the Spanish fleet returning homewards.

or unlawfully when shipwrecked, and the rest died of diseases such as typhus, scurvy and influenza. The coastal towns were overwhelmed with the problem of sick and dying men. On 10 October Philip appointed an official to supervise the situation in Santander. This man soon reported that 'If they are brought ashore the hospital would be so overcrowded that infection would spread, and if they are left to sleep in the stench and wretchedness of the ships, the fit are bound to fall ill. It is impossible to attend to so many'.

Medina Sidonia asked the king to relieve him of his command, arguing that his inexperience and incompetence had led to failure, as he had predicted when appointed.

The troubles and miseries we have suffered cannot be described to Your Majesty. They have been worse than have ever been seen in any voyage before. On board some of the ships that are in there has not been a drop of water to drink for a fortnight. On my own ship, a hundred and eighty men have died of sickness, three out of the four pilots succumbed, and all the rest of the people on board are ill, many of typhus and other infectious diseases. All the sixty men of my own household have either died or fallen sick, and only two remain able to serve me. God be praised for all He has ordained. Great as the miseries have been, we are now worse off than ever, for the men are all ill and the little biscuit and wine we have left will be finished in a week. We are therefore in a wretched state, and I implore Your Majesty to send some money quickly to buy necessities . . . Everything is in disorder, and must at once be put in competent hands, for I am in no condition to attend to business.

Reading this plea, and a statement from his doctor, the king agreed, excusing the duke the normal requirement of coming to kiss hands on relinquishing his post. So in October he set off for home. Knowing that he would be too easily taken as the scapegoat, the duke took care to travel home by a route which skirted towns and the houses of wealthy friends, who no doubt were mourning the loss of loved ones. In this way the possibility of hostile demonstrations was avoided, though when he spent a night at Valladolid, the crowd outside shouted, 'Here comes Drake'. By the following spring he was fit enough to walk and ride round his estates again. But his contemporaries, and many Spanish generations to follow, never forgave him.

When the full extent of the failure of the 'Enterprise of England' came home to Philip, he showed no sign of being overwhelmed by it. As a boy he had heard that his father received the news of the victory of Pavia with admirable self-restraint, and he had always perceived it the duty of a monarch to show neither rejoicing nor sorrow in public. In fact his self-restraint had become a legend in his own lifetime. Hundreds of popular stories were told of his behaviour in the face of adversity.

An account by Father Famiano Strada claims that Philip still held to a belief that the Armada was victorious, when a messenger from Santander brought news of the duke's return. The two royal secretaries were horrified and argued as to which of them should break the news to his majesty. Finally one of them entered the royal study and stammered out the news. Not showing any sign of reaction, the king replied,

> I give thanks to God by whose hand I have been so endowed that I can put to sea another fleet as great as this we have lost whenever I choose. It does not matter if a stream is sometimes choked, as long as the source flows freely.

He then picked up his pen and went on writing. A later version of this story makes the king add, 'I sent my ships to fight against men, and not against the winds and waves of God'. Elsewhere it is said that he turned on Admiral Diego Flores de Valdés with the words, 'I sent you to fight against men, not against God'. Don Diego was in fact imprisoned for giving bad advice to the Duke of Medina Sidonia.

In sharp contrast, Anthony Copley, an English spy, wrote that,

> When news of the disgrace of the King's late Armada was brought to him, being at Mass at that very time in his Chapel, he swear (after Mass was done) a great Oath, that he would waste and consume his Crown, even to the value of a [last] Candlestick (which he pointed to standing upon the Altar) but either he would utterly ruin her Majesty and England, or else himself and all Spain become Tributary to her. Whereby it was most evident that his Desire for Revenge was extreme and implacable towards England.

Probably none of these stories are true. He must have heard of the failure of the

Armada by stages, and can never have believed it was victorious until the return of the duke's ship. The duke had sent him a report and his diary on 21 August in any case. However, he no doubt took the defeat calmly, though it was noticeable that he was seriously ill that autumn. After 1588 his skin began to have a pallor about it and his beard finally turned white and became more neglected. Various reports refer to his health, but it seems likely that he suffered nothing worse than an attack of gout in his right hand.

He concluded that his sins, and those of the nation, had led God to disown the Armada. In so doing he was accepting Mendoza's eloquently presented argument that men's sins were so great and numerous that no punishment God could award would be unreasonable. Moreover, Mendoza argued, God punishes men for their own good, so as to make them humble before making them victorious. Religious though he was in all his thought, Philip did not fail to relate the practical to the spiritual, for he mused that God might have been more favourable to the 'Enterprise' if Spain had had a deep seaport, like Calais, already available, and if his ships had been designed like those of the English. His writings during the months that followed show that he had identified the mistakes of the 'Enterprise' of 1588 – lack of long range guns (more culverins and demi-culverins needed), ships too varied to sail together (more uniformity required), lack of a deep-water port opposite England (gain one), and so on. The conclusion was to make a greater, and more careful, effort next time. Divine support was only temporarily lost, and could be regained by the right response from the devoted.

When he wrote to his bishops on 13 October, he stated,

The uncertainties of naval enterprises are well known, and the fate which has befallen the Armada is an instance in point . . . We are bound to give praise to God for all things which He is pleased to do. Now I give thanks to Him for the mercy He has shown. In the storms through which the Armada sailed, it might have suffered a worse fate, and that its ill-fortune was no greater must be credited to the prayers for its good success, so devoutly and continuously offered. These prayers must have entailed serious expense and trouble on those who have conducted them. I wish you, therefore, all to understand that while I am, so far, well pleased with your exertions, they may now cease. You may wind up in the cathedrals and churches of your dioceses with a solemn Thanksgiving Mass on any day which you may appoint . . .

Clearly he felt that these prayers were no longer needed as no more ships were likely to return.

Marco Antonio Micea's *Advices from England*, *5 November 1588*, argues that there was 'bad management and the heavy loss of ships and men. I will only say that if the Armada had been conducted as it should have been, and its commanders had taken advantage of the opportunities offered to them, the King of Spain would now King of England'. The copy in the Paris Archives has 'This first is certainly lamentable' scrawled by Philip in the margin.

So far as the Duke of Parma was concerned, Philip noted that the duke had let him down and that he would only employ him in the Netherlands until he could find a replacement for him. This is not surprising when one recalls that the duke had written to the king's secretary, when requested to give a true explanation of what had happened,

> Notwithstanding all that has been said, or may be said, by ignorant people, or those who maliciously raise doubts where none should exist . . . the boats might well have begun to get out that night and joined those from Nieuport next day [8 August] . . . There was no need to supply water to the boats, whatever some people may say, because no cooking was needed for such a short passage and there was plenty of beer to drink. Nor was there any need, as others imagine, to waste time in fitting artillery in the warships, as we counted on the support of the armada.

His reference to August 8 is significant as that was the day on which he had insisted in no uncertain terms that the weather made it impossible to embark for England. When he heard mutterings of 'cowardice', he issued a challenge to any man who doubted his courage. He waited a whole day in the Grand Place of Dunkirk, with a rapier at the ready, but none came to take up the challenge.

For Spain it was a considerable blow to national pride, to say nothing of disbelief in the failure of God to support His Catholic Church. Inevitably the need for mourning was everywhere. Nevertheless cities were voting money for a new fleet almost at once. Castile offered eight million ducats, Toledo, one hundred thousand, and Milan a quarter of a million. By the end of 1588 timber from as far away as the Adriatic was being felled for further ship building at Cadiz, Lisbon, San Sebastian and Santander. Such generosity and activity can only have served to underline the popularity of the King of Spain at this time. The nation united behind him in its refusal to accept defeat.

So far as Protestant Europe was concerned, the Armada's defeat brought a feeling of great relief. Clearly God was not necessarily on the side of Catholics, even if they were powerful ones such as the King of Spain. In fact, it could be concluded that God had joined the Reformation and turned Protestant too. French Protestants, and the Dutch fighting against Spanish domination, were particularly heartened. In France Henry III felt the pressure on him lifted. At last he could reassert himself against Henry of Guise, whom the Spaniards had been subsidising. He rescinded his earlier decree banning all Protestants from holding office. The balance of power was welcome in Italy too. Elizabeth's standing in the Protestant world increased markedly. Perhaps even the Papacy was relieved at not having to pay the million ducats promised to Spain if the 'Enterprise' succeeded.

As for the propaganda document itemising the Armada's strength, which Philip had released when the fleet sailed, it was contemptuously dealt with by an English broadsheet entitled, *A Pack of Spanish Lies sent abroad into the world, translated out of the original and now ripp'd up, unfolded, and by just examination condemned, as containing false, corrupt and detestable wares, worthy to be damn'd and burnt*. It claimed that 'with all their great terrible ostentation they did not, in all their sailing round England, so much as sink or take one ship, bark, pinnace, or cockboat of ours, or even burn so much as one sheepcote on this land'.

By Easter 1589, Philip was bent on seizing the initiative again. Fearing an English invasion of Portugal that summer, he made plans to counter such an outrage. He had heard that Don Antonio of Crato, who had a claim on the Portuguese throne, had been in England for some time, staying with Drake himself it was said. Don Antonio had long wanted English support for an invasion of Portugal and now there was a real possibility of getting it. He even offered to pay the cost of the expedition within two months of coming to his throne, together with a further 300,000 ducats a year and full trade privileges. As Elizabeth had only £55,000 left in December 1588, this was indeed a temptation. Drake had proved he could raid the peninsula ports, and he and Sir John Norris persuaded her to accept the idea in principle. A joint stock company of £80,000, to which the queen contributed a quarter, the most she could afford, was set up. But it proved difficult to get the Dutch to release the 3,000 troops and six siege guns and necessary ships as Parma continued to press them hard. Finally they agreed to send 1,500 troops and 10 warships, and allowed England to withdraw her 3,000 troops – provided their own men were back by June.

However, squabbles between the leaders meant that the expedition did not finally leave the Channel until April. By then the queen had her doubts and the force was not up to that originally planned. While some wanted the Spanish fleet destroyed, investors wanted other priorities. The result was a fatal compromise, which in turn left Drake and Norris disobeying the queen and sailing for Lisbon on little more than a profiteering voyage.

The war was to drag on for fourteen years and end in what could best be described as a 'draw'. In all Philip dispatched three more armadas before he died in 1598. The first, in 1596, was for the invasion of Ireland. News of its coming left Elizabeth's War Council completely divided as to where it might land. Fortunately for her it sailed at the worst time of the year, November, against the advice of the admirals. A severe storm off the north Portuguese coast destroyed it.

The second, in 1597, was designed to land troops in Falmouth and capture Cornwall. Philip had had a careful survey made of the English coastline by an expert pilot sailing in a ship bearing a French flag. So detailed was his survey that the king knew not only harbour details, but what food was to hand and whether nearby inhabitants had Catholic leanings. Of Falmouth, the pilot wrote,

> In the middle of Falmouth harbour there is a rock named Falmouth which can be passed on one side or the other. There are four fathoms at the mouth at low water, and, within, it is eighteen fathoms. It will hold any number of ships. At the two points of the harbour there are two castles, one on each shore, with much artillery. On the right side it is flat, but both reach to the middle of the channel. Care must be had of some shoals on the right side after passing the isle. Almost all the artillery is emplaced outside of the two castles together with their gabions [earth-filled containers for defence purposes]. They can be taken by land with a small party of men. There is a large population, but it is not warlike. There is water, meat and grain.

As it turned out the fleet, with some six to eight thousand troops, was only stopped a few miles off the Lizard by a violent gale. But it shook England, which had failed to receive spy reports of its sailing, let alone its destination, as that was one of the best-kept secrets of the century. The panic on hearing of the ships off the Cornish coast was so great that there was a severe shock to the confidence the nation had in its queen and government.

The third armada which sailed just before Philip's death, reached Calais undetected by sailing up the Channel on the French side. It was simply to reinforce the Spanish army in Europe, and not to invade England. Looking beyond the king's death to the early years of Philip III, we find panic throughout England in the summer of 1599. A rumour went round in early August that the Spanish had actually landed. Hastily, chains were strung across London streets and coastal towns, troops were rushed to the old camp at Tilbury and a force of 30,000 assembled in London. Although it all proved a false alarm, it demonstrated just how confused a response followed yet one more threat of invasion. It also showed the nervousness of a country which had so nearly faced invasion in 1597. The expense of the hurried reaction to this false alarm led to much grumbling.

The last attempt in Elizabeth's reign came in 1601. It was targeted at Ireland, which was already experiencing a rebellion in the north. Although divided by storms on the way over, three ships did manage to land troops in Baltimore on the southern coast, while other ships landed 3,000 veteran troops at Kinsale. At the latter they were received in the town with open arms. Months of fighting followed, finally ending in the surrender of those who remained. They were repatriated without ransoms, a procedure which suggests a new spirit was now afoot.

Thus the Armada of 1588 was not to prove the end of the Spanish navy, but more its beginning. The English were unable to blockade the Spanish coast in the way they had done before it had sailed. Moreover, in the years 1588 to 1603, more *flota* treasure fleets returned safely to Spain than in any other fifteen-year period in the history of those fleets. In short, no one commanded the seas for the rest of Elizabeth's reign. The war finally ended as a result not only of exhaustion of men and money on both sides, but also of the growing respect each side had developed for the other during all those years of conflict.

CHAPTER FOURTEEN

The Findings of Underwater Archaeologists

The first man to find a sunken Armada galleon using the modern techniques available to underwater archaeologists was Sydney Wignall. With Joseph Casey and members of the St Helens Underwater Club, he began work in 1963. They searched Blasket Sound but found the conditions far from easy. Two years later, he got a licence for his work from the Ministry of Marine Affairs in Madrid, as the Spanish technically still owned any wreck in Irish waters. Fortunately he met Commander John Grattan, who was to solve the problem of locating the *Santa Maria de la Rosa* by using the swim-line underwater search system used by some diving teams in the Royal Navy. On one occasion this method had been used by thirty-five navy divers to search some 290 acres in half an hour. The system simply consists of the divers moving forward in a line while under control from the surface by means of the light-weight markers towed on the surface by each diver.

The team was completed by the arrival of the archaeologist, Dr Colin Martin, Director of the Institute of Maritime Archaeology of St Andrew's University, in 1968. Sydney Wignall described the swim-line technique as being like a visual vacuum-cleaner sweeping the 3,000 acres of Blasket Sound. 'It beats as it sweeps as it sees. We even picked up chicken bones. Believe me, we missed nothing in Blasket Sound'. Their finds included seven broken Armada anchors and cannon-balls. They also found an uncharted rock, which the *Santa Maria* must have struck, for otherwise she would have cleared the area comfortably at high tide. Further investigations followed some two hundred yards south east of Stromboli Reef, in spite of high waves and several capsizings of their inflatable craft. They were aided by Jeremy Green with his metal-detector which found a large pewter plate. The inscription, 'Matute', helped to identify the ship, as it was the name of the captain in charge of the 233 infantrymen on board the *Santa Maria*.

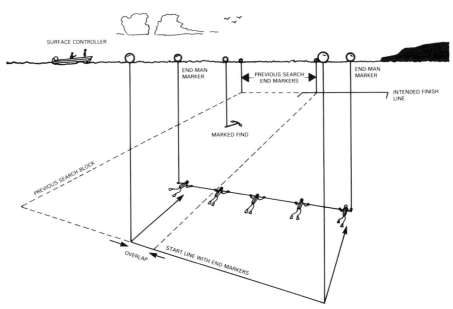

The swim-line technique used to locate the layout of shipwrecks. Eight to fifteen divers can be used.

In 1969 the shingle was airlifted and ballast stones removed to uncover the timbers at a depth of 110 ft., covering an area of some 100 ft. by 40 ft. Their findings seemed to indicate that the ship had lost her mainmast and broken her back. Lead ingots, pottery, a fire-lighting flint and a pewter goblet were found. Two coins were found in a cloth purse still attached to a skeleton in the ship's stern. Beside the skeleton was a pewter plate with 'A. H.' on it. There was a man called Augustin de Herrera who died on board, but also a poet called Antonio de Herrera, who survived. The lead bullets found were either ½ in. or ¾ in. diameter, weighing ½ or 2 oz. respectively. The former were arquebus, and the latter musket, bullets. Strangely no guns were found, but they may have been jettisoned earlier on when the ship was in difficulties. Certainly she fired two shots when she entered the Sound, but the swivel gun used then may well have been the one found by fishermen in 1839.

They found a great mound of ballast stones which marked the complete bottom of the hold which was left behind when the upper work of the ship broke apart and drifted away. Such ballast was needed as ships of her top-heavy design had to carry

a quarter of their own weight to keep upright. This would amount to a 2 ft. depth of 50 lb. rocks, which the divers found carefully packed one on top of another to prevent them shifting and destabilising the ship. Just as the crew would have had to systematically remove some stones to check for hull damage, so now the divers removed them to find the hull and calculate its size. As a result they learnt that the keelson (the section running directly above the keel, clamping down the ribs and forming, with the keel, the ship's backbone) was made up of jointed sections, 10 in. broad and 8 in. deep. Such light-weight sections suggested that the ship design was not as solid as had been supposed. Staunchions and two 20 ft. planks (each 1 ft. broad, 2 in. thick) were also found. A box fastened to the keelson puzzled the divers for some time, until they realised it must have been designed to give added support to the mainmast's fixing. They concluded that the mast had been stepped in a recessed wooden block which was bolted to the keelson. Furthermore, the box was clearly a temporary one, showing signs of rough-and-ready workmanship, and must have been put in during a 6-hour operation on 10 July 1588, when the *Santa Maria* lost her mainmast at Corunna.

They also concluded that the mainmast's collapse was a major cause of the ship being wrecked, and that when wrecked, she had broken into two parts. This suggested the ship struck the rock about midships on the starboard side. Then she sank quickly, stern first. Further investigations led to the finding of the main rib timbers, every second one of which was 8 in. wide by 1 ft. deep. The outer planking was 3 in. thick and was pinned to the frame with trenails (long wooden dowels). The makers preferred trenails as iron fastenings were liable to rust.

The whole operation had involved forty-three divers from twenty sub-aqua clubs doing thou-

Types of shot from the *Santa Maria*.

sands of dives. On behalf of the divers involved, Sydney Wignall was awarded the Duke of Edinburgh Prize of the British Sub-Aqua Club for this investigation. While he concentrated on research into Armada shot as a result of this investigation, Dr Colin Martin studied the structural design of the ship. He had to ask himself the question, was this 945 ton ship one of the new sleek race-decked Atlantic-line ships, or a large, beamy Mediterranean-style carrack. A major clue was that 'Atlantic' ships had their mainmast at the mid-point of the keel, while 'Mediterranean' ones had theirs set further forward for the sake of directional stability. As the mainmast box was placed 37½ ft. from the bow, this would make sense if the keel was 91¼ ft. long, so making the design a 'Mediterranean' one; otherwise the keel would only have been 75 ft. long, too short for a 945 ton ship. This was underlined by the directions given in a fifteenth-century Venetian treatise on shipbuilding, which said the mainmast's fixing point should be calculated by dividing 'the keel into five parts' and leaving 'three parts (less 1 foot) aft'. The fact that the ship was built for Mediterranean use may well help to explain why she was unable to cope with the voyage.

Meanwhile, the Belgian diver, Robert Sténuit, had spent some 700 hours in the libraries of five countries researching into the loss of the *Girona*. As a result, in 1967 he found the wreck at a depth of 20–30 ft. near Port-na-Spagna, adjacent to the Giant's Causeway, within an hour of diving there, in spite of the kelp and boulders covering everything. After numerous dives, bronze cannons, five breech blocks (powder chambers), countless cannon-balls, pieces of eight, a gold chain and other jewellery were found. He and his small team also raised an anchor using inflatable bags. Cannon-balls, 756 silver and 405 gold coins, 17 seals, 12 gold rings, 2 silver crucifixes, religious medals, 48 silver forks, 22 silver spoons, 2 silver ladles, 71 silver plates, 31 silver bowls, silver candlesticks, lead shot and copper rods were among a vast array of objects freed from a black concretion which had formed round them. A small gold dolphin designed so that its nose was a tooth pick and tail an ear pick was found. A ring inscribed 'Madam de Champagney, MDXXIIII' must have belonged to Jean Thomas Perrenot, her grandson, who died on the *Girona*, while a cross of a Knight of Malta must have belonged to the captain, Don Fabricio Spinola. Two small bronze guns were raised, both of which turned out to be still loaded. Another gun, a long-range cannon, had on it a levelling device only used on land artillery. It was probably one

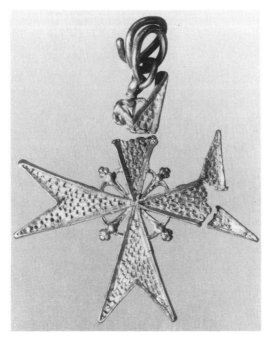

Cross of the Order of St John, later known as the 'Maltese' Cross, which belonged to Fabricio Spinola, captain of the *Girona*.

of the guns the Armada was carrying for use by the invasion army. Two astrolabes, 3 sounding leads and 5 nautical dividers were found too, as well as inkwells, basins, goblets and an anvil.

During the following winter Sténuit researched the coats of arms of knights who sailed with the Armada to see if the arms on the jewellery matched theirs. He found that some gold waistcoat buttons matched those on a contemporary engraving by Joss de Hondt of Sir Francis Drake, which suggests that Drake had used captured ones for his own waistcoat. In 1969, with bigger lifting bags, Sténuit and his team were able to lift huge boulders. They found a gold chain, at the rate of two links a day, totalling 1½ yd. in all. Another of 3 yds. was found. Probably the wearer would twist off a link to pay a bill, finding such chains a convenient way to carry his resources. In all eight such chains were found. Pewter plate, rings, and a gold reliquary in the shape of a book were located. This 'book'

A bronze astrolabe, from the *Girona*, a mariner's compass, its central steel pin now bent, from *La Trinidad Valencera*, and several pairs of bronze navigational dividers, those on the far right from *La Trinidad Valencera*, the remaining from the *Girona*.

The *Agnus Dei* gold reliquary possibly belonging to the Bishop of Killaloe, from the *Girona*. The hinged lid is decorated in relief, with a central area framed by pillars and topped with a pediment containing a representation of St John the Baptist.

opened to reveal a little tablet of red wax, an *Agnus Dei*. Such items were made as a protective amulet from the wax of an Easter candle mixed with holy oil, with Christ the Lamb stamped on one side and St John the Baptist on the other. They were blessed by the pope before he put them in the upturned mitres of bishops and cardinals present at the special mass. They would then be passed on to friends. It could have belonged to the Bishop of Killaloe who sailed in the *rata*. In all eleven gold frames with their lapis lazuli cameos of Byzantine emperors were found. Six thousand hours of diving resulted in 12,000 items being raised. To Sténuit's delight the Ulster Museum, Belfast, was able to acquire the whole collection by paying the Department of Trade and Industry £132,000.

In 1969, Colin Martin and Sydney Wignall decided to look for the *El Gran Grifon* off Fair Isle. When they began work in 1970 they found a bronze cannon, as well as several iron ones, in the southern gully of Stroms Hellier. A 60 ft. air lift pipe

A gold salamander pendant from the *Girona*, only three of the original nine rubies still surviving.

A lapis lazuli cameo portrait – one of a presumed set of twelve – with the profile of a Roman Emperor, from the *Girona*.

linked to an air lift compressor was brought in to aid the work of clearing the shingle from the wreck. Four wrought iron breech blocks for swivel guns were found, as well as five cast iron guns. One cannon had broken two feet from the muzzle at a point where the bore was obviously off centre as one side of the breech was 2½ in. thick and the other 5½ in. This would mean it was likely to blow up on being used. It was tempting to speculate that many of the Armada's guns were similarly badly made. The 6 ft. breech-loading iron guns found had been made by building up longitudinal strips of iron hammer-welded together on a mandrel to form the barrel, before being reinforced with hoops. Such a method was already obsolescent by the time of the Armada. It was significant that a front-line vessel such as the *El Gran Grifon* had to complete her armament with guns which were largely ineffectual and dangerous to use.

The archaeologists were able to make a number of calculated conclusions as to the overall armament of the ship, as they retrieved some 30 per cent of the guns aboard together with a considerable amount of ammunition. They suggested that the ship had 4 demi-culverins, 4 sacres, 3 demi-sacres, 6 quarter-cannons, 6 piezas, 9 large swivel guns and 6 swivel guns, a total of thirty-eight. This showed that the ship, although a flagship, was not armed like a front-liner. Its armament was purely defensive, as can be seen from the fact that demi-culverins and sacres are long range guns designed to keep the enemy off, rather than smash their hulls. In turn, this confirms Professor Michael Lewis' estimate of the armament for hulks in the front-line squadrons, and simultaneously points to the large gap between their armament and that of 'fighting-ships' such as the *Santa Maria de la Rosa*. One of Medina Sidonia's achievements had been to ensure that front-line fighting ships had the armament they needed for attacking with, while second-liners were left with the defensive, and partially obsolescent, armament available. In so doing he had remedied the chaos left by Santa Cruz, which included one ship having several new bronze cannons stowed between barrels and kegs, while other ships had no guns at all.

As expedition followed expedition, their team brought up cannon-balls, bar shot, 4,000 musket balls, and a leaden seal with Philip II's arms on it, as well as many other items. Among the lead musket shot they found a dozen flattened ones, which must have been fired by the English and buried themselves in the *El Gran Grifon*'s timbers. Probably they were fired when Drake's *Revenge* passed within 'half a musket shot' (about 50 yds.) range of her stern. A 15 in. viciously sharp steel shear hook was found. It would either have been tied to the yard-arm to tear down the enemy's rigging during a grappling operation, or fastened to a long pole to wield against an enemy's anti-boarding netting. This was a reminder that the Spanish still used such equipment as they expected grappling to be used as a fighting method. The English, however, regarded that tactic as obsolete. The items are now housed in the County Museum at Lerwick.

The City of Derry Sub-Aqua Club found *La Trinidad Valencera* 30 ft. down in Kinnagoe Bay (then Glenagivney or Glenganvey Bay) in 1971. Their first sighting was a cannon muzzle sticking out of a rock crevice. During the ensuing search, four bronze cannons were brought to the surface. Colin Martin was soon on the site, and found that two were a matching pair of 7¼ in. bore cannons, with lifting and breech dolphins, dated 1556, showing Philip II's arms encircled with the insignia of the Order of the Golden Fleece. One of the quarters on the arms bore the lions of England, which Philip was entitled to as husband of Mary I. The Latin inscription, the same on both guns, translates, 'Juan Manrique de Lara saw to my coming into being. The work of Remigy de Halut, 1556'. Juan was the Captain-General of Artillery for the Kingdoms of Aragon and Castile from 1551 to 1574, when he died. In 1556 he was serving as Captain-General of Artillery in the Flanders army. Remigy, Viscount of Burges Saint-Winoc and Master of the Royal Gunfoundry at Malines, was a famous cannon-founder with workshops near Antwerp. He introduced the idea of proof-firing, that is checking each new gun by firing it three times, while loaded with twice the normal powder load. Malines was considered the centre of the gunfounding art of Europe. Both guns were heavyweights, stamped 5,316 and 5,260 lb. respectively. But they were only two-thirds the weight and three-quarters the length of full cannons. Thus they were cut-down ('curtailed', hence 'curtails') versions of that class of gun. As Malines was also Philip's land artillery HQ, it seems highly likely that these two guns were part of a Spanish siege train of fifty-four artillery guns made there. This is underlined by the fact that Santa Cruz wanted to take that siege train for the invasion of England he was planning in 1586. When the Armada ships were being loaded in February 1588, the Venetian ambassador at Madrid informed his government that, among other guns, forty-eight siege guns with a double supply of carriages and wheels were loaded. Whereas it appears they were loaded simply as cargo for use on land when the invasion started, the fact that these two were found

The Remigy de Halut gun from *La Trinidad Valencera*.

on *La Trinidad Valencera* suggests that Medina Sidonia had decided to re-issue them to larger auxiliary ships to turn them into fighting ships.

Two smaller bronze guns were found in 1971. One was an 11 ft. 4 in. long, 6-pounder sacre, with a design of sea creatures, swans and flowering plants decorating the breech. The initials Z. A. showed it was made by Zuanne Alberghetti, a Venetian gunfounder. This suggests the gun was part of the ship's original armament when she was a Venetian cargo ship in need of protection from pirates. The other was a 9 ft. 7 in., 4-pounder gun which was probably Venetian too. A swivel gun was also found. Although its barrel was bronze, its breech chamber and other parts were wrought iron. It was found to be fully loaded with fine-grained powder and a 3¼ in. stone shot. A small piece of hemp was stuck in the touch-hole to keep the powder dry until it was necessary to fire it. Even the marks of the mallet used by the gunner to knock the wedge in place can be seen. It can be deduced that he used his left hand when hammering so as to keep his right free for aiming and loading the gun. Stone and iron shot was found in large quantities by the divers. It is possible that some guns were recovered by Sir James Stewart of Glasgow in 1610–11, as he raised 12,000 lb. (5,443 kg) of brass ordnance from some Armada wreck.

Six 5 ft. diameter wooden iron-reinforced guncarriage wheels were a major find. Santa Cruz's 1586 list mentions iron-bound wheels for cannons, demi-cannons, culverins and demi-culverins. Two of them were found beside one of the Remigy guns, which suggests that they belonged to it. If so, then the gun was mounted as an artillery gun and not as a ship-board gun on a small four-wheeled truck carriage. There was no trace of any truck carriage wheels. Although this may seem

An iron-bound wooden gun-carriage wheel from *La Trinidad Valencera* on the sea bed.

odd, the Spanish did in fact use field guncarriages on board ship at that time, possibly because they lacked the elm wood needed for the trucks. If so, they must have been much more difficult to handle on board ship than truck-mounted guns when placed in the ship's waist, not only in respect of their aiming, but also from their recoil. In view of their trail, they would need double their length, some 20 ft. in all. As the ship's waist width would be less than 40 ft., one gun would occupy over half the width when pushed out ready for firing. Uncontrolled recoil was impossible on board, so that the guns would have to be lashed to the ship's side. This in turn would put severe strain on the hull whenever firing occurred. Due to the shortage of gunners trained to fire such weapons, only ninety-five sailed with the Armada. On fighting ships this meant an allocation of two per ship. They would supervise a gun-captain and six soldiers per gun, none of whom would have had much, if any, experience in ship-board gun drill. Consequently they cannot have been as effective as the duke might have hoped.

Two wrought iron anchors, one 15 ft. long with an 8 ft. span, and the other 15 ft. 9 in., with a 9 ft. span, were raised. Twenty-two feet of 5 in. diameter hemp cable was found. Most of a copper kettle, a pair of brass navigational dividers, a boy's leather boot, steel morion helmets, muleteers' rope-soled sandals, a keg full of gunpowder, a blacksmith's bellows, hammers, barrel hoops, rope, canvas, pottery and pewter were among the numerous finds. A barrel-load of Baltic tar was found to be still sticky and pliable. Large pieces of timber were located, which was important as this was a Venetian design of ship, about which a lot of documentary material existed.

When Jeremy Green, of the Oxford Laboratory for Archaeology, carried out a metal-detector survey, it became clear that within 200 sq.ft. there was the biggest collection of Armada objects yet discovered. As a result, the BBC *Chronicle* programme, Irish TV and *Time-Life* decided to sponsor the work. Numerous other organisations also supported the costly work, which was to go on for years. It was discovered that in spite of a large number of ship's timbers being found, they did not present any coherent structure. All the planks and frames had been iron bolted, not trenailed, together, and this may explain why the hull totally disintegrated. This tallied with the known fact that such Venetian merchantmen were built to do intensive work over a relatively short working life of about ten years. Half-inch iron fastenings are quicker and easier for an unskilled man to fix than wooden ones. It was noticeable that the pattern of these fastenings was very regular, in contrast to the usual method of irregular patterning designed to avoid setting up weaknesses along the line of grain in the wood. Thus no attempt had been made when constructing this ship to allow for the grain, which in turn underlines the fact that it was a mass-produced ship.

Comparison of Santa Cruz's 1586 estimate for an Armada with the Armada which sailed in 1588

Ships Classes	1586 Number	Tons	1588 Number	Tons
1. Galleons	150	77,250	65	45,522
2. Urcas/hulks/storeships	40	8,000	25	10,271
3. Pataches/zabras/small ships	320	25,000	32	2,075
4. Galleasses	6		4	
5. Galleys	40		4	
Totals	556	110,250	130	57,868

Guns				
1. Guns for naval use	1,150		2,431	
2. Guns for army use on land	130		48	
Totals	1,280		2,479	

Men				
1. Sailors	16,612		8,050	
2. Oarsmen	9,800		2,088	
3. Soldiers	58,920		18,973	
4. Non-combatants, &c.	8,890		1,545	
Totals	94,222		30,656	

Victualling requirements in 1586 were calculated on feeding 94,222 men for 8 months, and in 1588 on feeding 30,656 for 6 months. The rations were virtually the same, but the water supply was doubled in 1588. The changes between the two estimates were largely due to the effect of superimposing Parma's invasion plan on top of Santa Cruz's Armada plan.

Composition of the Armada

The exact composition of the Armada as it sailed up the Channel remains difficult to be certain of. Figures given are usually 128 or 130 ships. Two counts were made, the first at Lisbon in May, just prior to departure, and the second at Corunna where reorganisation took place following the stormy journey there. The second list was hurriedly compiled and so contains discrepancies. In fact one of the urcas listed on it did not sail, so reducing the number to 130. The two muster figures, given by the unreliable Captain Fernandez Duro, are listed below.

LISBON MUSTER

Squadron	Classes of Ships	Ships	Men
Portugal	Ten galleons, two tenders	12	4,623
Biscay	Ten merchantmen, four tenders	14	2,800
Castile	Ten galleons, four merchantmen, two tenders	16	4,177
Andalusia	One galleon, nine merchantmen, one tender	11	3,105
Guipuzcoa	Ten merchantmen, two tenders	12	2,608
Levant	Ten merchantmen	10	3,527
Patches, zabras	Twenty-two patches and zabras	22	1,093
Urcas	Twenty-three urcas	23	3,729
Naples	Four galleasses	4	1,341
Portugal	Four galleys	4	362
		Other men	2,088

Totals: 128 vessels; 29,453 men
Totals by type: 21 galleons, 43 merchantmen, 4 galleys, 4 galleasses, 23 urcas, 22 patches and zabras, 11 tenders.

CORUNNA MUSTER

Squadron	Classes of Ships	Ships	Men
Portugal	Nine galleons, two zabras	11	3,705
Biscay	Nine merchantmen, four patches	13	2,374
Castile	Ten galleons, three merchantmen, two patches	15	3,808
Andalusia	Ten merchantmen, one patache	11	2,809
Guipuzcoa	Ten merchantmen, one urca, one patache, two pinnaces	14	2,936
Levant	One galleon, eight merchantmen	9	3,297
Urcas	Nineteen urcas	19	2,844
Pataches, zabras	One merchantman, two urcas, eleven patches, seven zabras	21	850
Naples	Four galleasses	4	1,336
Portugal	Four galleys	4	341
Carabelas	Nine tenders	9	125
Feluccas	One felucca	1	42

Totals: 131 vessels; 24,467 men

See also the composition published on the *Thankefull Remembrance* service sheet, page 152.

Spanish Losses

In about October 1588, two lists were published in Spain, one listing sixty-five ships that had returned, and the other a similar number of those that had not. The latter included 42 ships of major size, 3 galleasses, 1 galley and 20 pinnaces. The problem was that six ships appeared on both lists. This was partially due to the fact that several ships had the same names. A dozen of those which were due to set off are on neither list. Furthermore, some of those listed as missing were subsequently found to be safe. For example, the urca *David Chico*, was dismasted near Lisbon and so late in arriving; the galleass *Zuniga*, had been blown off course and ended up in Le Havre to await a year's repairs. Some of the 20 pinnaces had never rejoined the Armada after being sent off to carry messages. That did not mean they were not safe in some port. The list even included two ships which sank after they had reached Spain.

Consequently historians have argued ever since as to the exact figures. Professor Garrett Mattingley thought the figure for losses was too high, suggesting forty-four as more accurate. In doing so he included only ten ships as lost around Ireland, but this was disputed by Niall Fallon, who identified no less than twenty-six, including pinnaces, lost there. If one deducts the three ships listed as missing and known to have returned, and the six which appear on both lists, before adding five to the list of the twelve which are on neither list on the grounds that at least five are believed to have sailed, the resulting figures for losses are these:

Types of ship	Official list	Subtract/Add	Resulting revised list
Galleons	2	+ 2	4
Auxiliaries	20	− 3 + 1	18
Hulks	15	− 4	11
Pataches, etc.	22	− 1 + 2	23

Galleasses	3	− 1	2
Galleys	1		1
Totals	63	− 9 + 5	59

This means the greatest loss among particular types of ship was among the pataches, zabras and pinnaces, the small ships, as only thirty sailed in all. It has been argued by Michael Lewis that in view of this it would be wiser to assume that fifteen, rather than twenty, was the actual figure. If so this would reduce the overall loss to fifty-one. With this adjustment, the greatest losses, so far as groups were concerned, turns out to be among the flag and vice-flag ships carrying squadron leaders. Looked at another way, it is noticeable that the main losses were among the temporary warships (the hulks and armed merchantmen), rather than the Spanish royal navy. Among the latter only two galleasses, one galley and four major ships were lost.

ARMADA LOSSES IN IRELAND

In addition to the ships listed below, three unknown ships, all probably zabras, were lost in the area of County Donegal. Of the total of twenty-six ships lost, the losses per squadron are these:- Levant, seven; Castile, three; Biscay, two; Guipuzcoa, two; Portugal, one; Andalusia, one; Naples, one; urcas, five; zabras, four. As near as can be reckoned by Niall Fallon, 7,349 men connected with these ships were lost. Perhaps twenty per cent died in battle or at sea, which would leave a total of 5,904 cast ashore in Ireland. Some 760 of them returned safely to Spain. Of the remainder, 1,500 were killed by the English forces and the rest drowned or somehow killed when they were shipwrecked. At the time Sir Richard Bingham thought 15–16 ships had been lost, with 6–7,000 men involved, while Geoffrey Fenton, Secretary to the Irish Council, estimated the loss to be 16 ships and 5,394 men.

Ship	*Where wrecked*	*Probable date*
Barca de Amburg	Off Malin Head, Donegal	1 Sept.
Castillo Negro	Somewhere NW of Donegal	*c.* 4 Sept.
Trinidad	Valentia Island, Co. Kerry	15 Sept.

Ship	Where wrecked	Probable date
La Trinidad Valencera	Glenagivney Bay, Inishowen Peninsula, Co. Donegal	16 Sept.
San Nicolas Prodaneli	Toorglass, Curraun Peninsula, Co. Mayo	16 Sept.
Trinidad	Tralee, Co. Kerry	*c.* 18 Sept.
San Marcos	Reef nr. Mutton Island and Lurga Point, Co. Clare	20 Sept.
San Esteban	Doonbeg, Co. Clare	20 Sept.
Annunciada	Scattery roads, River Shannon	20 Sept.
Santiago	Inver, Broadhaven Bay, Erris, Co. Mayo	*c.* 21 Sept.
La Rata Encoronada	Fahy Strand, Ballycroy, Blacksod Bay, Co. Mayo	21 Sept.
Santa Maria de la Rosa	Stromboli Reef, Blasket Sound, Co. Kerry	21 Sept.
Ciervo Volante	Tirawley, north Mayo barony	*c.* 22 Sept.
El Gran Grin	Clare Island, Clew Bay, Co. Mayo	*c.* 22 Sept.
San Juan Bautista	Somewhere SW of Blasket Islands	*c.* 24 Sept.
San Juan	Streedagh Strand, nr. Grange, Co. Sligo	25 Sept.
La Lavia	Streedagh Strand, nr. Grange, Co. Sligo	25 Sept.
Santa Maria de Vision	Streedagh Strand, nr. Grange, Co. Sligo	25 Sept.
Concepcion Delcano	Duirling na Spainneach, Ards, nr. Carna, Co. Mayo	*c.* 25 Sept.
Falco Blanco Mediano	Freaghillaun South, Ballynakill, Co. Galway	*c.* 25 Sept.
Duquesa Santa Ana	Rosbeg, Loughros Mor Bay, Co. Donegal	26 Sept.
Girona	Lacada Point, Port na Spaniagh, Co. Antrim	28 Oct.
Juliana	Mullaghderg, Arranmore, Co. Donegal	unknown

Bibliography

Contemporary Sources

Calendar of the Carew Manuscripts
Calendar of State Papers (Ireland), 1586–92
Calendar of State Papers (Venetian), 1558–1603
Calendar of State Papers (Spanish), 1580–1603
Calendar of State Papers, Domestic Series: Mary and Elizabeth
Calendar of State Papers, Foreign Series: Elizabeth
Calendar of State Papers (Scotland), 1547–1603
Documents illustrating the History of the Spanish Armada, G. P. B. Naish, in *Naval Miscellany*, vol. 4, Naval Records Society, 1952. This includes the second version of *Discourse Concerninge the Spanish Fleete Invadinge Englande in the yeare 1588*, Petruccio Ubaldino
Pathway to Military Practice, Barnaby Rich
State Papers Relating to the Defeat of the Spanish Armada, 1588, vols 1 and 2, ed. Sir John Laughton, *Navy Records Society*, 1894, containing Howard's *Relation of Proceedings*
Calendar of State papers Relating to English Affairs, vol. 4, ed. M. A. A. Hume, 1899
King Philip's correspondence with Parma in *History of the Netherlands*, J. L. Motley, 1860
The Spanish War, 1585–87, J. S. Corbett, Naval Records Society, 1898
Captain Cuellar's account may be found in two books edited by (a) H. Allingham & R. Crawford, (b) Evelyn Hardy (translation by Frances Partridge) – see below.
Marcos de Aramburu's account, translated by W. Spotswood Green in *Proceedings of the Royal Irish Academy*, vol. 28, Dublin & London, 1908–9

Books

Allingham, H. & Crawford, R., eds, *Captain Cuellar's Adventures in Connacht and Ulster, A.D. 1588*, 1897

Andrews, K. R., *Drake's Voyages*, Weidenfeld, 1967; *Elizabethan Privateering during the Spanish War, 1585–1603*, CUP, 1964

Bradford, E., *Drake*, Hodder & Stoughton, 1965

Boynton, L., *The Elizabethan Militia*, Routledge and Kegan Paul, 1967

Crowson, P. S., *Tudor Foreign Policy*, A. & C. Black, 1973

Cruickshank, C. G., *Elizabeth's Army*, OUP, 1966

Dunn, R. S., *Age of Religious Wars, 1559–1689*, Weidenfeld & Nicholson, 1971

Duro, C. F., *La Armada Invencible*, 2 vols, Madrid, 1884–5

Elliott, J. H., *Europe Divided, 1559–1598*, Fontana, 1968; *Imperial Spain, 1469–1716*, Penguin, 1970

Fallon, Niall, *Armada in Ireland*, Stanford Maritime, 1978

Falls, C., *Elizabeth's Irish Wars*, 1950

Ffoulkes, C., *Gunfounders of England*, CUP, 1969

Flanagan, Laurence, *Ireland's Armada Legacy*, Alan Sutton Publishing, 1988

Graham, Winston, *Spanish Armadas*, Collins, 1972 and 1988

Hadfield, A. M., *Time to Finish the Game*, Phoenix House, 1964

Hardy, Evelyn, *Survivors of the Armada*, Constable, 1966

Howarth, David, *Voyage of the Armada: the Spanish Story*, Collins, 1981

Jenkins, E., *Elizabeth the Great*, Panther, 1972

Kenny, R. W., *Elizabeth's Admiral – Political Career of Charles Howard, Earl of Nottingham, 1536–1624*, John Hopkins Press, 1970

Kilfeather, T. P., *Graveyard of the Spanish Armada*, 1967

Lewis, M., *Armada Guns*, Allen and Unwin, 1961; *Spanish Armada*, Batsford, Pan, 1960

Lloyd, C., *Sir Francis Drake*, Faber & Faber, 1957

Lynch, J., *Spain under the Hapsburgs*, vol. 1, Blackwell, 1965

Martin, C. M., *Full Fathom Five: Wrecks of the Spanish Armada*, Chatto and Windus, 1975

Martin, C. M., and Parker, G., *Spanish Armada*, Hamish Hamilton, 1988

Mattingly, Garrett, *Defeat of the Spanish Armada*, Jonathan Cape, 1959

McDonald, Kendall, *Treasure Divers*, Pelham, undated; *Wreck Detectives*, Harrap, 1972

Ortiz, A. D., *Golden Age of Spain, 1516–1659*, Weidenfeld & Nicholson, 1971

Parker, Geoffrey, *Dutch Revolt*, Penguin, 1979

Petrie, Sir Charles, *Philip II of Spain*, Eyre & Spottiswoode, 1964; *Philip of Spain*, 1961

Pierson, P., *Philip II of Spain*, Thames & Hudson, 1975

Pope, D., *Guns*, Weidenfeld & Nicholson, 1965; Spring Books, 1969

Robinson, G., *Elizabethan Ship*, Longmans, 1956

Rowse, A. L., *Froude's Spanish Story of the Armada*, Alan Sutton Publishing, 1988; *Tudor Cornwall*, 1941

Rule, J. C. & TePaske, J. J., *Character of Philip II – The Problem of Moral Judgements in History*, D. C. Heath & Co., 1963

Smith, Captain John, *A Sea Grammar, 1627*, Michael Joseph, 1970

Sténuit, Robert, *Treasures of the Armada*, David & Charles, 1972

Thomson, G. M., *Sir Francis Drake*, Secker & Warburg, Book Club Associates, 1973

Uden, Grant, *Drake at Cadiz*, Macdonald, 1969

Waters, D. W., *The Art of Navigation in England in Elizabethan and early Stuart Times*, Hollis & Carter, 1958

Webb, H. J., *Elizabethan Military Science*, University of Wisconsin, 1965

Wernham, R. B., *Before the Armada, Growth of English Foreign Policy, 1485–1588*, Cape, 1966; *After the Armada, Elizabethan England and the Struggle for Western Europe, 1588–95*, OUP, 1984

Whiting, J., Roger S., *Handful of History*, Alan Sutton Publishing, 1978

Williams, N., *Elizabeth, Queen of England*, 1967; *Francis Drake*, Weidenfeld & Nicholson, 1953

Williamson, J.A., *Age of Drake*, A. &. C. Black, 1938; *Hawkins of Plymouth*, A. & C. Black, 1949; *Sir Francis Drake*, Collins, 1957

Woodrooffe, T., *Enterprise of England*, Faber & Faber, 1958

Articles

Appointment of the Duke of Medina Sidonia to the Command of the Spanish Armada, I. A. A. Thompson, vol. 12, *Historical Journal*, 1969

Armada Losses on the Irish Coast, K. Danaher, *Irish Sword*, 1956

Armada Ships on the Kerry Coast, W. Spotswood Green, *Proceedings of Royal Irish Academy*, 1909

Armada and administrative reform: the Spanish council of war in the reign of Philip II, I. A. A. Thompson, vol. 82, *English Historical Review*, 1967

Armada pilot's survey of the English coastline, October, 1597, A. J. Loomie, *Mariner's Mirror*, vol. 49, 1963

Armada Shot Controversy, S. Wignall, *Marine Archaeology*, Colston Papers 23, 1973

A Commander for the Armada, P. O'M. Pierson, *Mariner's Mirror*, vol. 55, 1969

Drake's Game of Bowls, C. Lloyd, C. E. Carrington, D. W. Waters, *Mariner's Mirror*, p. 144, vol. 39, 1953; p. 160, vol. 40, 1954; p. 64, vol. 41, 1955

El Gran Grifon – an Armada wreck on Fair Isle, C. M. Martin, *International Journal of Nautical Archaeology*, vol. 1, 1972

Elizabethan Navy and the Armada Campaign, D. W. Waters, *Mariners' Mirror*, vol. 35, 1949

England's War Effort against the Spanish Armada, O. F. G. Hogg, vol. 44, *Society for Army Historical Research Journal*, 1966

Franco-Spanish Diplomacy and the Armada, De Lamar Jensen, *Diplomacy and Dogmatism*, Cambridge, Mass., 1964

Guns of the Jesus of Lubeck, M. A. Lewis, *Mariner's Mirror*, vol. 22, 1936

How to find; the divers' swim-line search, J. Grattan, British Sub-Aqua Club Paper 2, 1972

If the Armada had Landed, G. Parker, vol. 61, *History*, 1976

Ireland, the Armada, the Adriatic, J. de C. Ireland, *Colston Papers*, 1974

La Trinidad Valencera and Underwater Exploration, C. M. Martin, vol. 8, *International Journal of Nautical Archaeology*, 1979

Metal detector survey on the wreck of the Santa Maria de la Rosa, J. N. Green and C. M. Martin, *Prospezioni Archeologiche*, vol. 5, Rome, 1970

Papers relating to the Navy during the Spanish War, 1585–87, J. S. Corbett, vol. 12, *Naval Records Society*, 1898

Shape of Ships that defeated the Spanish Armada, T. Glasgow, *Mariner's Mirror*, vol. 50, 1964

Some Survivors of the Armada in Ireland, M. Hume, *Transactions of the Royal Historical Society*, 1897

Spanish Armada and the Ottoman Porte, E. Pears, *English Historical Review*, vol. 8, 1893

Spanish Armada Expedition, 1968–70, C. M. Martin, *Colston Papers*, 1971

Spanish Armada Prisoners' Escape from Ireland, D. Quinn, *Mariner's Mirror*, May 1984

Underwater Search Systems, S. Wignall, *Surveying in Archaeology Underwater*, Colt Monograph V, 1969

Wrecks of the Spanish Armada on the Coast of Ireland, W. Spotswood Green, *Geographical Journal*, 1906

Playing Cards

Whiting, Roger, *Spanish Armada* facsimile playing cards, Past Times, 1988

Index